Life Lessons
from the Cat

Chicken Soup for the Soul: Life Lessons from the Cat
101 Tales of Family, Friendship and Fun
Amy Newmark

Published by Chicken Soup for the Soul, LLC www.chickensoup.com
Copyright ©2019 by Chicken Soup for the Soul, LLC. All Rights Reserved.

The publisher gratefully acknowledges the many publishers and individuals who granted Chicken Soup for the Soul permission to reprint the cited material.

Front cover photo courtesy of iStockphoto.com/cynoclub (©cynoclub)
Back cover and Interior photo of cat sitting on books courtesy of iStockphoto.com/milarka (©milarka)
Back cover photo of cat with glasses courtesy of iStockphoto.com/CasPhotography (©CasPhotography)
Photo of Amy Newmark courtesy of Susan Morrow at SwickPix

Cover and Interior by Daniel Zaccari

Distributed to the booktrade by Simon & Schuster. SAN: 200-2442

Publisher's Cataloging-In-Publication Data
(Prepared by The Donohue Group, Inc.)

Names: Newmark, Amy, compiler.
Title: Chicken soup for the soul : life lessons from the cat : 101 tales
    of family, friendship and fun / [compiled by] Amy Newmark.
Other Titles: Life lessons from the cat : 101 tales of family, friendship
    and fun
Description: [Cos Cob, Connecticut] : Chicken Soup for the Soul, LLC,
    [2019]
Identifiers: ISBN 9781611599893 | ISBN 9781611592894 (ebook)
Subjects: LCSH: Cats--Literary collections. | Cats--Anecdotes. | Human-
    animal relationships--Literary collections. | Human-animal
    relationships--Anecdotes. | Cat owners--Literary collections. | Cat
    owners--Anecdotes. | LCGFT: Anecdotes.
Classification: LCC SF445.5 .C454 2019 (print) | LCC SF445.5 (ebook) | DDC
    636.8/088/7/02--dc23

Library of Congress Control Number: 2019900484

PRINTED IN THE UNITED STATES OF AMERICA
on acid∞free paper

25 24 23 22 21 20 19   01 02 03 04 05 06 07 08 09 10 11

Life Lessons
from the Cat

101 Tales of Family,
Friendship and Fun

Amy Newmark

CSS

Chicken Soup for the Soul, LLC
Cos Cob, CT

Changing the world one story at a time®
www.chickensoup.com

Table of Contents

❶
~Meant to Be~

❷
~Wild Thing~

❸

~Who Rescued Who?~

❹

~My Very Good, Very Bad Cat~

❺

~A Natural Therapist~

❻

~Who's in Charge Here?~

❼

~Making Better Humans~

8

~Smart Cat~

9

~Learning to Love the Cat~

10

~Miracles Happen~

Meant to Be

Aye, Captain!

In ancient times cats were worshipped as gods;
they have not forgotten this.
~Terry Pratchett

Today started like any other Sunday. I woke up, made coffee for my boyfriend and me, and took out our pack of dogs. I say "pack" because, well, there are four: three Cocker Spaniel females and a male Jack Russell Terrier. It is a fun-loving, furry zoo of animated proportions to say the least, each one with its own unique personality. However, they are my boyfriend's dogs, not mine. I love them, but I am a cat person. However, we just couldn't see getting a cat with four dogs at home.

I noticed soon after taking out the dogs that their focus was directed toward a tree. It was not unusual for them to circle, sniff, and claw at the dirt around the trees, especially if they smelled a squirrel, but today was a little different. They paid extra attention to this one tree. The sun was not up entirely, so it took a minute to focus in the dwindling darkness on what was commanding their attention. Then I heard it: a mew. Just one, but a mew. A kitten was somewhere near that tree!

The dogs were frantically trying to find the source of the sound. They ran in circles around the tree, under the nearby bushes, and back and forth to me as if to say, "Mom, where is it? I can smell it. I can hear it, but I can't find it." I stood still for a moment, staring at a blank space in front of our outdoor shed when I noticed a little shape coming toward the dogs. My heart raced. I had no idea what they would do to a small animal they had never seen before. The dogs formed a tight circle around the animal, with noses to the ground and tails hanging low, and I ran toward them to save the little creature.

Suddenly, a gray-and-black-striped kitten popped out from between one of the Cocker Spaniel's legs and came toward me. I realized the dogs were merely curious, and not about to attack the little thing. I picked him up and he started mewing louder and rubbed his little cheeks against my hand and arm. He was about six weeks old, and he had the loudest purr I'd ever heard. It was like listening to a Mack Truck idling.

The dogs, still not sure what to do, clamored for me to show them the kitten, so I did. To my surprise, the wee kitten jumped out of my hands, right into the center of my pack of dogs, allowing them to sniff and lick him all over. This little one had no fear! I said to the kitten, "Well, I guess this means you're the newest member of our pack. Welcome home, little one!"

I took him inside and yelled out to my boyfriend, "You won't believe what the dogs just found in the back yard." I showed him the kitten, and he laughed. He said, "Looks like you got yourself a cat. What are you going to name him?"

That decision didn't take long. I looked the kitten over and noticed that his right eye was a little pink and swollen, and he had no hair on his bottom. I had no idea how long he had been surviving in the woods, but he seemed to be commanding the pack already, so I knew I had to give him a fitting name. Being that one of the hit movies out at the time was about pirates, and that my boyfriend loves to dress like a pirate on Halloween, I decided on a pirate name. I took the kitten, looked him in the eyes and stated, "Ye shall be known as Captain Jack Lickinbottom, ye scoundrel!" His response was a loud purr, an even louder mew, and a paw tap on my nose as if to say, "I approve. You've done well, so I think I shall keep you."

Twenty-four hours and a trip to the vet later, my six-week-old commander was taking his role seriously. He would slap a nose if he didn't want to be bothered, climb across furry bellies when he wanted to play or snuggle, and climb up our legs to get attention or demand food. And when he wanted some solitude from all the ruckus and chaos, Jack could be found curled up inside the pot of my Camellia plant, napping soundly.

That was eleven years ago, and I still have Captain Jack with me today — all fifteen pounds of him. He no longer has the company of a pack of dogs, but he does have a sweet, feisty feline companion, Little Bit, upon whom he showers daily kisses and baths. She was found under similar circumstances as Jack. And, like Jack, she chose me to be her scullery maid, kitchen staff, massage therapist, and all-around underling as they plot world domination from their window perch. I wouldn't have it any other way.

As Mel Brooks once said, "It's good to be the king!" But, in this instance, it's good to be Captain.

— Danielle Stephens —

Bonded Brothers

There is something about the presence of a cat...
that seems to take the bite out of being alone.
~Louis J. Camuti

Denny and Checkers were nine-year-old, brown tabby brothers. They looked almost exactly alike, except that Checkers was slightly bigger. They did everything together and slept in the same large cage at floor level in our shelter. We would always find them curled up with each other when they were not cautiously examining and rubbing against potential adopters. We knew they had been together all their lives, so they were a bonded pair. Whoever adopted one had to take the other.

Checkers went in for routine surgery and did not wake up. It is a rare occurrence, but it happens. Denny was left alone in his cage, wondering where his brother went. He became depressed and would no longer come out to play and say "hi" to people looking to adopt. Not even treats or wet food would coax him out. He would barely let people touch him. People asked about his story and felt bad for him, but never put in an application to adopt him. For weeks, he sat in the cage he and his brother had shared. We did not change the blanket Checkers had lain on so Denny could always smell his brother.

A small, blond woman came in looking to adopt one day. When she heard about Checkers, she said, "I have to call someone," and rushed out to make a phone call. She returned a half-hour later with a somber-looking gentleman and led him to Denny's cage. Denny looked up at him for a while, and then stood up and came out of his cage. We all gasped and gave them space. Denny sniffed the man before rubbing his face against his hand a few times. He stood there next to him, sniffing and slowly rubbing against the man.

"I have to have this cat," said the man. We were near tears as we handed him an application. He filled it out immediately, and we pooled our resources to call his vet and references to get the adoption approved by the evening. Usually, it takes days to process an application.

The man came and got Denny the next morning. We waived the adoption fee since we were so happy that Denny had come out of his shell for someone. As the man began to leave, he set down the carrier gently, got down on his knees, and cried. We ran over to see what was wrong.

Through fractured breaths, he said, "I lost my brother to cancer six months ago. We were two years apart, and we were inseparable. He was my best friend. We talked every day. I miss him so much. This cat knows what that pain feels like. He knows I have lost a brother, too. It's like we need each other, and we will take care of each other. Together, we will be alright." Then he walked out with Denny in his carrier. I had to take a moment in the bathroom to splash water on my face and wipe my eyes before returning to finish my shift.

We received an update a month later with a photo of Denny. He was relaxing in his bed, looking out the window. He was happy. It was a miracle those two broken-hearted brothers found each other and formed a new bonded pair.

— Sarah LM Klauda —

My Angel

*Our perfect companions never have fewer
than four feet.*
~Colette

The morning was not going well. My one-year-old son sat on the floor screaming, his face red and his features contorted with frustration and despair. We'd spent a sleepless night, and at sunrise I took him for a long walk around the neighborhood. I hoped that the fresh air and rising sun would calm him down, leading to a nap for both of us.

But a nap was obviously not in his plans. I gave him a bath, changed his diaper, attempted to feed him, brought toys and blankets, and put on soothing music. Nothing worked. He was inconsolable, and the screaming just got louder.

I was getting tired, cranky, and frustrated myself, and we entered into a bizarre feedback loop where we fueled each other's frustrations. I felt like a failed mother, doomed to spend my life with a screaming toddler. Suddenly, to top it all off, our cat Angel jumped down from her perch up on the couch, startling both of us. She opened her mouth and started meowing at the top of her lungs.

Just what I needed: another loud creature. "Great job, kitty," I said. As if understanding my sarcasm, my son stopped wailing and giggled.

Angel moved closer and brushed her furry tail on my son's face. He laughed and tried to catch her tail. Angel moved the tail away but did not leave. My son stretched his hand out and petted her. She purred. He put both of his little hands on her, and she purred louder.

"Thank you, Angel," I whispered, relief washing over me. "I'm glad you're here."

I had never planned to have a cat, and it was by mere chance that Angel ended up with us. A few years prior, I was a graduate student, sharing an apartment with a roommate. Days after we moved in, Janet asked if I would mind if she got a cat. I'd always liked cats but did not want to commit to having one until after I finished my studies and found a permanent place to live. Having a cat who wasn't my responsibility sounded like a great idea, and I agreed happily.

The next day, Janet and I were at the Humane Society, looking at rows of cages with cats in them.

"What do you think about this one?" Janet asked when we stopped in front of a black-and-white cat with huge eyes and soft fur. I put my finger through the bars and petted the cat's head. It was beautiful and very friendly.

"I like it, but I'm not the one getting a cat," I reminded her. "You need to choose."

"Give me a few minutes," Janet said and walked off.

I stayed in front of the black-and-white cat, petting its head. A printed page was taped to the wall next to the cage explaining that the cat's name was Angel. She preferred dry food, was housebroken, and was good with kids.

Janet ended up choosing Angel. It took her a few days to get used to our apartment and us. But then, while Janet was at night classes, Angel would wander into my room, jump on my lap and purr.

I enjoyed Angel's company and did not look forward to the end of the school year. Janet was graduating and would move, taking Angel with her. I kept reminding myself that Angel was never my cat, and I should simply enjoy these moments with her.

Weeks turned into months, and soon it was time for both of us to move. Janet found a job in a different city, and I was planning to move closer to campus.

A few days before her big move, Janet came into my room holding Angel. "We came to say goodbye."

I didn't understand. "I thought you weren't leaving until Saturday. And we still have your farewell party on Friday."

She nodded. "I'm leaving on Saturday, but I don't know what my new situation will be, so I'm not taking the cat with me."

For a moment, I thought she was joking. She had to be.

"What are you going to do with Angel then?" I asked.

"Take her back to the Humane Society. I'm sure someone will pick her up."

She handed Angel to me to say goodbye. She climbed onto my shoulder and grabbed on to me, as if she knew something was wrong.

"I'll take her," I said without hesitation.

"All right," Janet said. "She's yours. Thanks. I'll go pack."

She walked out. I stood in the middle of the room with Angel still clinging to me. As I petted her soft fur, I felt a momentary panic. Many places around campus did not allow pets, and those that did were expensive. Would I be able to afford her? What if Angel got sick? How would I pay the vet bills?

I sat down on my bed, and Angel jumped on my lap, immediately relieving me of all anxiety. The choice was clear. There was no way I was letting Janet take her back to the Humane Society.

Now, my son's giggling interrupted my thoughts. I smiled at the memory of how this cat came into our lives, and I watched as she performed her magic. She took a couple of small steps away from my son, and he leaned forward, grasping her with both hands. Then she lay down on the carpet, and my son lay down, too, still holding her. I wondered if she would run away. What cat would let a toddler use her as a pillow?

But Angel stayed still as my son put his head on her. I lay next to them, watching my two favorite little creatures enjoy each other's company. A moment later, all three of us were fast asleep.

— Julia Gousseva —

On the Outside Looking In

*Thank you… for gracing my life with your lovely
presence, for adding the sweet measure of your
soul to my existence.*
~Richard Matheson

At age fifteen, I had a petit mal seizure while out with friends. My life changed instantly. I was put on numerous medications and denied a driver's license.

Finally, long after I graduated from college, I was declared seizure-free. As soon as my doctor said it was safe to drive, I got my license and a car. Now that I could get around town more easily, it was time to get the pet I had always wanted. I had grown up with Siamese cats, and they had always been there for me when I needed comfort. I did my research and found a breeder with a litter of Siamese kittens. I headed right over.

A woman with frazzled hair opened the door. "Are you here about the cat?" she asked.

"Yes, my name's Danielle."

"Yes, yes. Come on in. You're first, so you have the pick of the litter, my dear."

I followed her into the basement where a furry mess of white-and-gray kittens lay in a cat bed. I knew I wanted a female because my parents' male cat ended up being an outdoor cat because he sprayed in the house. After seeing how often my parents had to clean up the furniture, I wasn't sure if I was up for dealing with that.

I told the woman that I'd like a female, and she pointed them all out to me. I tried to pick one up, but she leapt out of my hands. I tried again, and the next female wiggled out of my palm. I was starting to worry that I would walk out of there without a cat!

"You know, you don't have to get a female," she said. "You are the first one to 'reserve' a cat, so if you want to take home a male, you can." She pointed out the two males, and I picked one up gently.

The kitten settled into my chest and purred deeply, his little sapphire-blue eyes squinting as if to smile at me. After about five minutes, the woman's voice broke my trance. "Looks like you found your cat," she said, smiling at the instant bond I had with the kitten.

When I returned home to my husband, I joked about the expectations I had for what kind of cat he would be. Fittingly, I named him Pip after Charles Dickens' character from *Great Expectations*.

About the same time I took Pip home, I had started a new job that included a forty-five-minute highway commute. I was still fairly new to driving, but I felt confident in my abilities. Still, my husband, friends, and family were always concerned because of my prior history with seizures. They told me how frightening it had been to see me staring off into the distance and unresponsive. I waved away their concerns, thinking that the doctor wouldn't have signed off on me getting my license unless she thought it was okay.

Then the day came when I had a breakthrough seizure while driving home. Nobody was injured, and I didn't hit any other cars. Other than a bruise from the seatbelt, I was fine. However, I had totaled my car and I lost my license. Upset, I spent the next few days recovering from my accident with Pip curled into a "Sonic the Hedgehog" ball on my chest. I was glad to have Pip to distract me from the guilt and blame I put myself through.

I never knew the emotional pain my seizures caused others until about a year after my accident. I woke suddenly when I felt Pip fall off the bed. Rubbing the sleep from my eyes, I heard an odd noise in the dark and reached over to use the flashlight from my cellphone. Pip's body was thrashing all over the floor, and he was foaming at the mouth. This went on for what seemed like forever.

My husband and I looked at each other in shock. We kept an eye on him and called our vet first thing in the morning. The vet confirmed that Pip did, in fact, have a seizure and promptly put him on phenobarbital (a medicine I had once used) to get them under control. I would have to give him medicine twice a day for the rest of his life.

My husband and I were shocked that Pip had seizures like me. Now I was on the outside looking in. I was the person witnessing someone I loved so much suffer from the same illness I had. Feeling the same emotions that others felt for me, I no longer brushed off their concerns or got irritated when they voiced their opinions about what was safe and what wasn't for me.

I believe animals choose their owners, not the other way around. There was a reason Pip melted into my arms that day.

— Dani Watkins —

Taming Mighty Mouth

*Are we really sure the purring is coming from the kitty
and not from our very own hearts?*
~Emme Woodhull-Bäche

My retired husband sits in his recliner talking to the long-whiskered roamer who walks all over him. "You are not a lightweight, Buddy. I just want you to know that."

He and the orange-and-white cat are inseparable. The cat snoozes in the crook of Bill's right arm, stretches his torso up Bill's chest until they're nose to nose, or looks out the window from the back of Bill's chair.

Our kids and grandkids knew how heartbroken we were after our beloved gray-and-white cat passed away prematurely from heart failure. They kept offering to replace him, but neither Bill nor I was ready for another pet.

"Grandpa, statistics say having a pet to stroke and love makes seniors live longer."

"By seniors, do you mean me or an old cat?" Bill laughed off their suggestions and refused their offers.

Then in December, we noticed this very skittish cat nosing around our backyard shed. We usually throw cooked egg yolks out each morning for the blackbirds, but as soon as the egg hit the ground, the cat came bounding out to devour it. I put out food and a bowl of water. The cat ate ravenously and ran off.

"That cat isn't going anywhere if you keep feeding it," Bill warned.

I tuned him out and sweet-talked the kitty.

One cold morning, the orange cat was huddled at the edge of the shed waiting for me. Its chest and cheeks were white. An orange, heart-shaped patch of fur covered its mouth and chin. Despite its cuteness, it yowled like a terrified wildcat. My goodness, that cat had a mouth!

Bill watched from the kitchen window as it came closer each day. "That cat is not coming inside," he grumbled.

When I opened the back door, and the cat stepped cautiously across the threshold, Bill said, "That cat better not have claws… or fleas!"

I reminded him that fleas wouldn't survive in sub-zero temperatures.

The cat devoured its food, and then yowled endlessly as I sat beside it, trying to pet it.

"No wonder it's on its own. Nobody could put up with Mighty Mouth," Bill complained.

"It's freezing out," I explained. "This is a scared cat with trust issues."

Bill ignored us and went to sit in his recliner. Before he knew what hit him, that orange fur ball jumped into his lap. Exhausted and on high alert from having been outside, that poor kitty snoozed soundly.

"Why me?" my husband asked.

"He recognizes a softie."

Finally, my husband took pity on it. "You're exhausted, and you do need me right now, but soon we're going to find your owner. You're not living in this house, so don't get too comfy."

The cat stayed in the same position until both nightfall and snowfall coincided. Bill looked at me. "I guess it's not going back out?"

"We'll take it to the vet tomorrow and see if it's been micro-chipped," I said.

Bill slept in bed that night, and I slept on the couch with the loud mouth that yowled off and on all night long. Tense, it jumped at every sound and shadow. I doctored the fresh battle scratch on its nose. There was no way I was returning it to the perils of outdoor living.

The next day, the vet provided contact information for the cat's owner. The phone number had been disconnected, so we drove to the address two miles away. No one answered. I put a note and our phone number in the mailbox. Two weeks passed without any word from the owner. When my husband asked what I wanted for Christmas, I smiled and said, "This loud-mouthed cat."

Bill and the cat continued to bond. We purchased equipment and toys, and enough cat food for one month. We called our temporary cat "Kitty."

Weeks later, the phone call came. A man said he had been busy, had just gotten around to reading his mail, and found my note on the bottom of the stack. My heart fell.

"Do you want your cat back?" I asked, my voice quivering with emotion.

"I guess I'd like to see him. He disappeared at Thanksgiving."

"What's his name?"

"Fitz. He's three years old, and he's been fixed."

"Was he an indoor cat?" I asked.

"Well, he really liked going outside, but he just never came back."

I wondered how the man could allow Kitty to roam in winter, so I expressed my concern. "Sir, I'm afraid you'll allow him outside again, and it's going to snow and be bitterly cold all week. What if he gets lost or beat up again? We are an older couple, and we've made him an indoor cat." My voice broke, and I wept. "We don't want to worry about him. We've gotten pretty attached to him during this month."

The man said in disbelief, "You mean you *want* him?"

"Oh, yes, we love him. He and my husband are best friends."

"Well, okay then. I have a bag of food here if you want it," he offered.

I thanked him, but decided to let sleeping cats lie… right in my husband's arms.

We changed his name to Sassy because he's quite a talker, although he no longer yowls. Bill calls him Whiskers, Thumper, Sweet Boy, and Mooch. He does not answer to Fitz or any of his names. But he does answer to the rattle of his food bag, and he bunks on the foot of our bed at night.

Our cat of many names taught us that trust is earned, the depths of love are unknown, and the benefits of touch do reap great rewards. Bill's blood pressure is down and his mood is up, thanks to the cute cat with a heart-shaped patch of orange fur on his mighty mouth.

— Linda O'Connell —

Always Grateful

Cats choose us; we don't own them.
~Kristin Cast

My days always started with a two to four mile run on a nearby greenway. For about two years, I had a very faithful running buddy. I could count on him to be waiting at the white wooden fence come rain, snow, sleet or hail.

This giant, orange tabby cat was probably the most social feline I had ever encountered. It was remarkable for a stray. He would see me cresting the hill and join in, running alongside me for about a quarter-mile until he meowed enough to get me to stop and pet him. I'd give him a stroke on the back, and then he would flop over for a belly rub. A few minutes later, when I would attempt to resume my run, he would wind around my ankles to keep me longer. I was a pushover, so it worked.

Although he was a rather stout fellow, I always brought him some cat food, figuring that might supplement whatever he caught on his own.

On fair-weather afternoons, I would pick up my four-year-old granddaughter from preschool and we would visit the tabby together. She would insist on bringing him an afternoon treat. Before long, he started winding around her little ankles as well.

Sometimes, our feline friend would be accompanied by a crony that was quite clearly his opposite. This long-haired female calico wanted nothing to do with a belly rub or back scratch. It was obvious she showed up for one thing and one thing only: the food.

One day, while my granddaughter was pouring out the plastic baggie full of cat chow mixed with leftover chicken nuggets, she brought up a good point. In a matter-of-fact way, as if this logic had come to her four-year-old mind in a crashing thunderbolt, she cried out, "Ne Ne! How long have we been visiting this kitty?"

She spoke as if she were scolding me. "And we don't even know *his* name! *Their* names!" she continued. "We've got to call them *something*!"

She was right. For months, I had been sharing my morning runs with this generic "Kitty," the same moniker that we used for his sidekick and every other feline we would meet along the way.

My granddaughter then stepped back and, deep in thought, studied both cats carefully as they devoured the remains of her Happy Meal.

Then she announced, "I've got it! Tom Tom and Rose!"

I looked at her, puzzled.

"He's Tom Tom, and she's Rose! *That's* what we'll call them!"

And so began the adventures of "Tom Tom" and "Rose," literally.

All the regular runners, walkers, bikers and visitors to the greenway soon came to know the big, friendly orange tabby as "Tom Tom" and his reclusive sidekick as "Rose."

My granddaughter loved these two cats, even as unlovable as Rose may have been. She looked forward to our greenway walks and visiting Tom Tom and Rose, something simple that the two of us did together.

With her birthday approaching, I wanted to do something extra special. I collaborated with a local college art student and produced a self-published children's book for my granddaughter about our two greenway friends. My only real intent was to print a copy or two for her birthday, so I was pleasantly surprised when several copies were sold!

I was given the opportunity to use the book as a means to fundraise for a local animal organization that helps stray and feral cats by providing spaying and neutering services as well as a pet-food assistance program. Soon, Tom Tom became the most famous cat in town!

On a Friday in January, when the forecast was calling for bad weather, I went to the greenway and left extra cat food in the event that I was unable to make it back out for a few days.

Later that night, as I watched the almost blizzard-like conditions, my heart sank as I thought of my greenway buddy. More than a foot and a half of snow blanketed the ground after the storm passed, which was far more than had been predicted.

Tom Tom was found the next day barricaded under a bridge between two heaping piles of snow and ice. I was so thankful he was alive! At this point, I knew what I had to do.

Tom Tom has been part of our family for the past three years. Of all the cats I have ever had, I can honestly say that he has taught me the most.

He consumes his freshly poured cat food enthusiastically, as if it were a different daily delicacy instead of the same dry morsels I offer up in his bowl each morning.

Next, he eagerly races to dig around in his clean litter box, whether he needs to go or not.

Much like a faithful canine, Tom Tom listens for my car to pull up in the driveway. I can sometimes see him jumping down from his upstairs lookout window and hear him running down the steps as I'm unlocking the door, making sure he beats me to the kitchen by the time I enter.

He is my shadow around the house, often prompting me for that same familiar belly rub with that same persistent meow.

No matter how deep a cat nap he's in, he always comes when called.

Tom Tom likes to play "biting" gently in a playful and comical manner, but refusing to do the same with either one of the grandchildren, only softly pawing at their little hands.

He's made it clear he loves being an indoor family cat. As far as going outside, he wants no part of it.

As I sit at my desk finishing this tale of my faithful tiger-striped running buddy, I realize that he chose me, not the other way around, and I'm so glad he did.

Smiling, I notice that aside from my clicking computer keys, the only other background noise I hear is that of the soft, steady, and satisfied purr of a once-stray orange tabby cat turned children's picture-book hero, who now lays curled up in a chair beside me, taking absolutely nothing for granted.

—Valerie Archual—

7

My Garden's Bumper Crop

One must love a cat on its own terms.
~Paul Gray

One summer, a gray tomcat settled into the small garden patch that ran along the side of my garage. Each morning, he would lie on the ledge beneath my garage window, soaking up the sun's early rays. Although he wouldn't let me pet him, he gladly accepted the food and water I put out. Everyone assumed he was my cat since he was always in front of my house, so I named him.

Lion had white paws and face markings, and a muscular, barrel-chested body. Rather than walk, he seemed to swagger. He appeared to be a tough guy with a neck that vanished into his shoulders. A friend of mine hinted that he was probably getting into a lot of fights, and on his peaceful nights siring far too many offspring. "You should have him neutered," she advised.

As he wouldn't let me catch him I rented a humane trap. I found an opossum in the cage on my first morning out. The opossum, true to its reputation, played dead and refused to leave when I opened the cage. Finally, using a hanger, I lifted the cage until the opossum tumbled out and dashed toward the bushes.

Lion resisted entering the cage for his regular cat food. It took a can of albacore tuna to entice him. Once I had, we were off to a vet for the procedure and shots. After I paid, the vet suggested callously that I not get attached to Lion. She said he was a street cat — too tough to

Meant to Be | 21

be domesticated. I was incensed and baffled by my vet's inability to see what a treasure Lion really was.

I returned him to his little garden and continued feeding him. Occasionally, he allowed me to stroke his head lightly while he ate, but he still refused to be held.

About this time, he was joined by a companion who was heard long before he was seen. Sometimes, as Lion lay calmly and majestically on his ledge, a mournful wail would come from inside the dense bushes below. Thinking an injured animal was crying out for help, I'd try to peer in at it, but all I could see was a dirty, cream-colored thing slinking farther back out of my view.

I began watching from my kitchen window after I fed Lion. He'd eat his fill and stroll over to the lawn. Next, a Siamese-looking cat would dart out to devour the meal's remains, always managing to disappear before I could open the door.

This strange couple continued their relationship for some weeks before the Siamese, who I called Winetta in honor of his loud, pitiful cries, ventured out more boldly. I began to put out two plates, and the pair soon ate side by side. Eventually, Winetta occupied the ledge along with his mentor — both in calm repose, which made me feel especially proud when I walked past them.

Winetta became quite tame and welcomed my pats. Without the drama of capturing him in a humane trap, he was shortly off to a new vet to be neutered.

Around Halloween, Lion showed up with one eye swollen shut. I tried to capture him for treatment, but he ran off every time I approached. Naturally, I returned to the humane trap since it had worked before. No dice! He remembered what had happened the last time he went in and wasn't about to be fooled again.

Days passed, and his shut eye bulged and watered. I had to get him! The vet gave me some kitty tranquilizers to put in his food. He ate heartily and appeared ready to fall asleep, but each time I tried to pick him up, he ran. Two hours later, with the help of a friend, I had him. Actually, I lured him with more food — first on the porch and then on the threshold of my house. Right at my door, he sort of slumped, finally succumbing to the relaxers.

Rushing him to an emergency veterinary clinic, I was distressed to see the bloody pulp that should have been his eye when the vet pulled back his swollen eyelid.

The efficient vet's prognosis: "It's a foxtail in there. Been there a while working its way through the eye. May not be able to save his sight," he concluded.

I imagined how painful this must have been for Lion. The doctor removed the foxtail quickly and sent me home with some eye ointment. "You'll have to apply it four times a day, and then we'll see if he has any vision left in that eye."

I agreed to the treatment but immediately panicked, realizing that Lion wouldn't want me to handle him.

As it turns out, it wasn't half bad. I kept him in an extra-large cage in my garage so I wouldn't have to chase him again. The ointment must have felt soothing to him because, after the first application, he stopped fighting me. I took advantage of his newfound dependence on me by cuddling and petting him as much as he'd allow. A week later, his eye was open, no longer a bloody mess. The vet instructed me to continue with the ointment for ten more days, which I did gladly. Miraculously, even though the foxtail left a scar just above his retina, it didn't impair his vision at all.

Throughout all this, Winetta continued to be fed, rubbing up against my leg as I put down his food. He'd peer into the garage through the window to check on Lion. Occasionally, he'd let out his trademark wail just to let Lion know he was there for him.

In mid-November, with the temperatures near freezing, Winetta moved into the garage with Lion. They adjusted well, cuddling up on the comforter I'd given them.

At last, they became tame enough to move into the house. They now share the back bedroom. To this day, they continue to be the best of friends, wrapping themselves around each other whenever the temperature drops.

The loyalty and support they offer each other made me recognize friendship in its purest form. Now I know what to look for in a two-legged friend for myself.

— Marsha Porter —

Home Is Wherever I'm with You

I love cats because I love my home, and after a while
they become its visible soul.
~Jean Cocteau

In the middle of the night, a cat appeared in our bed. We recognised her as "the garden cat" that spent a large part of her day sitting in our herb garden since we had moved into the beachside rental a few months earlier. Usually, she stared at the compost bin; a couple of mice lived inside. Occasionally, she'd wander over and let me give her a scratch on the ears.

The morning after the cat-crashing, we investigated how she might have got in. We discovered paw prints on the sill of the window above our bed. It seemed she had leapt onto our bed over our heads as we slept!

Quickly, it turned into a habit. "The garden cat" became "the window cat." Each night, we would settle into bed with our books and tea, and then hear the cat jump up onto the windowsill. We'd see her little face poke through the opening in the curtain, followed by her leap onto the bed.

Nighttime sleepovers soon extended into daytime visits as well. She became a regular part of our lives, curling up on the couch with us in the evenings and in our bed each night. Our window was open all the time, so she came and went as she pleased. She spent the majority of her time with us, leaving every morning, presumably to return home for breakfast. We didn't feed her, knowing that if we did, she wouldn't likely go back home again, and we didn't want to steal someone's cat. We took to calling her "You don't live here."

After some time, we noticed she was looking a bit skinny and her fur was dull, so we started feeding her. We didn't make this decision lightly, but since she spent the majority of her time at our place, our consciences couldn't abide seeing her malnourished. We started calling her Alice because *Alice in Wonderland* is one of my favourite books. It seemed appropriate since she arrived through the window and found a whole new world to live in. (It was also clear that "You don't live here" wasn't sinking in.)

We assumed she belonged to the big house next door, along with a few other cats, dogs and kids, including a baby. It was a busy house with a lot of activity. I didn't blame her for seeking the calm sanctuary of our garden and then our home. One day, the woman who lived in the house was outside, and we asked if she had a tortoiseshell cat.

"Oh, you must mean Rosie," she said.

We explained that "Rosie" spent most of her time at our place, and we had just started feeding her as we were concerned she had gotten thin.

The woman replied that they hardly saw Rosie anymore and had assumed she found someplace else to live. She and her husband got her when some friends asked them to watch their kitten while they were away and turned up with wee Rosie with a cast on her leg. Our neighbour owned Rosie's brother and offered to keep Rosie. So Rosie joined their bustling family some years back and was now about eight years old.

Things carried on as they were for a few more months until we received notice that our landlord had sold our place, and we would have to move. We found a new rental across town. We could barely speak about what this meant for our relationship with Rosie/Alice, who had been a regular in our home for nearly two years.

We had to ask the impossible question. My partner, Rew, had had many cats dear to him throughout his life and knew the gravity of what we were asking. He built up his courage and went next door to discuss the issue with the neighbour. He explained that we had grown quite attached to the cat, but we had to move. Would they consider allowing us to have her?

The man explained that Rosie/Alice didn't come home much since their baby had become a toddler, and they had hardly seen her for the past year. He said he would rather the cat live where she was happy, but he would have to discuss it with his wife before he could give us an answer.

We waited anxiously as we moved out over the next few weeks. We thought that when we started moving, Alice might be put off by the commotion and disappear. Quite the contrary, she sat on our suitcases or in our moving boxes every day. It was as if she was telling us not to forget to take her.

Finally, it was our last day in our old home. Everything had been moved to the new place; cleaning up was all that was left. I went to the new home to begin unpacking. The neighbours hadn't said a word since we had asked, so I could only think that the cat would stay behind. She had never actually been our cat, so I had to accept that. I busied myself with setting up our new home while Rew did the final cleanup at the old one.

I was in the kitchen unpacking pots and pans when I heard the car pull into the drive. The front door opened, and there was Rew — holding Alice in his arms! Tears sprang to my eyes as I went over to pat her. All I could say was "Really?"

He had a huge grin. "She's all ours. The neighbours said to take her with their blessing."

I sat on the floor with tears streaming as I petted her. My little Alice was with us for good.

Alice inspected the house, explored her territory (around the perimeter of the fenced-in yard, then over the fence — I waited nervously for a half-hour before she returned) and settled right in. We found a window we could leave open so "the window cat" could come and go.

She decided the beanbag would be her daytime bed. She played with toys as if she were a kitten, batting them around and leaping in the air. Her new granddad made her a scratching post, which became part of her daily routine.

I had been nervous that she would try to find her way back to the beach. However, Alice clearly chose us, and she wasn't going anywhere. If I went out to the garden, she followed. If I sat on the couch, she did, too. When I read outside in my swing, she'd jump into my lap.

We have since moved to an island, back to a different city on the mainland, and to a different home in our original town, but Alice has made herself at home wherever we go. We don't ever worry about her running off. She's found her home with us, wherever that may be.

— Mindi Picotte —

Shoebox Kitten

Who would believe such pleasure
from a wee ball o' fur?
~Irish Saying

On a sunny afternoon in July, my husband Lenny decided to make a garbage run. Living on a farm where no pick-up service was available, we burned what we could and took the rest to the town's landfill.

After unloading, Lenny walked around to see what others had thrown away. Being a person who finds treasure in what others call trash, Lenny would sometimes bring home what he called "great finds." He'd say, "You'll never know when this will come in handy," or "Look at what someone actually threw away," or "I can fix and use that." As a young family on a tight budget, we appreciated his finds.

Since it was a small-town landfill, it was never monitored, and the gates were locked only at night. As Lenny walked around that day, he picked up a few items and threw them on a large pile of garbage. He heard a "meow" and looked around for what he thought would be a feral cat but he saw nothing.

Then he saw a shoebox in the garbage pile move slightly, and he heard the cries again. He picked up the box, which was sealed with tape. When Lenny cut the tape and cautiously tore open the shoebox, he found a black-and-white kitten, approximately eight weeks old. He will never forget the terrified look in the kitten's eyes after he removed the lid. It was so frightened that it jumped into his arms and clung to him with its tiny claws.

The kitten was not wild and was already acquainted with humans. It was not afraid of him. The poor thing was very thin and had probably been taken away from its mother only recently. It's unfathomable that someone had cruelly left that kitten to die there on the landfill.

My husband has never been a great cat lover. Even though Lenny grew up on a farm where cats were necessary to keep the mice and rat population down, he did not feel they should be household pets. Our two daughters had a different perspective as they had recently been the recipients of another kitten from a local farmer.

Lenny knew he couldn't leave the kitten there, even outside the box. It would probably be eaten by a fox or a coyote. So, he decided to add another kitten to our growing pet population along with the rabbits and dog. The shoebox kitten sat on his shoulders meowing and purring while he drove back home.

Our five-year-old daughter, Cindy, was ecstatic to see another kitten because now she did not have to share with her sister, Jodi. We determined the kitten was a male and Cindy named him Whiskers.

Whiskers thrived on the loving attention from our daughter and despite the fact that he was a house pet, and not a farm cat, he became our best mouser. During the day he would hunt and stay around the farmyard, coming inside at night.

Lenny and Whiskers became the best of friends, too. The cat would follow my husband around the farmyard and drop presents of mice at his feet. When we were in the house during the evening, relaxing in front of the TV, Whiskers would abandon the girls and sit on the back of the sofa behind my husband where he could touch him or wrap his body around Lenny's neck and purr contentedly. We believed that Whiskers was forever grateful for the rescue on that fateful day, and we often talked about "the treasure" that Lenny found at the dump.

—J. A. Rost—

A Fearful Introduction

*We go on and on about our differences. But, you know,
our differences are less important than our similarities.*
~William Hall

My husband Randy had come with me to help clean out my locker at the end of my last summer lab class. All the other students had left. As we were finishing up, the professor came out of the back room, which housed supplies and experimental animals.

He said, "We have one rat left over from the summer session. He hasn't been used in any experiments. Would you like him? Rats make great pets."

That sounded like a bad idea to me. We had a cat, and not a particularly brave one.

Randy said, "Can I see him?"

"Sure. Come on back."

The professor led the way. When Randy returned, he sported a big white rat on his shoulder. "Look at him! He's great — and he likes me. Check him out!"

I reached out and petted the rat, half expecting one of his big, long teeth to take a chunk out of my hand, but he just sniffed me. I stroked his head. He closed his eyes and pushed his head against my hand. Maybe this would work after all.

We went home with that large white rat. Even though I had made friends with the animal, I shuddered as I listened to him rustling in

Meant to Be | 31

the cage in the back seat of the car. What we were about to do seemed insane. Why had I agreed? True, Randy had fast reflexes and should be able to rescue our pretty cat — or the rat — if necessary. But maybe Randy was taking too big a risk this time, one that threatened the life of one or both of these animals.

Kitts, our cat, outweighed the newcomer, but she was lazy — and that was one big rat! His body was at least eight inches long, and his tail was just as long as his body. His front teeth were enormous. I was sure they could do significant damage to anyone or anything.

When we entered the house with the rat, Kitts lay sleeping on our soft, royal-blue couch, as usual. It was her favorite spot, and she always looked so pretty there, with her long white fur and bright blue eyes. I didn't want to see that white fur covered with splatters of blood.

I sighed. "What are you planning to do?" I asked Randy. "Just put the cage on the floor and open the door?"

"Yup," he said, his brown eyes sparkling. "But it's going to be all right. You saw how friendly the big guy is. And if anything goes wrong, I'll grab him and stick him back in the cage."

"I'm not sure I can watch," I said.

"It'll be fine. You'll see."

"Yeah, right," I said in a mumble, expecting fireworks punctuated with blood and guts.

Randy set down the cage about ten feet from the couch and opened the cage door. The rat approached the door, his nose wiggling and his head bobbing as he took in everything. He stuck his snout outside the cage.

Kitts was awake by now, watching alertly. As the rat stepped out of the cage, she stood, jumped down from the couch, and stalked, stiff-legged, toward the rat.

They stopped and stared at each other, and then continued their slow march forward.

I held my breath. They scrutinized each other as they got closer, but neither one showed any signs of aggression. Kitts didn't growl or hiss, and her tail remained upright. The rat showed no change in his behavior.

The two animals sidled up to each other, snuffling.

I relaxed a little and took a deep breath.

After the initial sniffing ceremony, Kitts jumped back onto the couch, taking up her position as queen cat, and went to sleep. The rat continued to explore his new home.

Over the next few weeks, Kitts and Rattles became best friends. Sometimes, they'd sleep together, curled up on the blue couch. Sometimes, they'd lick each other, closing their eyes contentedly. When Rattles licked Kitts, she'd purr as well.

And they'd play. Rattles often initiated playtime. He'd clamber up onto the couch and begin nipping Kitts's tail. Typically, that didn't result in a response, so he'd work his way up to her nose or ears, nipping all the way. She'd wake up and bat him around a little. If she got too rough, he'd scamper off the couch and hide behind the drapes.

In spite of his frightening teeth, Rattles never hurt anyone. Randy carried the rat around in a big pocket, and Rattles sometimes stuck his nose out for a breath of fresh air. As a result, he startled more than one person.

After about three years, Rattles developed a malignant tumor on his face. Randy took him to a vet, who showed Randy how to lance the growth himself, a task that he had to do several times. Even then, Rattles never tried to bite. Eventually, we had to put him down because the tumor grew and began to interfere with his brain function. That was a sad day because he had become part of our family.

I had been wrong to think that two animals of different species, instinctive mortal enemies, wouldn't accept each other. Certainly, introducing these two animals to each other could have gone either way. Yet, they became friends.

Why can't we do that? After all, people are all the same species, except for some physical and cultural differences.

My life has become richer because of what I learned from the friendship formed between those two animals.

— Susan Cooper —

Wild Thing

11

The Uninvited Playmate

*Always the cat remains a little beyond the limits we try
to set for him in our blind folly.*
~Andre Norton

I t was finally spring, after a long, hard winter. Our three dogs galloped around the house acting delirious. And when our normally taciturn gray tabby, Sergeant Tibbs, scaled the couch, zoomed across the top of it and launched himself, flying-squirrel style, onto the back of our unsuspecting sixty-five-pound black Labrador dog, I knew it wouldn't be fair to sequester him in the house any longer. I worried about letting him outside, but our vet gave us the thumbs up. "You can't fight how God's designed him," she said. "When he's going nuts like that, you've got to indulge the poor guy once in a while."

The following morning, I slid open the patio door and called to Tibbs, who was in some secret location in the house going through his post-breakfast grooming ritual. Within seconds, he appeared like Houdini, slid across the kitchen floor and tore into the family room. But he screeched to a halt midway into the room. He eyeballed the open door and big, beckoning outdoors, and then gave me a this-is-too-good-to-be-true, so-what's-the-catch look.

"Come on!" I coaxed, waving him outside with my wholehearted approval. Tibbs sprinted across the carpet and through the open door into cat paradise. At the end of our patio, he stopped and looked back to make sure I wasn't pursuing him. Satisfied that I was keeping my word, he treated himself to a couple of pancake-flip rolls in the dirt to mask his cat scent and then bounded across the grass and disappeared over the block wall into the desert. "Have fun!" I called.

Inspired by Tibbs's enthusiasm to enjoy the gorgeous spring day, I decided it would be a good time to start working on my tan for our upcoming trip to Hawaii. Soon, I was garbed in my flowered bikini and armed with every expert tanner's supplies: comfy towel, water bottle, sunscreen, sunglasses, a watch to keep track of my scheduled flip time, and a juicy novel. Within minutes, I located a perfect spot on the patio, slathered up and stretched out, holding my book at just the right angle to shield my eyes from the sun.

Twenty minutes later, my watch timer indicated it was time to flip and work on my back. Since every experienced sunbather knows how to avoid embarrassing tan lines, I unhooked my top, slid the straps down, and lay facedown. Then I closed my eyes and let the sun-induced lethargy relax my body. It was nice. Tibbs had the right idea.

I wondered what cats like him did for entertainment on their spring outings. And then, ten minutes into my personal catnap, the wooden gate leading to the front yard slammed against its hinges.

It must have been Tibbs returning. I wondered why he was back so soon.

I sensed him race by me. "Hi, buddy!" I called out and waved at him without opening my eyes.

Then the gate thudded again. How did Tibbs go back out and come back in?

He raced by me again. By the time I managed to prop myself up several inches on my left elbow and crack open my blurred right eye, he was near my head, close enough to reach out and grab.

But it wasn't Tibbs. As I struggled to prop myself up higher, the strange, four-legged intruder realized the figure on the ground had moved. The animal froze mid-stride, one forepaw raised, tail stiffened in alert. Its blue eyes met mine before I made a quick visual scan. Tan body… Light black spots… Compact ears with black fur tufts… Black-banded tail. "Oooooh, aren't you a cute kit…"

Finally alert, my brain processed the situation in a nanosecond.

I let out a screech before yelling, "Bobcat! Oh, no! No, no, no!"

My heart pounded. I scooped up my top and leapt to my feet as my eyes searched frantically for Tibbs, who peered at me from around a corner of the house. The bobcat sprinted another several feet to come alongside Tibbs and then turned back to look at me — left arm pressing my unhooked bikini top to my chest, right arm flailing at Tibbs and the bobcat, back straps flapping behind me.

I pointed at Tibbs and yelled, "Stay right there!" Then I ran toward the bobcat, shrieking at him to vacate my property. After scurrying to the edge of the patio, the bobcat turned around to take another quick look at us. It seemed to be assessing whether it was going to confront the two-legged animal with the flailing limb and flapping straps to enforce his play date, or surrender the fun and go home. In one effortless leap, it sailed over our block wall.

I opened the patio door, and Tibbs shot into the house. Then I re-attached my bikini top, gathered my tanning supplies and strode in behind him. After dropping my items on the couch, I waggled my finger at him. "You're grounded. Indefinitely!"

When my son, Cory, returned from high school that afternoon, we laughed as I recounted the story. But when I got to the part where I theatrically described the feline's long, thick, black-banded tail, my arm froze mid-air, my mouth dropped open, and our eyes widened.

"Bobcats don't have long tails," Cory and I cried out in unison.

"Oh — my," I stuttered as reality registered.

Cory did a quick Internet search on his phone and handed it to me. "Did it look like that?" he asked. I stared at the screen. Tan body. Black spots. Compact ears with black fur tufts. And a long, curving, black-banded tail.

A photo of an adorable mountain lion cub. A little bigger than a large house cat.

I looked at Cory. He grinned at me, and his eyes sparkled in astonishment.

"Oh, my goodness." I shook my head. How could I have missed it? Although rare, mountain lions were seen occasionally in people's back yards in our mountain foothills neighborhood. When we had lived in

California, our country home sat in the middle of the mountain-lion migration path. It wasn't as though I'd never seen a cub in the wild before.

And I knew I could count on one thing: Where there's a cub, there's a mountain-lion momma. Quickly, I thanked Tibbs for not bringing her home, too!

After that, I didn't venture outside again — to sun or sit — without my three dogs. And Tibbs got a stern lecture about who he was allowed to bring home for a playdate, spring fever or not.

— Andrea Arthur Owan —

Shoe Bonanza

If a cat spoke, it would say things like,
"Hey, I don't see the problem here."
~Roy Blount, Jr.

Life was a whirlwind as my husband's time in the Navy came to an end. Preparing to move was stressful enough, but we also needed to put our townhouse up for sale. We met with a real estate agent and discussed how best to present our home. Matters of money and timing weighed heavily on my mind, but I worried foremost about our cats.

"Palom and Porom are completely indoor cats," I told the agent. "When these potential buyers are walking through our home, I'm really scared that someone will leave the door open. If they get out…" My imagination filled in the blanks.

She reassured me that she would flag the listing so that all the agents would know to be careful, and we could also post a sign on the door as a reminder. Even so, I was left ill at ease.

Palom and Porom were true Navy family cats. We adopted them as kittens from a shelter in South Carolina. We were dirt poor, but I was happy to live on ramen noodles and cake mix in order to afford our rambunctious tabby kittens.

Seven years later, the cats had already done one cross-country move from South Carolina to my husband Jason's new duty station north of Seattle. They had been my stalwart companions through two deployments. Palom was my vivacious, loud-mouthed buddy, the kind of cat who stuck his nose into every grocery bag and would jump five feet to rip tacks out of the wall. Porom was more subdued. She liked to hang out and cuddle, but she'd wallop her larger brother in order to commandeer the kibble at feeding time.

Palom and Porom weren't just pets to me. They were my family, and I knew they loved and trusted me. I couldn't let them down. I had to keep them safe.

I heeded the agent's advice, but I didn't simply make one warning sign about the cats. On every door leading outside, I posted, "INDOOR CATS! Please be careful that they don't get outside!" On the doors to bedrooms, I taped fliers instructing that the doors be kept closed so the cats didn't get in and become trapped.

A few days after our house was posted for sale, our agent called. "We're doing a big monthly meeting today with the company real estate agents in the area, and we're carpooling to visit our new houses. Can we come by? You don't have to leave."

A short while later, we heard a discordant symphony of car doors slamming. I looked at Jason, wide-eyed. "How many of them are coming?"

Real estate agents flooded our house, all attired in their business best. They all grinned, laughed and said "hello" as they entered and kicked off their shoes.

I stayed by the front door, and not simply to play greeter. I knew my cats. Porom would hide from the invasion, but not Palom. Not only did he love people, but he adored shoes and purses. As soon as the first visitors came in the door, he was there, yowling and rubbing against their calves. Then he proceeded to dive into their discarded shoes like Scrooge McDuck swimming through his money bin.

"I have never seen a cat do that!" said a woman, laughing as Palom rolled, writhed and wormed his way through five square feet of footwear. He bounded from shoe to shoe, nuzzling decorative bows and applying quick licks of inspection to laces and completely immersing his head in a select few shoes.

Instead of touring the house, a small audience gathered to watch Palom. That gave them a chance to see the sign I had posted inside the front door, too.

"Indoor cats only," said a man, nodding. "Good to know."

"What a sweetheart!" cooed a woman as she rubbed Palom's head. He yowled "hello."

"He acts like we walked in catnip!" said a fellow.

"How many cats are here?" asked another.

"Two. Both black tabbies. The other one is hiding," I said.

"Almost all cats hide when we go around in a mob to tour our listings." A woman laughed. "We usually don't get a welcome like this!"

They all completed their circuit of the house and returned to put on their shoes again. Within ten minutes, they were gone. Palom stayed by the door, sniffing and yowling in dismay at the absence of his precious shoes.

Over the next few days, we had more visits, this time with potential buyers. As I headed out into the driveway one day, a woman parked at the curb. By her crisp pantsuit, I knew she had to be an agent.

"Hi, you're the owner?" she asked as she shook my hand. "My clients will be here in a few minutes." She glanced at her clipboard and then back at the house. Her eyes went wide. "Oh. Oh! This house!"

"What?" I asked, suddenly alarmed. Why did my house have a reputation?

"This is the house with 'The Cat'!" She said it like a distinct name, and then laughed. "You know, we've been talking about your cat ever since we came by. We'll never forget how he went crazy for our shoes."

I grinned as I walked away from the house. Suddenly, I wasn't as worried about someone letting out the cats. Palom was famous! The agents wouldn't forget him anytime soon.

A few days later, we were delighted to get an offer for our house. I took down the door signs.

"You know," I told Jason, "I think only one member of the household is disappointed that we found a buyer so quickly." I motioned to Palom, who was lounging in a sunbeam.

Palom yawned and stretched out his front paws. The move would be scary and exciting for him — for all of us — but we would handle this change together, and he'd have all kinds of new smells on our shoes to enjoy soon.

—Beth Cato—

13

The Christmas-Tree Kitty

Taking down the Christmas tree makes it feel official:
time to get back to joyless and cynical.
~Greg Fitzsimmons

My five-year-old son came running frantically into the kitchen. "I can't find Zorro, Mommy!" I dropped my dishtowel to help in the search. Zorro was an indoor-only cat and did not know how to fend for himself.

Together, my son and I made a thorough search of the house, but still no Zorro. As my son grew closer to tears, and I edged toward his earlier panic mode, I remembered that we had decorated for Christmas the night before.

"Did you check under the tree?" I asked my son. He looked up at me with wide eyes, and then dashed into the living room to check as I followed him. Sure enough, we found a very sleek and elegant black-and-white gift underneath the tree. His green eyes blinked up at us with a look that could only be described as pure rapture. My son petted him happily, and we were relieved that the crisis was over — for the moment!

Despite all the colorful Christmas toys and stocking stuffers that our kitties received each year, Christmas for Zorro wasn't about the wrappings and tinsel, expensive presents and fancy feasts. It was about the artificial tree.

That year, I put away the tree a few weeks after Christmas, and I learned just how important our little tree had become to Zorro. After my son and I removed all the ornaments, we started to unfasten the branches. A restless Zorro seemed to guess what we were doing, and he lay down on the tree skirt, latching onto it with his claws and giving me the most pitiful look I had ever seen. I could almost hear his desperate pleas in my mind as he begged me silently with his eyes not to take away his "Christmas present." I wondered how it must seem to him, to think he had been blessed with such a wonderful toy, only to have it snatched away just a few weeks later.

We were moving that year, though, and I had no choice but to take down the tree. When it came time to put away the last fixture — the soft tree skirt — I attempted to distract the rather morose cat with one of his favorite toys. It didn't work. He simply lay there and stared at me. Then I tried calling him from the kitchen while shaking his favorite treat bag — a trick that always worked. It seemed he wasn't hungry for treats that day, as he held his ground fiercely.

Finally, I was forced to remove him physically from the red fabric — a dance of wills that left me struggling for breath and Zorro's claws eventually extracted from his beloved tree skirt. Quickly hiding it in the box where it would be stored, I dusted off my hands, relieved that I had accomplished my goal — for this year, at least. My son had enjoyed the intense battle between Mom and cat immensely, giggling the entire time. But we did not have the last laugh over the next few weeks, as we were forced to endure hateful glares and an extremely depressed cat who spent the majority of his time lying in the exact same spot where the tree had been.

Eventually, he seemed to forget about this major catastrophe — or at least chose to forgive us — as he gradually began to slip back into "normal cat" mode and found other interests, like pestering us for more attention or bossing the other cats around. When we moved not long afterward, his attention became focused on the huge changes in our daily schedule. He also no longer had a "tree spot" to lie on at our new place.

Eventually, Christmas rolled around again, and the first part of decorating for the holidays was, of course, the grand entrance of the tree box from the storage shed. Despite the fact that it had been many months and there had been many changes since he'd last seen this box, Zorro's ears perked up, and his eyes grew huge as he watched me carry the box into the living room. He sat down nearby to watch the proceedings while my son and I put the tree together and decorated it.

When we took a break, Zorro snuck over in his catlike way and proceeded to examine the tree. The ornaments were of little interest to him, strangely enough. It was the tree that had always intrigued him. Zorro chose a spot underneath the tree and claimed it for his own, lying there while we finished decorating, his face a picture of pure happiness. My son picked him up eagerly from underneath the tree as I added the final decoration — the much-loved and well-worn tree skirt. When the now-six-year-old placed him back down on the ground, Zorro ran over to the skirt and promptly curled into a ball, laying his little head on the fabric and looking like he had found a long-lost family member.

From that moment on, he became a permanent Christmas decoration. Whenever I was looking for him, my son would automatically run to the tree to find the soft, little Christmas present that was always underneath it.

When Christmas passed as swiftly as it always did, the time soon arrived to put away the tree. But when I dragged out the tree box to begin the proceedings, Zorro became almost desperate in his attempts to latch onto the tree and tree skirt. He looked so miserable and pitiful that I did not have the heart to take down the tree, and we decided to put the box back in storage and wait for a while.

That year, we left the tree up until Easter. Zorro didn't care which holiday it was, though. To him, Christmas was every day that the tree was there. To this sensitive, little cat, Christmas was about enjoying the things we have with a fierce intensity that sometimes defies all logic. He reminded us to take a step back and quit rushing through the holidays, something we all tend to do in our hectic lives. It didn't really matter if the tree wasn't put away by New Year's. In fact, it brought so much happiness to one caring heart that having a Christmas tree at Easter made perfect sense to us.

— H.M. Forrest —

14

Chicken Soup
for the Soul

"The Talk"

*Everything becomes a little different as soon
as it is spoken out loud.*
~Hermann Hesse

Through the fifty-eight years we have been married, we've had many dogs but only one cat. Our four-year-old daughter Karen discovered the cat in the neighborhood, apparently abandoned, and named him Tiger. We were in the process of moving from Kentucky to Southeast Georgia, and were feeling a bit guilty that our kids had to leave family and friends, schools and church buddies, to relocate to a place they had never seen. So when Karen asked sweetly, "Can we bring Tiger?" we agreed reluctantly.

Tiger adapted well to the new surroundings and even gained some weight. It was not long before we discovered that Tiger should have been named "Tigress" because she was pregnant.

One evening, we left our very pregnant cat at home while we went to church. We could tell she was restless, so we prepared a space in a bottom dresser drawer, putting in towels to make it comfortable for her in case she was making preparations for birth.

As we were riding in the car, our young son said, "I wonder if those kittens will look like me."

A little perplexed and not sure what he was thinking, I said, "Son, why would you think that?"

He replied, "Well, you said she would have to be with a male, and she's been with me more than anyone else."

I looked at my husband and said, "Perhaps it's time for 'The Talk.'"

It was Good Friday, and we had to get to church to prepare communion and all the other chores a pastor and his wife do, so we put off the discussion until later. Throughout the service, we thought about Tiger going through the stages of birth all alone, wondering and praying that she was okay and eagerly awaiting what we would find when we returned home.

Tiger was just fine. She was out of the dresser drawer, but close by as we all peered in to see the three little kittens snuggled together, seemingly doing well.

Not long after, my husband did have "The Talk" with our son. As parents, we learned not to assume our children understood our vague explanations — especially when it concerns how kittens come to be!

— Donna W. Adkins —

Daisy the Holstein Cat

When I play with my cat, who knows if I am not a
pastime to her more than she is to me?
~Michel de Montaigne

One summer afternoon, my husband and I took our younger son, Mike, to the Humane Society to visit the kittens and puppies. We stood at a window where a black-and-white cat was housed. She leapt around, pawing at the window as if to say, "Pick me! Pick me!" The name on the window read, "Sassy."

We already had Pepper, a seven-year-old gray cat.

"Can we get her, Mom? Dad? Please, please?"

We couldn't resist our nine-year-old's plea. The kitty came home with us that day.

We changed our new kitty's name to Daisy. We joked that she was our "Holstein cat" because her black-and-white markings looked like those found on cows.

Over time, standoffish Pepper accepted her. Daisy groomed Pepper, mothering the older cat. We'd find them asleep, snuggled in a small cardboard box. They enjoyed basking in the sunlight that beamed through the front door glass. Pepper's tags caught the sunlight and reflected on the carpet, catching Daisy's attention. She'd pounce on the light. Pepper would turn her head. The light would reflect elsewhere. Daisy would pounce again. Sometimes, Pepper looked at Daisy as if to say, "You're such an idiot."

While Pepper preferred her solitude, Daisy loved being around the boys and their friends, hanging out in the basement where they played video games or watched television. A load-bearing pole covered with carpeting became Daisy's exercise pole. She'd run around the basement and jump on the pole, climbing to the top, entertaining the boys and their friends. Sometimes, the boys would scratch the carpet on the pole, and Daisy would dash up and swat at their fingers.

She explored the basement, jumping up on the bar, going into the small bathroom, and nosing around the laundry room. She'd travel the areas as if on a quest. Then, just when the boys would be at the height of their video game, she'd jump up in front of the screen, disrupting their play. She climbed on their backs, going from shoulder to shoulder, making it difficult for them to maneuver the game controllers.

One evening, our sons, Joe and Mike, were in the basement watching TV when I heard, "Mom! There's a snake in the window well."

"A snake? How do you know?" I stood at the head of the stairs to the basement, listening.

"It's near the window."

Curtains covered the windows. How could they see a snake?

"We can hear it."

"Hear it? What do you mean?" I grabbed the flashlight and headed downstairs.

"There's a strange sound. Listen." Mike pointed to the ceiling.

I paused at the foot of the stairs. "I can't hear anything with that beeping going on. Turn off the game."

Grabbing a plastic grocery bag to capture the snake, I climbed onto a footstool near the window well. It was difficult to see.

I turned on the flashlight and peeked gingerly through the curtain. I saw nothing but a few spider webs.

I listened. Suddenly, a loud clanging echoed from the ceiling. "What in the world?"

Something was in the ductwork.

The sound grew louder and more frequent. I paused. What was making the noise? Could it be a snake like the boys suspected? Pepper had killed a few garter snakes and brought them home to show us. I told myself that, if it were a snake, it was probably harmless since rattlesnakes aren't prevalent in Omaha, Nebraska. It seemed too noisy to be a little garter snake. Was it a bull snake or rat snake? Maybe a hognose snake?

Harmless or not, the thought of capturing any kind of reptile repulsed me.

It was apparent my sons would be no help. They'd scooted to the edge of the couch. Joe had drawn a blanket up to his shoulders and Mike stared at me wide-eyed.

I took a deep breath and pointed the flashlight toward the spot where I'd heard the sound. An echo followed by a scratching sound startled me. I reached to catch my balance, nearly dropping the flashlight as I braced myself against the cold cinderblock wall.

The creaking grew louder and more intense as I aimed the flashlight toward the window well. My heart raced. The ductwork popped and echoed. The curtain moved. The snake was close. I leaned back, hoping it wouldn't drop from the ledge. With the flashlight still beaming toward the window, I saw something move.

I breathed a sigh of relief when a little white and black paw reached down, swatting the beam. "Daisy!" She'd seen the light and followed it, making her way to the window well.

We all laughed at the scare she'd given us.

When my husband got home from a late meeting at work, I said, "We're going to have to change Daisy's name to Python."

— Susan Grady Bristol —

Frankie and Squirrelzilla

You can't be friends with a squirrel! A squirrel
is just a rat with a cuter outfit.
~Sarah Jessica Parker

Frankie caught his first squirrel at 7:08 a.m. on a crisp October day. In a directly related incident, he released his first squirrel at 7:08:13 that same morning, after a brief but terrifying tussle involving claws, teeth, growling, yowling and possible squirrel karate. Looking back on that pivotal moment, it would probably have been best for Frankie to stick it out, lick a few wounds, and declare a victory, no matter how brief. Instead, he yowled in a most panicked way, banged through the pet door (dislodging a curious Chihuahua in the process), and hid under the bed. The squirrel never forgot this and developed a pattern of feline abuse.

I should explain that Frankie, a tabby, was born a runt and matured with minimal growth. When the squirrel incident happened, he was a year old and only the size of a large kitten. Not only did this incident stunt his growth even further, but he may have actually shrunk.

Frankie took the squirrel incident as a lesson to never attack anything bigger than him, and for the next year busied himself with stalking bugs and attacking dandelions. Meanwhile, I had taken to feeding peanuts to the squirrels, a fact I hid from Frankie for he would never have forgiven me. Actually, I was just feeding one squirrel because a particularly large squirrel with a bad attitude declared the backyard feeding area as his own, not even allowing other squirrels in the vicinity.

And woe be to the household pet who came too near; it would soon run away while the squirrel shouted squirrel obscenities from a low-hanging branch. The legend of Squirrelzilla was born.

Squirrelzilla was Frankie's declared nemesis, the undisputed champion of their encounter the year before. Whereas Frankie's size was stunted, Squirrelzilla grew to enormousness, at least by squirrel standards. Frankie avoided the feeding area (a picnic table) and the overhanging limb that the squirrel used as a guard post. The few times Frankie strayed, he was rudely threatened via angry chirps and growls from the squirrel.

I had never heard a squirrel growl like that, but this was no ordinary rodent. He had no fear and would come within a foot of me to get a peanut. My original intention was to try to hand-feed him, but after the growls I decided that we should forgo any actual contact lest he mug me for the remaining peanuts just inside the door. I suspected that he was only a missed nut away from being a man-eater.

But time heals all wounds, and even a squirrel fight eventually becomes a dim memory to a cat. While Frankie generally avoided squirrel encounters, he eventually decided to stand up for his right to snooze in the sunshine on the railing beside the picnic table. Squirrelzilla began to accept this arrangement grudgingly. Sometimes. But every so often, he would decide that Frankie should relocate and would lunge at him as if to charge. It worked. Terrified, Frankie would leap from the railing into the yard, seeking shelter under a nearby garage.

One day, though, Frankie decided that he'd had enough. I had long before decided that the safest approach was to throw peanuts toward the picnic table, and then run inside and watch through the windows. I also locked the door because one can't be too careful when dealing with rodents with bad attitudes. As was routine, the squirrel lunged from a few feet away, and Frankie leapt from the railing. But this time, he landed beside the picnic table and went no farther, instead looking up at Squirrelzilla from only a couple of feet away. Squirrelzilla took this as a great insult. He stood on the table, ignoring the nuts, and looked down at Frankie while chattering insistently. Their eyes locked. The katydids and crickets became silent. Then came the squirrel growls.

Still, Frankie refused to budge. It was on.

Squirrelzilla leapt over Frankie, clearing the cat's head by mere inches. But instead of retreating in fear, Frankie stuck up a paw, slapping the squirrel in mid-flight. I saw a look of utter shock on the rodent's face as the cat's paw connected. Squirrelzilla hit the ground, tumbled, and then in a reversal of past history, ran up the tree with Frankie right behind him. I could only see about ten feet up the tree from the safety of the window, but I was content in knowing that Frankie had finally made a symbolic stand against bullies everywhere, or at least this particular squirrel.

It didn't matter that Squirrelzilla was almost his size, had threatened him on numerous occasions, laughed at him to his face, or even cursed him in Squirrelese. An era of rodent bullying was ending, and I was there to see it. They remained out of sight for several seconds, and my only fear was that Frankie would climb so high in his pursuit of the rodent that I'd be required to rescue him later. I shouldn't have worried.

Falling chunks of bark were my first clue, and then I saw a panicked tabby scooting down the tree trunk at a speed I didn't think was possible while going backwards. The squirrel followed close on his heels. Frankie hit the ground butt first, bounced once, and then charged through our pet door, disappearing into the confines of the great indoors. Fearing an invasion, I blocked the pet door as Squirrelzilla stood just outside of it growling. I'm not exactly sure what he was saying, but I do know I couldn't repeat it in a family-oriented publication anyway.

I soon found Frankie under the bed in his safe space. He was terrified, but his close encounter had taught me an important lesson in life: Stand up to adversaries, but also know when to stand down. And never forget: Nuts will always be involved in life's trials and tribulations.

— Butch Holcombe —

The Midnight Shift

Cats are designated friends.
~Norman Corwin

Sitting alone in an empty lobby each night was getting increasingly boring and a tad lonely. As the residents slept in their condos above me, I sat downstairs at the front desk acting as a barrier between their resting heads and the hoodlums of the city. It was an effortless job in a quiet, posh neighborhood. I didn't see a human soul all night — neither in the lobby nor on the cameras.

All the action was outside. A rustle in the bushes. A shadow darting across the grass. Skunks, rabbits, and one big raccoon kept the outdoor cameras buzzing each night. More importantly, they kept me entertained.

No one knew why I chose this job. Friends were confused. "Do you sleep at work? Isn't it difficult to stay awake?" I had my reasons. I was single for the first time in twelve years. No kids. No major assets. The split was more civil than others. However, being on my own for the first time in over a decade was a harder adjustment than I anticipated. During the day, I was living the clichéd life of a newly single woman in her mid-thirties. I traveled to other continents for the first time. I started a new fitness routine.

During the night, though, life wasn't as rosy. I wasn't sleeping enough. The unfamiliar quiet hum of an empty apartment left me completely awake most nights. So I took this night job. It gave me the flexibility to travel, freelance, and avoid sleeping alone five nights a week.

One night, while watching the familiar neighborhood critters go about their nightly routine, I noticed the big raccoon waddle across the screen quicker than usual. A tiny shadow, half the raccoon's size, was giving it a scare. The raccoon waddled as fast as it could while this tiny shadow kept up just behind its tail. With a quick shimmy up the fence, the raccoon was gone. The sassy shadow slinked around the courtyard. I had to take a peek.

I opened the back door. Through the darkness, a slender black cat with the largest green eyes I'd ever seen glared back at me. "Hi, kitty!" I called out softly to the little feline trespasser. She (I always assumed she was a she) jumped into the bushes.

For the next few nights, I watched this stealthy black cat chase away all the usual animals. She did quite the job keeping prowlers off the property. Each night, I opened the back door and called out to her. Gradually, she became less startled by my voice and moved closer to the door.

Over the next few weeks, I became enchanted with this dark little night prowler and decided she needed a name. I called her "Midnight" to match her dark coat and solidify her status as my partner on this quiet overnight shift.

I started to leave little trays of cat food by the back door for Midnight. Eventually, she trusted me enough to sit near my feet and eat while I talked to her. She never let me pet her. She was feisty, and I respected that. We became hands-off friends.

One night, I saw the big raccoon steal the tray of food I had left for her. *She's gonna get him this time,* I thought. Within minutes, the giant raccoon speed-waddled past my window, and Midnight was right on its tail, swatting her little paw as the giant food thief shimmied up the fence.

After the raccoon disappeared, I put some cat treats at the back door and called her name. She ran over, gobbled the treats and ran away. She appeared briefly on the camera twenty minutes later and then disappeared again. I opened the back door. My heart swelled. A large, bruised crab apple was sitting on the ground where I usually leave her food.

I burst out laughing and looked around. There were no crab-apple trees on the property. I didn't know where Midnight found it, but I was charmed. She considered this human food. I took it as a "thank you" and a solid seal on our budding friendship.

After several months, Midnight stopped coming around. I was worried. She seemed too smart and quick to get hit by a car and too feisty to be caught by anyone. But anything was possible. I scoured the city's animal-shelter sites and lost-and-found animal pages. I asked around. No one had seen her.

Every night, I called out to her. Occasionally, a different cat would appear. I wondered if one of these cats had scared her off. But Midnight was the queen of the streets. She would've chased them all off in a heartbeat. The night shift became boring again without my little friend, and the lack of sunshine in my daily routine was affecting my overall mood. I decided it was time to find a job during the day and give life amongst the living a second shot.

The final days of my time at the posh condo came during an unusual warm snap in the middle of winter. I glanced out the window one morning as the sun started to rise and saw a little black shadow in the bushes. The shadow disappeared. The leaves rustled. Could it be? My expectations were low, but I opened the back door anyway.

"Midnight?!" I called out. I waited. Nothing. I knew it. I sat back down and stared at the bushes. They sat still, too. Moments later, a little black cat appeared on the cameras, slinking around the back door. I ran and opened the door. Staring back at me were those gigantic green eyes only one kitty could have.

"Midnight!" I squealed. I almost cried. Did she know I was leaving soon? Was this just the craziest coincidence ever? It had been months. I was so happy to see her. She was healthy. She was okay. Maybe she did have a family, after all.

I always kept a bag of treats in my locker, just in case. I poured a handful for her, just like old times. Quickly, she gobbled them up. I thanked her for coming to see me, as if she could understand. I tossed her a few more treats. She nibbled them quickly, gave me one last look with those giant green orbs and took off.

I had three nights left at the condo and didn't see Midnight again, but I felt better. I knew she was safe and getting by in this crazy world. She was my tough little sidekick during one of the more difficult transitions in my life, and it seemed that I needed her more than she needed me.

As my nerves got to me that first night of sleeping alone during the week, I thought of sassy little Midnight and that big raccoon. If she could get by in this crazy city, maybe I could, too.

— Leslie Silver —

Rascal

My daughter Sarah and her best friend Lauren were sitting in the back seat of my car. Both were four years old, and Lauren was coming to our house to play. Pulling into our driveway, I noticed something lying on the sidewalk. It was our cat Rascal, and he wasn't moving. A quick look in my rearview mirror assured me that neither girl had seen him. Wanting to keep it that way, I hurried them into Sarah's bedroom. Then I went and told my husband.

"Maybe he's just sick," I ended hopefully. "Would you check?"

After confirming my worst fear, my husband asked me what I wanted to do. "I don't know," I said. "Give me a minute."

Heading down the hallway, I couldn't stop thinking about how small and helpless Rascal looked lying on a cold, indifferent sidewalk. Then there was knowing I had to tell the girls. I went into my daughter's bedroom and sat down on her bed; both girls looked up. Choosing my words carefully, I said, "Girls, I have some sad news: Rascal has died. I think he was hit by a car."

"Let's take him to the vet," Sarah reasoned immediately.

"I'm sorry, sweetheart, but when an animal dies, the vet can't make him better. We're not going to see Rascal anymore. We'll miss him a lot."

"My grandpa died," Lauren said.

"Yes, Lauren, people die, too. But when people die, they're usually very old, like your grandpa."

"We had a funeral for my grandpa."

Having never been to a funeral, Sarah asked what it was.

"It's a way of saying goodbye when someone you love dies," I explained.

"Can we have a funeral for Rascal?" she asked.

I paused and then responded, "I guess we could have a funeral after the vet buries him."

"Can't we bury Rascal?" Sarah continued.

"Where?" I asked.

"In the back yard, in our flowerbed. That way, whenever we play outside, Rascal will always be with us."

"Hmmm, I think we should talk to Daddy about this."

My husband said he would bury Rascal, and while he was doing that, I kept the girls inside by suggesting we write a eulogy.

"What's a eulogy?" Lauren asked.

"It's when you write down loving memories about whoever died, and then you share those memories at the funeral."

"Let's write a eulogy," Sarah said.

Lauren nodded.

I helped the girls compose Rascal's eulogy. When we finished, I asked if they wanted to go into the empty field next to our house and gather rocks and wildflowers to place on Rascal's grave as a memorial. They did, and as I watched them from a distance, I thought once more about Rascal — how he looked so much smaller in death than in life.

"Everything's ready." My husband's voice interrupted my musings. I called the girls. We all drifted into the back yard, and there, amid tears of grief, we said goodbye to our beloved cat. After an appropriate amount of time, I ended the funeral by asking if anyone wanted a snack.

"We had food at my grandpa's funeral," Lauren said.

Patting her on the shoulder, I led the girls toward the back door. Just then, a faint mewing sound came from the garage. "What was that?" Lauren asked.

"It sounded like Rascal," Sarah answered.

"Meow." We heard another plaintive cry; this one came from underneath my car, Rascal's favorite hangout spot. With an uneasy feeling, I approached guardedly. Bending down, I stared into the darkness beneath the car. There, staring back at me, were two green-golden eyes. "Meow," said a tabby that could have been Rascal's twin. The cat crawled out from under my car. He walked over to the girls and began sidling in and out, around and through their legs, purring softly... just like Rascal.

"Rascal!" the girls shouted as the cat bolted out of the garage. Jumping onto the top of our fence, the ghost cat walked its perimeter, passing through each diamond opening, until he reached the corner post and leaped straight up into the air, landing surefootedly on top of our roof and strutting from one end to the other... just like Rascal.

"Rascal?" I asked aloud.

"Meow" was the cat's enigmatic response.

Could it be? Was it possible? Was this cat Rascal? And if it was, then who did we bury in the flowerbed?

We spent the rest of the day canvassing our neighborhood, knocking on doors and asking everyone we met if they were missing a cat, a tabby, one that looked exactly like Rascal... only a little bit smaller. No one was missing a cat, and to this day the mystery cat remains buried in our back yard. At least, I think he's still there, but sometimes I can't help but wonder if that age-old myth about cats having nine lives isn't a myth after all. Maybe, just maybe, cats really *do* have nine lives.

— Deborah Leandra —

Cat in a Box

The cat is the only animal which accepts the comforts
but rejects the bondage of domesticity.
~Georges-Louis Leclerc, Comte de Buffon

Rain. All day. All night. For weeks, sometimes months. It was late April, the beginning of monsoon season. As a young Navy wife accompanying her pilot husband to a base in southern Japan, I quickly learned what the term "monsoon" meant.

We lived off-base in a Japanese house overlooking rice paddies with a sweeping view of the Inland Sea. It was beautiful and quaint, but so cold when wet. The constant gray skies made the world look like an old black-and-white movie, and the cultural differences of Japan added a sense of the surreal. Within weeks, though, it took on a fairytale quality — all because of a cat.

We heard a mournful cry through the steady rain one evening not long after we settled in. At the front door sat a forlorn-looking, bobtailed, trying-to-be-white cat holding up its swollen and bleeding left front paw. My husband leaned down to look at it.

I hung back, not sure if the cat was rabid or feral or just wanting to sneak into the house. However, he seemed genuinely in need of attention and expected us to provide it.

As I watched the cat stare into Bill's eyes, I realized this had nothing to do with me. Cats have always come to my husband — not to live with him necessarily, but to be near him. How that cat knew we were living there was a mystery, but there he sat, unmoving, yowling off and on to make sure we didn't try to ignore him. There was little chance of that.

Gently, Bill checked the oozing paw. "It's infected." He shook his head. "We don't have any first-aid supplies."

He rummaged around the small house looking for something, anything that might work, while I stood guard at the door. Finally, he grabbed a bottle of mouthwash and a clean towel and returned to doctor the paw. I stepped farther back because I figured the stinging antiseptic was going to cause a real ruckus. However, the cat surprised me by accepting the treatment without a whimper. He didn't move except to lean away from us, seemingly reluctant to leave, yet showing an intense aversion to going into the house. We were at an impasse. We couldn't just leave him out in the cold rain.

"Ah. The crate!" Bill exclaimed suddenly.

"What crate?" I glanced at him quickly before returning my gaze to the cat.

Bill reminded me that the large wooden crate the Navy used to ship our refrigerator from San Diego along with our other household goods sat in the yard behind the kitchen waiting to be cut up and carted away. "Perfect," he said.

I nodded, a bit embarrassed that I had forgotten it was still there.

The cat stepped off the porch and followed us around the house through the mud and slick leaves. Then he watched as we stood the crate on end, open side to the front, and slid it under a tree. Back inside, I gathered some towels to use as bedding while Bill opened a can of tuna. As we returned to the back yard, I wondered if the cat would still be there — he was. We placed everything in the bottom of the box and stepped back. The cat sniffed the can cautiously, lapped a bit of the liquid, eyed the towels, and then curled up in the farthest corner, sheltered from the rain. We checked on him several times during the evening as he slept soundly.

He stayed there for days, and we began calling him "Neko San," Japanese for "Mr. Cat." He allowed Bill to check his paw regularly and treat it with the mouthwash. There was usually a fresh can of tuna for him as well! After a few days, Neko wandered through our yard, which let us know he was feeling better. It was almost as if he and Bill had a professional-only relationship.

Not a "rescue cat" in the usual sense of the word, Neko demanded to remain independent and free. He never pretended to be a loving cat, but acted like an appreciative one at times as he spurned our touch but sought our assistance and care. We learned that the Japanese in rural areas such as ours didn't even consider bringing their pets into the house.

After healing and abandoning his shelter, Neko San visited us occasionally, announcing his arrival with his signature yowl. He would clean himself casually with the healed paw to prove to us that he was healthy.

The big box remained in place under the tree behind our house until Bill's two-year tour of duty was over. Occasionally, we saw signs that other animals slept there, as well as the cat. Perhaps its existence was like a beacon that indicated animal-loving people lived there. We'll never know for sure, but I like to think so.

Sometimes, I wonder if Neko San relayed the information to them. He certainly communicated his needs to us. And he taught us that, despite being in a foreign land with distinct cultural differences, none of it mattered when it came to caring for and understanding others, whether animals or humans.

As we became familiar with our new off-base home and neighbors, we realized gradually that we are alike in our most basic needs and wants. We all seek shelter, food, and safety. No matter who we are or where we live, we crave love, face fears, and strive to care for our loved ones.

Language and cultural barriers drop away in light of those basic needs, and we find a way to overcome them in order to communicate with each other. It's been over fifty years now, and we still marvel that our understanding of our connection with people everywhere all began with our encounter with a loud and wily, independent and communicative cat.

— Jean Haynie Stewart —

Cat Karma

Time spent with cats is never wasted.
~May Sarton

I accidentally fed a cat treat to a senior citizen. I know I've let the cat out of the bag by admitting this, but it was not my objective to have the poor old fellow ingest the kibble. In hindsight, my intentions were good — for both the cat and the elderly man in question — although Pumpkin the orange cat would have been dismayed that one of his tidbits went astray.

It was my second year working at a retirement residence. I was the front desk administrator. I answered phones, collected rents and sold items from our shop. I was also asked to do everything from accounts payable to gardening. Seniors even asked if I would give them an enema! (Of course, I sent them to a qualified care aide for that request.)

In addition to my duties, if the kitchen staff had a shortage, I would be called in to help serve. On this particular day, things were very busy. I was greeting tours and trying to get payroll finished among other things. I already felt like I was herding cats when I was advised that the dining staff was down a person. I was asked to fill in over the lunch hour.

I recall hustling to help out so I could get back to my front-desk duties. For the noon meal, my role was to hand out spinach salads to residents as their first course. No sooner had I set down a bowl of greens in front of ninety-two-year-old Bill when he had the audacity to pinch my butt! I looked at him in shock. He looked at me like the cat who swallowed the canary.

It turned out that this particular senior had also very recently patted the rear end of a highly respected elderly "matron" who lived at the home. Her family was well regarded, as they ran the largest car dealership in town. The eighty-nine-year-old lady was up in arms with indignation over the violation of her person. She even threatened to sue the residence over the uninvited grope.

Thus, when word got to the managers that I was also the victim of having my behind dishonored, they were on high alert. My direct supervisor came to see me and asked if I was all right, but I shrugged off the incident. I understood that such inappropriate behavior happened at times when working with the elderly. My supervisor was relieved, and he said, "If it is any consolation, old Bill pinched my butt last week, too."

Now, enter Pumpkin, the resident cat of the seniors' home.

When hired at the residence, I was thrilled to discover a kitty was on premises. I truly considered this feline benefit a perk to my job.

While working, I watched sleepy, orange Pumpkin snooze the day away in the lounge chair. He was petted and fussed over constantly by residents and staff alike. At will, Pumpkin would simply go in and out of the building as people came and went. This frisky feline's life was definitely the cat's meow.

As I got to know this sociable orange tabby more, we bonded. When I arrived for work, Pumpkin would be waiting for me. I fed him low-sodium tuna or other gourmet, gravy-style cat food. In addition to this constant, tender loving care, spoiled Pumpkin got special kitty treats from me. My devotion to him was rewarded. Pumpkin now often slept on top of my desk.

To make him more comfortable, I purchased Pumpkin his very own kitty bed. He even acquired his own name tag that said, "Hello, my name is PUMPKIN." I suppose it was a form of preferential treatment, but I gave my furry friend the important job title of "Resident Relations."

Yet Pumpkin started slacking off on the job. Or maybe he went on strike? I'm not sure which, but Pumpkin became so attached to me that he decided the residents' laps were not nearly as good as the gig he had going with me at my office. It took time for me to realize it, but sassy Pumpkin had stopped mingling as much with our seniors.

One morning, a group of residents was sitting in the lounge, calling out in raspy, aged voices, "Here, kitty, kitty, kitty!" But lazy Pumpkin did not budge from his special spot on my desk. He was too content to sleep the day away right where he was. Finicky feline! I should have fired his furry butt on the spot, but Pumpkin was utterly protected by the union of my heart.

Yet I felt remorseful about Pumpkin now ignoring calls to be sociable and cuddly — especially to those who paved the way for our younger generations. To appease my guilt and remedy the situation, I walked quickly over to the residents and passed out cat treats. This was in hopes that Pumpkin would be food-driven enough to cease his cat nap and come visit the lonely seniors again.

No sooner had I passed out the last cat treat when I heard ninety-two-year-old Bill exclaim, "Hmmm… This tastes kind of blah." Speechless, I realized that the elderly man had eaten Pumpkin's food instead of giving it to the cat! Truly, the cat got my tongue.

So, yes, I fed a senior a cat treat. And it was to Bill, the same gentleman who liked playing cat-and-mouse by pinching people's bottoms!

As nervous as a cat in a room full of rocking chairs, I just couldn't bring myself to tell the old fellow what he ate. Instead, I offered him a mint candy to placate him, which he accepted gladly.

Funny, though, along with other adages, they do say, "What goes around, comes around." I wondered if old Bill had been given a little payback for his recent butt-pinching episodes. He had also told off the manager's mother the week before, rudely saying she could take her kind offer of giving him an umbrella and "shove it where the sun don't shine."

In the end, after placing me in such a predicament and for his newfound indolence, Pumpkin the cat never got that promotion to

"Manager of Resident Relations." He did at least go and visit the seniors when they had treats for him. To get the job done, if all else fails, bribery works. Sigh.... It is so hard to find good help these days.

— Irish Beth Maddock —

Here Kitty, Here Kitty

A well-balanced person is one who finds
both sides of an issue laughable.
~Herbert Procknow

As is often the case in my career as a Realtor, I was given strict instructions by the sellers: "Never let out the cat." Through numerous showings, I obeyed their instructions successfully. Then we had a buyer, and the home inspection was taking place. Five people were present: the home inspector, the couple buying the home, their Realtor and me. All of them were definitely cat people who petted and fussed over the cat. Even before we went inside, I gave them the dictum: "We must not let out the cat."

Everyone got busy and somehow, you guessed it, the cat got out. I was the only one who noticed and knew it was my responsibility to catch the cat. I went outside and saw him rapidly circling the house. It was impossible for me to run in the grass in high heels. I felt panic rising just when he decided to sit down at the end of the driveway. I crouched and coaxed in my most alluring voice, "Here kitty, here kitty," over and over again.

It seemed to be working. He crept slowly toward me. I was not a cat person, but I had this. *Stay calm and sound inviting*, I told myself. I was in luck as he got closer and closer. When he was close enough, I made my quick move, sweeping him up into my arms. I was so proud of myself and felt as if I'd won the Fight of the Century. I didn't even have any experience wrangling cats, and I had pulled this off. The cat

Wild Thing | 69

and I went back inside, and no one was the wiser. Another victory for this Realtor and another notch in my Top Producer belt.

The next day, I learned that I had put the neighbor's cat in the house. The owner's cat was still in hiding.

— Barbara S. Foster —

Chapter
3

Who Rescued Who?

The Cat No One Wanted

What greater gift than the love of a cat?
~Charles Dickens

I was hesitant when my niece called to ask if I would foster a pair of cats until she could find homes for them. My husband and I had already adopted several strays and felt we had reached our limit. Although we live in the country where there's plenty of room for our cats to roam, there are still quite a few costs involved in caring for pets.

"I found them in the hollow of a tree at the campground," my niece told me. "They're both declawed."

Immediately, I was swayed. Most cats can't survive in the wild without claws. They need them to hunt for food and defend themselves against predators. After consulting with my husband, we agreed to keep them temporarily.

When my niece showed up with two long-haired calicos, we were shocked to see how emaciated they were. At first, they were both skittish, but the male cat soon realized he was in a safe environment and overcame his fear. The female cat, on the other hand, dashed down the hall and disappeared into our son Benjamin's room, huddling against the far wall under his bed.

My husband named the male Sam and the female Hal (an acrostic for Hides A Lot). Though identical in appearance, Sam and Hal's personalities were as opposite as night and day. Sam was playful, curious, and affectionate. Hal was fearful, cautious, and aloof.

We placed posters on the vet's bulletin board. Within days, Sam found a wonderful home. Hal, on the other hand, wouldn't venture out from under Benjamin's bed other than to eat, drink, and use the litter box. No one wanted to adopt the sullen cat.

After almost a week, Hal finally ventured out to nap on Benjamin's bed while he was at school. But as soon as my husband or I entered our son's room, she would dash back under the bed. Gradually, she began to sleep with Benjamin, curled up next to his pillow — near enough to sense his presence, but not close enough to touch.

Almost two weeks after Hal arrived, Benjamin experienced a full-blown meltdown. Our son has high-functioning autism, also known as Asperger's. When his sensory issues trigger a meltdown, he goes to his room, lies on his bed, and covers himself with his favorite cat blanket to block out all sensory input. Unfortunately, it still takes a while for him to calm down.

Although he'd slammed his bedroom door, we could still hear him ranting about the unfairness of life. I was about to enter his room to check on him when his tirade stopped suddenly. It was as if someone had flipped a switch. Ear pressed to the door, I heard nothing but silence.

Carefully, I opened his bedroom door and peered in. Hal was lying on the blanket covering Benjamin. Our son's breathing was slow and regular. Spent after his meltdown, Benjamin had fallen asleep with the cat resting on his chest.

Over the next few weeks, we witnessed the same phenomenon happen every time Benjamin spiraled into a meltdown. As soon as he lay down in bed and covered himself with his blanket, Hal would settle on his chest and, within seconds, Benjamin would transition from agitation to complete calm. My husband and I had read about weighted blankets, which often help individuals with autism to relax and calm down. Now it seemed the cat was providing the same type of effect.

It soon grew quite apparent that Hal had come into our lives for a reason. The frightened, aloof cat has developed an unusual bond with Benjamin. She seems to sense his special needs and appears to have her own sensory issues to boot. She doesn't like to be touched, hates loud noises, and favors solitude over boisterous games with the other cats in our house. But none of that matters to Benjamin because he shares the same sensory issues.

Benjamin and Hal are best friends. When she's not eating or taking a walk around the garden, you will find Hal napping on Benjamin's bed, curled up beside his pillow, or lying on his chest when he's feeling stressed.

The cat no one wanted has blessed us beyond expectations. We gave her a home, but she has given our special son so much more.

— Renée Vajko-Srch —

Best Buddies

A meow massages the heart.
~Stuart McMillan

I t was Friday morning when I received my daughter's e-mail at work. "Mom, there's a new kitten at the shelter."

"How old?" I asked.

Within seconds, she replied, "Six weeks, I think. Name is Raven. Gray. There's no picture."

We'd spent the week going back and forth to this animal shelter looking for a kitten. In frustration the day before, we had decided to take a break from our search.

Clearly the break was over. I asked, "Do you want to go back to the shelter this afternoon?"

Immediately, she responded, "Yes."

It had been years since we had a pet. When my daughter was in grade school, our cat, Peanut, passed away. We all mourned, but it was worse for Kelsey. Peanut had been part of our family before Kelsey was born, and life with a cat was all she knew. For years, she grieved deeply.

Finally, we felt ready for a new kitten. We did our research and visited different animal shelters, but it wasn't easy. My daughter has an even bigger heart for animals than I do. So to see a cat frightened when we wanted to hold it, or to sense that a cat we liked was uninterested in us was emotionally exhausting.

The day we found Raven was different. This adorable, tiny gray kitten curled up in my daughter's lap, never making a sound. Kelsey looked up at me with tears in her eyes and said, "Mom, this is the one." But I already knew. I could see they were meant for each other.

Raven took to Kelsey immediately, the way a duckling imprints on a mother duck. For Kelsey, it wasn't as easy. I could see it before she said anything. After wanting a new kitten so badly, having Raven with us now seemed to make her miss Peanut even more.

Kelsey struggled. She loved Raven, but kept her at arm's length emotionally. In tears, Kelsey confided that she couldn't let go of Peanut. If she let Raven in her heart, it would be like taking Peanut's place. She felt guilty for loving Raven, but at the same time, she felt guilty for not loving her enough. I didn't know what to do or how to help her, but I prayed.

Raven just kept loving Kelsey. She followed her around the house and sat with her while watching television. When Kelsey needed some time alone, Raven looked for her and waited in the hallway until Kelsey opened her bedroom door.

One day, Kelsey told me she felt God nudging her. She explained that maybe she didn't have to let go of Peanut, but she could still move forward. Raven wasn't there to replace Peanut. She was there to love her and help Kelsey through her grief. I thanked God silently and kept praying.

Meanwhile, Raven kept trying to find her place. The unconditional love from a pet can be like healing balm on a wound, and Raven loved Kelsey unconditionally. Slowly, something began to change — a melting of sorts.

Kelsey started to respond to Raven with a little more ease. They snuggled together watching television, and Raven let Kelsey hold her like a baby. Every day, more selfies were taken, which she would e-mail to me at work. Raven slowly but surely worked her way into Kelsey's heart, and Kelsey let her in.

They are now best buddies. Some days, they are inseparable. Other days, they get on each other's nerves, just like real family members. But, no matter how their day went, I always find them cuddled together by evening.

We still talk about what led us to find Raven at the shelter that day and how God worked through one tiny kitten to begin the healing process. Raven needed her forever family, but for so many reasons, I know Kelsey needed Raven even more.

— Laura Rath —

BeBe's Last Blessing

Who hath a better friend than a cat?
~William Hardwin

I wasn't thrilled about shopping on that busy Labor Day weekend. However, my darling daughter had convinced me that she needed a few more outfits to begin her freshman year of high school in style.

Hours later, exhausted from walking miles through the malls, I looked forward to a quiet night. However, when we were stopped at a red light on our way home I caught sight of a massive man, laughing and screaming as he hosed down a little waif of a cat.

Without thinking, I turned into his long driveway, got out of my car and told my daughter to lock the doors. I'm not sure where my strength came from. I had survived an abusive marriage, but I still feared a man's strength. Yet here I was, standing in front of a huge man, who was tormenting a mother cat while she tried to rescue her kittens.

"What are you doing?" I shouted at this heartless giant.

"Getting rid of a mangy cat and her kittens," he said, laughing hysterically. Then, with a threatening tone, he screamed, "Get off my property before I turn the hose on you."

Our eyes met, and I never flinched. It was a defining moment for me, but as a single mom who had fought to protect her child, I felt that mother cat's desperation. I confronted not only this cruel man, but also my personal fears.

Taking a deep breath, I said calmly, "Please put down that hose.

I'll take the cat and her babies if you give me two weeks to rescue her."

After an uncomfortably long pause, he dropped the hose and gave me an ultimatum. "You've got your two weeks. One day more, and I'll finish them off." I thanked him quietly. I had no clue how to handle a rescue, but watching this precious mother cat hide her babies in the old tires on this man's property gave me confidence that I could.

My neighbor and dear friend was a pro at cat rescues, and she volunteered to help us. That night, we returned to the darkened property to put our plan in place. With flashlights and opened cans of tuna left strategically by the old tires, we waited patiently to lure the mama cat to us.

It didn't take long for the spirited mother cat to run across the lot. She was barely able to stay upright as she raced from the diner next door with a slice of pizza in her mouth. She placed it gently near the old tossed tires and called to her babies one by one. The kittens slowly crawled out and she cleaned their faces. Ignoring our tuna, she took a few bites of the pizza and then stepped aside and stood guard as her four kittens devoured it. After they ate, she played with her babies and then led them back to the old tires, placing each one carefully inside.

Then she saw us. Without any trepidation, she trotted over as though she knew us, as though we were neighbors visiting. She was a tiny cat, no more than seven pounds, with uneven tiger stripes, but a captivating personality and hypnotic, green eyes. With a tilt of her head, she shared her story vocally. After witnessing her abuse, I was amazed at how she trusted us.

This scenario continued to the very last night of the second promised week. That night, I found myself driving home from a junkyard with a mother cat, now christened BeBe, and her four kittens.

God had sent us a blessing at the perfect time. My divorce had been brutal, exposing the scars of physical and emotional abuse from my marriage. I no longer believed in others or myself. But this little abused cat showed me how to trust again.

BeBe always knew when I needed a kiss to wipe away a tear or a happy cat dance to share a moment of joy. She was my brave protector, insisting I follow her as we walked through dark, creaking corners of my house. When nightmares awakened me, she would join me patiently in bed until I was able to sleep.

She seemed to know all my thoughts, and she knew when I needed to relax. I had installed chimes on her favorite windowsill, and when I heard their melodious ring, I knew BeBe was inviting me to take a break from the pressures of the day. I would sit next to her, calmed by her soothing purr, and watch the seasons come and go through her window.

For twenty years, we shared a special love for each other as we grew old together. Her children matured as my daughter did, claiming their own pathways and growing independent from their moms.

In her own courageous way, BeBe let me know when it was time to say goodbye as well. On a clear and crisp winter day. I scooped up my precious little mama cat, wrapped her gently in her favorite worn blanket, and drove her to the veterinarian's office. With my last kiss, I held her close to my heart, thanking her for all the blessings she gave us. She took her final breath in my arms.

Returning home that day with her empty carrier and my empty heart, I felt lost. Life would never be the same without my precious BeBe. No more blessings from a little cat who believed so much in life. Then, miraculously, I heard the chimes inviting me to her favorite place to rest. As I stood in front of BeBe's window, I caught the reflection of a woman staring back at me. She was strong, confident, trusting and loving, ready to take on the world. And then I realized that BeBe's last blessing would stay with me forever: it was my restored belief in myself.

— Lainie Belcastro —

Speed Bump

You learn something every day if you pay attention.
~Ray LeBlond

For weeks, I checked the shelter website daily to see if her photo was still there. I had mixed emotions every time I began scrolling through the photos. I always hope that animals at shelters are adopted into loving homes. But this time, in my heart, I wanted our home to be the one this adorable cat moved into. If her photo was gone, I'd always wonder what happened to her. I'd also feel terrible knowing I didn't follow my heart and adopt her.

I didn't need to adopt another cat. It hadn't even crossed my mind until I saw the picture of this precious cat with short legs and an imploring expression that tugged at my heart. With all her cuteness, I was certain she would be adopted quickly. I was wrong. I'd been checking the website for at least two weeks, and she was still there. I knew her time was limited. When I couldn't resist the temptation to adopt her any longer, I called the shelter and told them I'd be there the following morning to adopt her.

My husband and I were at the shelter when it opened the next day. As we were walking to the area where the cats were kept, the shelter employee told us he stopped by every morning to visit with the cat we came to adopt. He described her as a real sweetheart.

As we approached her cage, it was easy to see why he started each morning with a visit to her cage. She wasn't bashful about wanting attention. As soon as the cage door was opened, she stepped right into

Who Rescued Who? | 8

my arms and secured a permanent place in my heart. Needless to say, she never returned to the cage.

After we brought her home, I decided to name her Smores. Her coat had all the colors of a s'more, and she was indeed a sweet treat. I soon realized that I should have named her Speed Bump, instead.

Smores came into my life at a time when every day seemed overly hectic. I felt rushed and overloaded with obligations. Smores brought a change to my daily routine. She made it impossible for my mornings to begin in their usual hurried manner. As soon as I got out of bed, she insisted I stop and pet her for a while. Just like the shelter employee, I couldn't disappoint her. She slowed down my morning routine just like a speed bump slows traffic. From the day of her arrival, Smores began creating beneficial "speed-bump moments" for me.

I have health problems and my husband had been trying to get me to take better care of myself and rest periodically throughout the day. Smores solved that problem. She has become my motivation for slowing down and taking breaks. She seems to sense when my energy level is getting low or my pain level is intensifying. During those times, she vocalizes her desire for attention or paces back and forth from me to the chair I typically sit in when reading or relaxing.

I used to put relaxation and quiet time at the bottom of my priority list. Days often ended without me ever getting to that last item on the list. Smores took care of that. The day we brought her home, she needed grooming desperately. Although I wasn't sure how she would react, I sat her on a footstool, talked to her softly and brushed her hair for a long time. She loved it. Every day since then, she has jumped onto that same footstool and waited for me to brush her hair. Brushing Smores is never at the bottom of my priority list. That time we spend together is calming and soothing for both of us. That's just one of the ways that Smores acts as the speed bump I need to reset my daily routine to a manageable pace.

I was mistaken in thinking I didn't need another cat. I needed help in getting my out-of-control days under control. I needed motivation to slow down and stop pushing my body beyond its limits. Smores helps me with those needs. I'm certain Smores and I experienced a dual rescue. Living with us, she receives the love and attention she desires and deserves, and I have a lovable, furry speed bump to keep my days from getting out of control.

—Veronica Bowman—

Mocha

Beauty is not in the face; beauty is a light in the heart.
~Kahlil Gibran

everal months after my mother passed, and with more animals than I really needed, I was definitely not looking to adopt another pet, especially not another cat. But Mocha was different, completely unlike anything I, or anyone else, had ever seen. And she was only a couple of days away from being euthanized when I adopted her.

I always say she was the best rash decision I ever made, and I make a lot of them when it comes to animals in need. Mocha was normal when I first saw her, with wide eyes staring at me from behind the bars of a kennel. She was cute and sweet, so I didn't pay much attention to her, convinced she'd be adopted in no time. I had no idea how wrong I'd be.

Mocha grew into her deformities like most people go through puberty—fast and ugly. At first, we at the Humane Society thought she had injured herself in the isolation room, but it soon became obvious that something wasn't right with her. Honestly, if she had started barking like a dog, I don't think anyone would have been surprised. Her wide eyes became bug-eyed and watery; her severe overbite gave her vampire teeth; and her soft fur began to fall out in clumps. Suddenly, she had my—and everyone else's—full attention.

No one knew what was wrong with her, not even the many vets I took her to. She was ugly and had problems, and it was suggested, strongly and repeatedly, that I have her euthanized. Luckily, I'm known to be very stubborn, and I became determined to look after her.

She was only about two months old when I adopted her, but she was very smart and well behaved. Her favorite place to sit was on my shoulder, and she would climb up my shirt to perch there like some disturbing parrot, something she had learned from the other kittens she had become friends with. But unlike them, she stayed there and watched everything and everyone. She even allowed me to place a harness and leash on her. It had started as a joke to have a cat on a leash, but Mocha enjoyed going to pet stores and riding in my car with me. I became known around town as the girl with the cat on her shoulder.

Many people would stop me and ask what kind of animal she was. A monkey? A lemur? There was no way she could be a cat. There were a few wary, and some disgusted, looks sent her way, but most people were charmed by her unique appearance and by the person who adored her. I was complimented many times simply for choosing to have a cat like her in my care, as if I had to be extraordinary just to give her a chance.

Mocha never cared. She was happy and relatively healthy. She demanded her usual breakfast of mushed canned food every morning at six, and the same meal at lunch and supper. Almost every night, she'd curl up in my arms and under the blankets.

For some reason, I began counting down to her first birthday. I was warned that she'd have a short lifespan, and that she probably had a heart condition, but a part of me believed we could prove them all wrong as long as she made it to a year. It sounds silly now, but I was very attached to her and willing to hope. More than anything, though, I was determined to give her the best life I could.

Slowly but surely, a year passed, and her birthday arrived on a rainy day in March. She wore a small birthday hat that was still too big to fit properly, and everyone pitched in to wish her a happy birthday although the rain kept us both from socializing.

Two months later, I knew something was wrong when she let me sleep past six and refused to get out of bed for her breakfast.

I buried Mocha just as the sun was setting beneath our favorite tree, and I stayed before the freshly dug grave until I was alone in the darkness. It may sound strange, but it was as if I was getting the news of my mother's death all over again. It felt like that same heartbreaking moment when nothing made sense, and I couldn't go back inside and pretend that nothing had changed. To many, she was just a cat, and not even a pretty one, but I had lost my best friend.

Mocha had come into my life right when I needed her the most, when I was still struggling to return to my normal, everyday life in the wake of losing my mother. But I had this idea that if I loved her enough, if I did everything right, then I wouldn't lose her. I know that things don't work that way, but part of me didn't want to admit it.

Mocha used to look up at me like I was the best thing that had ever happened to her. The amount of overwhelming love I felt from that tiny cat was incredible. I still feel it now when I think about her, show people her picture, and talk about her like she was the best thing in the world. Because she was. It's been over a year, and I still hold her memory close to my heart. I'll always be grateful for that rash decision that brought us together. In the end, she was the one rescuing me, and I'll never forget her.

— Ashley Ledlow —

27

Jimmy Carter McGill

*There are few things in life more heartwarming than to
be welcomed by a cat.*
~Tay Hohoff

Jimmy Carter McGill had just passed his behavioral evaluation, the final step to being approved as a therapy cat in the College of Veterinary Medicine's HABIT (Human Animal Bond in Tennessee) program at the University of Tennessee. *Wow*, I thought, *I'm so glad I finally said "yes" to this little fella.*

Jimmy, named after the former president and my favorite TV character, had wandered through the woods into my friend's yard one cold March evening and parked himself, emaciated and shivering, on her stoop, insisting she let him in.

"Betsy, I think I have your cat," read Celeste's late-night text.

"No, you don't," I replied. Still raw from the death of my seventeen-year-old cat Phoebe six weeks earlier, I was in no mood to accept a "replacement" for my sweet girl.

Phoebe's passing threw her eighteen-year-old sister, Maggie, into a grief that manifested as aversion to the litter box and loss of appetite.

Additionally, my brother was losing his battle with cancer. I had enough going on emotionally; the answer to Celeste's implied question was a resounding "No!"

But Celeste was not deterred. Her second text that Monday night included pictures of a skinny, gray creature standing at her feet, looking up with an attitude that plainly begged for some nurturing. Her third text brought the news that it was declawed and a female. Surely, someone was missing this poor thing!

During the next few days, Celeste and I hashed over what to do about this cat. "Skinny Gray Stray" lived in the comfort and safety of the apartment attached to Celeste and Bob's house while I coached her through cat-feeding and litter-box issues. Celeste felt sympathetic to the little gal, but she and her husband are dog people, and she felt sure their six-year-old Misty would not take kindly to this feline intruder in her domain.

I, too, felt sympathetic. But I just didn't have any room in my heart to take on another emotional project. Besides, I was deeply concerned for my ailing Maggie and couldn't imagine diverting any of my love and time nursing Maggie through her old age to bring a young whippersnapper into our home. Maggie and I had our routines. It hardly seemed fair to her to upset those comfortable routines at this point in her life.

Celeste's efforts to identify Skinny Gray's owner proved fruitless. Apparently, for whatever reason, no one was looking for her.

Finally, I agreed that when I went to Celeste's later in the week for a church meeting, I would bring my cat carrier and take this sad, homeless critter to my house — just to have my vet check her for a microchip that might lead us to her owner. I could set her up in my guest bedroom with water, food and a small litter box for a few days. Maybe Maggie wouldn't even notice. And, hopefully, fingers crossed, the scanner would find a chip, and Skinny Gray would be reunited with her family. If not, well, I would take her to the local no-kill shelter to be adopted. End of story.

Toward the end of our Service Team meeting Thursday night, Celeste brought Skinny Gray in from the apartment. Clearly delighted by the attention, she darted from person to person, rubbing against legs and presenting herself to be petted. Several times, she jumped up into laps and even onto the back of the couch to get closer. She was even skinnier than she looked in Celeste's texted pictures. But she was a lovely silver-gray and had a sweet face. In fact, she looked a lot like my Phoebe.

On Saturday morning, the techs at my vet's office—who had endeared themselves to me with the loving, gentle care they gave Phoebe during the last few months of her life—"oohed" and "aahed" over this visitor. "How pretty!" exclaimed one. "This is a very loving cat," observed another. "You're keeping it, right?"

I had to admit their observations were accurate. She was pretty—or could be with a little proper nourishment and a serious dose of TLC. And during the couple of days since I had brought her home from Celeste's, I noticed how friendly she was. As much as I loved Phoebe and Maggie with all my heart, this cat was sweeter than either of them had ever been!

"No… no, I just don't see anything," my vet said, putting down the chip scanner. "And, you know, I think this is actually a male," she announced, doing a bit of exploring while a tech held Skinny Gray upside down. "Yep, this cat is a neutered male. Judging by the condition of his teeth, he's three or four years old. You are going to keep him, right?" she asked, handing the cat to me.

"Well… um…"

Neutered. Declawed. Skin and bones. Out in the cold for who-knows-how-long. And nobody looking for him. I sat in my car in the parking lot and started sobbing uncontrollably.

There is just too much pain in the world, I thought. Phoebe was gone. Maggie was fading fast. My brother was dying. And now there was this pitiful, little thing that somebody must have cared about at one time, but apparently no longer did. What would become of him? And sitting there in the parking lot, cat carrier buckled into the passenger seat and Skinny Gray meowing at me, I started talking to Phoebe through my tears.

"Phoebe," I sobbed, "I just don't know what to do! I miss you so much, and you will always live in my heart. Maggie, too. But this sad, little thing has shown up in my life, and…"

"Well," the snarky Phoebe-voice in my head retorted before I could finish my thought, "I sent you that cat!"

Oh. Oh! Oooohhhhh! That settled it.

By the time Jimmy Carter McGill and I had completed the half-mile drive home from the vet's office, I had his name figured out.

Celeste had been right; she did have my cat.

Two weeks after I adopted JCM, my brother died. Six weeks later, Maggie's body was shutting down, and I made the heart-wrenching decision to have her put to sleep. I was plunged into a depth of grief I had never known before.

Then one Friday afternoon at the end of a trying week at work, I took Jimmy to my office so my co-workers could meet the new little man in my life, whose saga — and mine — they'd lived through with me. Their sheer delight in him reminded me how wonderful it feels to bring happiness to others. I felt joy for the first time in many months.

Now Jimmy and I visit nursing facilities as a HABIT therapy team, where we comfort patients whose broken bodies are mending. It's a win-win-win situation: Jimmy has a home. The patients get a few moments of distraction. And bringing healing to Jimmy's life and theirs is slowly healing my heart, too.

I'm so grateful this miraculous cat wandered into my life.

— Betsy Boyd —

28

Feline Premonitions

Cats are mysterious kind of folk — there is more
passing in their minds than we are aware of.
~Sir Walter Scott

We were celebrating because my spouse and I had both just landed dream jobs at a NATO air base in Europe. We would be working in Aviano, a small town in northern Italy with a large military presence. The climate was warm and pleasant enough that cats thrived there, often seen in the back alleys slurping spaghetti fed to them by kindly grandmas.

While house hunting, we stayed at a quaint hotel in town, where the delicious food was amazingly cheap, the staff was cheerful, and espresso coffees and cappuccinos from the café gave us a delightful jolt to perk up our day. A glass of wine after evening dinners on the restaurant terrace was a wonderful way to end our workdays. It was paradise.

We were so enchanted with the hotel that we were thrilled when we found a house to live in right across the street. Living so close by, we could continue to enjoy everything that the hotel had to offer. We rarely made coffee at home after that, preferring to enjoy the fine brews at the café instead. We loved getting to know the local folks as we eased into the Italian lifestyle.

Not long after we had settled into our new home, we accumulated a band of felines at our house. Cats can readily identify cat people, so when a pregnant female had her litter in our woodshed, our kitty family was born. Other ragtag strays joined them, and we had a dozen cats in our family group before long.

The stray cats became extremely attached to us, with several of them tagging along as we crossed the street to the hotel to have a coffee and croissant in the mornings or a pleasant dinner in the evenings. The animal-friendly staff welcomed our cat escorts, while spoiling them with snacks and plenty of fresh water to drink. The hotel guests found it fascinating and joined in by pampering the felines.

The cats enjoyed the attention so much that they started taking the lead as we went through our daily ritual of having meals and snacks at the hotel. While they trooped in front of us, we started to notice that they would take a curved route to traverse the street, instead of going straight across. At first, we didn't realize what they were up to, so we didn't pay much attention. But as time passed, the curved pattern they walked became more pronounced and noticeable. Instead of walking directly across the road, they would walk off to the left or to the right, curving back in to finish up at the hotel terrace. Going home, the same thing happened in reverse. We were stumped but intrigued.

Time passed, and the route the cats took to the hotel terrace became even more circular. They walked a half-circle outline going across the street to the café and another half-circle going back home. It was becoming very odd. We kept trying to figure out why the cats wouldn't go straight across the road. Soon, we made a game of it, giggling as we followed the spherical route that the cats took to the restaurant terrace, and then back home again.

Over dinner one evening on the terrace, while relaxing and enjoying ourselves, watching the world go by, we were shocked by an unbelievable explosion as a passing car disappeared into a cloud of dust right before our eyes. Running to the road with other dining guests, we found ourselves looking into a gaping hole, about six feet deep, with the car crumpled inside it. It was a sinkhole, collapsing in the very spot our cats had been circling for months. We now realized that they had detected the anomaly and had been avoiding it, thus leading us around it, too.

The emergency services personnel later told us that a leaking water pipe had caused the earth to erode under the street, leading to the sinkhole that collapsed the road. Somehow, our brood had sensed the danger. Happily, no one in the car that fell through was gravely injured.

Back home, we congratulated our feline family as we rewarded them with extra treats. Their intuition about that imminent disaster reminded us to trust their instincts, as well as our own in the coming days.

— Sergio Del Bianco —

29

Flower

*Who among us hasn't envied a cat's ability to ignore
the cares of daily life and to relax completely?*
~Karen Brademeyer

The phone call came late at night. A friend of mine was reaching out about a stray cat that was "in pretty bad shape and really needs a home." I quizzed my friend for more details, only to discover that the injured cat was female, Siamese, declawed, and scared. She'd been found almost unconscious in someone's back yard. Without hesitation, I said, "Bring her to me."

A week later, I met my new cat after she spent several days recovering at the vet's. From the moment we made eye contact, there was a connection. Within a few minutes of being in her new home, she found her way into my arms and fell asleep for hours. The next morning, my friend called to check on her and asked, "What did you name her?"

I looked down into her beautiful blue eyes and said impulsively, "Her name is Flower."

"Flower?" my friend repeated. "That's a strange name for a cat."

"No," I said. "It's perfect for her. She's a little damaged, but she's adorable. All she needs is a little love."

Flower became attached very quickly. She didn't want to leave my side. I became worried that she was suffering separation anxiety when we were apart. I took Flower to my vet for a checkup and to get some advice. There, the vet shared with me just how badly Flower had been treated. She had burn scars on all four paws, her tail had been broken twice, and some of her teeth had been knocked out. I was overwhelmed with emotion, angered and saddened by the cruelty my sweet cat had endured. She had probably never been loved by a human before.

"This is why she's so attached to you," the vet explained. "Many Siamese bond with one human in their lifetime. For them, the bond is quite intense. Given that you rescued her and are taking care of her, she might be afraid of losing you." The vet gave me some techniques that might lessen Flower's anxiety, most of which worked over time.

Before Flower and I found each other, I had allowed my life to become pretty hectic, putting work above everything else and never taking the time to enjoy the world around me. It seemed impossible for me to be present in the moment. Yet, I soon found myself anxious to get home and sit with Flower on the sofa. No longer was busyness appealing. I wanted to spend time with my cat, and she wanted to spend time with me.

I thought about the horrible experiences Flower had gone through before she was mine, and how she was still willing to trust and love. I couldn't help but be impressed and inspired by her resilience. She was a survivor in the truest sense of the word.

I soon realized how affectionate Flower was. She loved to cuddle and rub noses, and insisted on being kissed on the top of her head whenever the need struck her. I discovered what food and treats she preferred, what toys she loved, and the quirky traits that made her unique. In other words, Flower and I became best friends.

Now, a year later, Flower has taught me the importance of slowing down and taking the time to enjoy every moment. No longer am I rushing from place to place, completing endless tasks or speed-walking through life. Instead, I'm enjoying quiet moments with my beautiful Siamese Flower, who has taught me the importance of stillness and love.

— David-Matthew Barnes —

30

Healing in the Company of a Cat

A beating heart and an angel's soul, covered in fur.
~Lexie Saige

I felt the familiar uneasiness that always accosted me when around homeless animals. The meows to get my attention echoed out of the cages, but I didn't take my eyes off the volunteer who was describing the shelter's money woes. Although I was usually the one to cave in and bring home a needy critter, this day was different. I was an emotional wreck. Since the untimely death of my daughter six months earlier, I hadn't gotten my footing. The reality that someone I cherished could be taken away was causing me bouts of fear and anger. Bringing more life into my life was the last thing I wanted. I was only at the shelter to drop off stuffed animals and books to be sold in their thrift shop.

"I hope these items will sell," I said to the volunteer. "My daughter would be pleased to know her things are being donated for a good cause."

"They're just perfect," she said, no questions asked. "And thanks so much for helping us out."

The mewing echoing through the converted barn was beginning to bother me, so I said my goodbye and turned to leave. And then it happened — a gentle, feather-light touch came from the cage behind me. A faint mew whispered in my ear. Holding my breath, I flashed a quick look toward the volunteer, hoping she had missed the encounter and praying she wouldn't feed my weakness with a sad kitty tale. I exhaled in relief when I saw her with her back to me, pricing donations. But now the touch became a tapping on my shoulder, and although I remained still as a post, I caught sight of a fluffy gray paw and pale pink pads out of the corner of my eye. Then came another delicate mew. I stood there urging my body to push onward — and then I melted there weeping as a fragile gray waif chose me, with my fractured gray spirit.

Outside the shelter, I zipped my jacket around the kitten, who nestled tightly against my chest. "Now what?" I said out loud. The low buzz vibrating from inside my jacket calmed me, but as we got closer to home, reality kicked in. I would have some explaining to do. "Our house is so busy with kids and critters. Maybe Jim won't even notice," I reasoned out loud to no one.

My husband Jim was stretched out on the couch in the family room, the back of his head deep into the green plaid corduroy pillow, newspaper arms-length in front of him. "Hi, babe," I mumbled as the cat and I entered the room.

"Hi, yourself, sweetie," he replied. "Did you do okay at the shelter?"

I slid the kitten out of my jacket without answering and tucked it in the bend of my arm like a tiny football. I lowered myself to the hearth on the side of the couch right behind Jim's head. Then the kitty plopped onto the red brick hearth and leaped onto the green plaid couch pillow. He rolled down over Jim's shoulder, landing on all fours right in the center of his chest. The two were nose to nose when boys and dogs tumbled in. Their surprised faces went from kitten to Dad to me and back to the new wee critter.

"You'd never believe the story…," I began, and then our younger son chimed in.

"Can I name him? Please, Mom."

In the silence that ensued, our little boy's eyes showed a hint of their old sparkle. We hadn't seen much of it since we had lost his sister.

"I think that's the perfect job for you," Jim acquiesced. "You're in charge of naming."

Our newest family member was dubbed Cooshie, and his rehabbing of me began immediately. That evening, as sleep again eluded me, a new comrade curled quietly in my lap, a friend who provided acceptance when others had grown weary of my isolation and anger. I resisted the urge to push him away as I had everyone else. Instead, I chose to stroke his little gray body. And with the simplicity of that connection, my recovery journey was set in motion.

Cooshie meshed well with our other pets and genuinely liked his human family. He curled on Jim's chest, and supervised homework and the construction of Lego skyscrapers. But he stayed clear of my inane daytime busywork. It was at night, when my heartache was its worst, that Cooshie would seek me out. Plunking down in my lap, he'd place a paw on my arm and tap me the way he had at the shelter. The light strike of his paw would continue until I acknowledged his presence. Then he'd curl up in my lap, looking into my face.

This nightly exchange kept me linked to the present. And in those vulnerable hours, I rallied from numbness. Every night, Cooshie would stay with me, licking away my tears, his loyalty diffusing the poison of anger. Slowly, with each nightly meeting, the pain of death ebbed and my soul was rejuvenated.

One night, after months of our ritual, there was a test. I sat in my usual spot next to the family-room window, staring out at the blackness. Cooshie did not join me. I began to succumb to my old bitterness, but suddenly, miraculously, I wasn't at all comfortable functioning in self-imposed isolation. Bolting forward, I squared my shoulders and called for Cooshie. He did not come. I called again. From across the room, under the ruffle of the couch, a small, black nose appeared. Desperately wanting the living he had brought to my dying, I called yet again. The couch ruffle gave way to a fuzzy, gray face and a lightning-streak jump, landing him up near my face. I stroked him as gently as he had stroked me. Cooshie turned and directed wide, smiling eyes at mine. His student had passed the test. I felt close to happy, on the verge of survival, healing in the company of a cat.

— Carole Marshall —

Chapter
4

My Very Good, Very Bad Cat

31

Kitty Is a Thief

Way down deep, we're all motivated by the same
urges. Cats have the courage to live by them.
~Jim Davis

Zipper was a nondescript gray tabby, but her personality made up for that; once anyone met her, she was rarely forgotten. She practically raised my sister and me. My parents referred to her as "The Nanny Cat." She walked us to school, slept in our beds, and consoled us whenever we cried. In return, we dressed her in doll clothes, nursed her with baby bottles of milk, and fed her under the table.

Thanksgiving was Zipper's favorite time. This was the only day she was not constantly by our sides. Instead, she stayed next to my mother, making sure to be underfoot, especially as my mother transported the bird from counter to oven and back again. She'd meow, beg and plead, but she'd have to wait patiently for the diced-up gizzards to be split between her and the dog.

More than once, we'd hear our mother yell at her for tripping her or jumping on the counter. Normally, Zipper was very well behaved, but the rules were different on Thanksgiving.

At dinner, when the turkey was carved, my sister and I eagerly awaited a glimpse of the wishbone, which was put on the window ledge to dry and saved for Christmas Eve. We ate only one turkey a year, so this was super special.

Every Christmas Eve, though, the wishbone would have gone missing. My mother always assumed she must have accidentally thrown it in the garbage.

I was twelve when we discovered the truth. Late one night, Zipper was caught red-handed by my father, chowing down on the wishbone. She showed no regrets, growled and completed her meal while he watched.

Over the years, we gave up on that wishbone. It was still put on the windowsill, but with full knowledge that Zipper was going to have her traditional, late-night, after-Thanksgiving snack.

Zipper passed when I was nineteen. It was like losing a family member. We all grieved her, but she'd lived very comfortably to a ripe old age.

Our younger cats, Kinda and Felicia, had relied on her during their time with us. She set the rules for them, showed them how to protect themselves from blue jays and mice, told them where they could sleep and, most importantly, taught them how to take care of her people.

That Thanksgiving, my mother put the wishbone on the windowsill as usual. I knew how sad she felt; I could see it as her eyes welled up. She missed her turkey-cooking companion. That offering had become a tradition, and now it was over.

The following Thanksgiving, we all figured that wishbone would stay where we left it, but one day I realized it had disappeared. It seems that Kinda and Felicia had picked up where Zipper had left off.

It's been almost forty years since I met Zipper, and I still I leave a wishbone on my windowsill at Thanksgiving, just like my mother does.

About ten years ago, a nondescript gray tabby walked into my apartment and made herself at home. Mommy Cat became a great nanny; my children became hers. She used to walk my older son to school, and she is always willing to be carried and coddled by my six-year-old daughter. When the turkey goes in the oven, she is always directly underfoot, trying to trip me up. She meows and complains while it cooks and would hang off the counter if I let her. She has now taken over the traditional wishbone heist, as well. She's everything I want in a cat!

—Nicole Ann Rook McAlister—

32

Meowy Christmas

Tree decorating with cats. O Christmas tree,
O Christmas tree, your ornaments are history!
~Courtney VanSickle

My sister-in-law Carol said she'd already picked out a kitten for me. I agreed to go with her… just to look. I made no promise to take one home. After all, only two months had passed since I lost my beloved calico, Mandi. Maybe I needed to be pet-free for a while.

When we got there, three of the four tuxedo kittens remained in the litter. Carol picked up one and handed it to me. The beautiful face and white fur on the right side of her nose reminded me of a harlequin mask. How could I resist? Then another kitten, with a more symmetrical white face, jumped into my lap and purred.

Driving home in my British sports car proved difficult with two rambunctious kittens. One clung to my left arm and shoulder, watching the scenery zip by from the window. The other paced back and forth from my lap to the passenger's seat, hindering my ability to shift gears. Both mewed in a loud duet of protest. Of course, I hadn't brought a cage. I had not planned to take home a kitten — or two.

The harlequin-masked female earned the name Squeakette with her tiny voice squeaking about each new discovery as she explored her new home. The male, lacking only a black tie in his formal attire, took the name Sebastian for my favorite composer, Johann Sebastian Bach.

A few weeks later, a neighbor helped me carry down my six-foot artificial Christmas tree from the attic. I thanked him with a batch of cookies, and then set up the tree in the corner of my living room.

Sebastian and Squeakette knocked it down before I opened the box of decorations. Propping it up, I straightened the few bent wire branches back into place. As I checked for any other damage, a flash of black-and-white fur zipped past me. Up they went, branch by branch. The tree danced a jig as the two kittens climbed it in tag-team fashion. Sebastian made it to the top a moment ahead of Squeakette.

He lunged at me from the top, paws stretched out like wings. I didn't know cats could fly. Landing on my shoulder, his hind claws dug into my upper chest. The gashes bled only for a moment and didn't require stitches.

The tree teetered from side to side, with the little female clutching the top branch. It came to rest upright, and Squeakette allowed me to pluck her trembling body from her perch. A few moments of cuddling calmed her fears.

Among the decorations, I found the eighteen-inch synthetic tree I had planned to take to my office. Aha. On the opposite side of the living room, an empty place next to the wingback chair looked perfect. I dangled assorted cat toys from the branches and topped it with a stuffed yellow mouse.

I played their game of "we knock it down — you pick it up" enough times to amuse them and divert their attention from the large tree. A sprinkle of catnip on the branches helped, too. How many kittens could boast about having their very own Christmas tree?

I made an appointment that Saturday to have their Christmas picture taken at the local animal shelter. As a fundraising activity, they brought Santa in to pose with families and their pets.

Wrestling Squeakette into the cage for transport seemed easy compared to the fight Sebastian gave me. The cardboard box, with inch-and-a-half holes on each end, served as a temporary cage. It now bore slashes from Sebastian's claws. So did my hands. Note to self: Next time, wear gardening gloves.

After doctoring my wounds and changing my clothes, we headed for the photo shoot. Squeakette emitted a few protests, crouched in the back of her cage and scowling at me. Sebastian caterwauled from his box, digging at the hole with his paw. Every traffic-light stop gave me a chance to check on him. Yowling, then digging. Yowling, then digging. Each time, he pressed his nose in the hole. By the time I drove into the facility parking lot, he had made the hole large enough to get his little white face through it.

I carried my two kittens into the building and set their carriers on the table to sign in for our appointment. Laughter exploded from the small crowd nearby. I looked down to see Sebastian's head protruding from the hole like a mounted moosehead.

With a volunteer's help, we eased Sebastian's head back through the hole. The ordeal left him in a more cooperative mood. He sat still while I put the red-and-green plaid hair scrunchy over his head and around his neck. He even let me fluff it out.

Squeakette issued a mild complaint when I slipped a red-mesh scrunchy over her head. With their colorful collars in place, I realized this would be the closest I'd ever come to dressing them in festive costumes.

Santa waited in his makeshift sled. He appeared almost agreeable as I handed him Squeakette. She gazed up at him with wary eyes and then, surprisingly, nestled in the crook of his arm and purred.

I took my assigned seat in front of Santa and hugged Sebastian against my chest.

The photographer held up a stuffed toy. "Look this way, please." Click.

"Thank you very much."

Santa remained unscathed, at least from my kittens. Later, I wondered how he fared the rest of the day when I caught a glimpse of the Great Dane next in line.

I ordered a five-by-seven for framing and a packet of photo Christmas cards to send to friends and family.

With the kittens back in their respective carriers, Sebastian shied away from the head-trapping hole. Smart kitty. On the way home, he inched his way close enough to peek out at me and uttered a soft mew. Note to self: Get him a cage of his own.

The pictures arrived in the mail a few days later. I grinned with pride when I looked them over. My kittens had posed like professional models. They faced the same direction, holding their little heads up as though sporting angelic halos. No smiles, but neither showed any fear.

Each day, Sebastian and Squeakette gazed with wonder at the tree in my living room, decorated with blinking lights and shiny ornaments. Then they trotted to their own tree and batted the toys on the branches.

Sipping a cup of hot cocoa, snuggled in my favorite chair, I took in my surroundings. The framed picture of Santa with my kittens and me, Sebastian and Squeakette's carefree mews as they played with their tree, and classical Christmas hymns flowing from the radio reminded me of the simple joys intended for this season.

Mandi the calico would have approved. True contentment comes in moments like these.

—Janet Ramsdell Rockey—

33

Mama's Little Doll

The smart cat doesn't let on that he is.
~H.G. Frommer

We often had friends over for dinner and a movie or game, accompanied by a glass, or three, of wine. It wasn't unusual for a friend to stay the night in our guest room or on the couch afterward, rather than risk the dark drive over the dam. Blaze, our half Maine Coon cat, was used to it all. He kept mostly to himself during the early part of the evening, unless we had shrimp with dinner, but he was always out and about by bedtime, making friends and hoping to get some extra love and treats before we all called it a night.

I came out of my bedroom one morning, after just such a night, half expecting to see my long-haired kitty curled up on the couch with my friend. They had a nice relationship. She would stroke his silky, orange fur for hours, and he would curl up on her head while she slept. That wasn't the case this morning, however. My friend was sitting up in the corner of the couch, her knees drawn up to her chest, hugging a pillow and looking quite frazzled. I knew our night hadn't been that raucous, so I doubted it was from that, but something was definitely wrong.

"Are you okay? I mean, no offense, but you look awful."

"No! I am not okay," she snapped at me. "That freaky little doll of yours kept me up all night, and it was not funny!"

I was clueless. "What are you talking about? What doll?"

"You know exactly what I'm talking about! I know you like to play little jokes, but that was just too creepy, and it kept me up all night."

My family had been known to play a prank from time to time, and some of them had been pretty good, but I really didn't have any idea what she was talking about. I continued to protest my innocence, and she went on to explain.

"It's one of those dolls that says 'Mama.' You know the ones I mean. You turn them over or lay them down, and they say 'Mama' in that funny little voice."

I knew exactly the type of doll she was talking about, but I still had no idea what that had to do with the previous night and me, so I encouraged her to continue.

"First, it sounded like it was coming from down by your room, so I thought it was you being silly. Then it was behind the couch, and in the kitchen, and downstairs. And just about the time I thought it had stopped for the night, it would start all over again. It was the creepiest thing I've ever heard! It was like the doll was crawling around your house all night saying 'Mama'!"

I tried to reassure my friend. "I swear that I don't have any doll in this house that says 'Mama' or anything else. The only doll I have is an old stuffed one that can't say anything at all. Maybe my son left a game or something on downstairs...."

"This was no game downstairs! It moved around your house!"

I tried to calm my friend down, but she wasn't having it. She was up and heading home with the threat that if the talking doll had been a prank, she was never speaking to me again.

I was thinking about everything the next day, trying to figure out what my friend might have heard, so I asked my son, "Is there anything in your room that says 'Mama'?"

"Sure, Blaze does."

Through the years since we had adopted Blaze, my son granted him great powers. I would enter my son's room to find drawers emptied in the middle of the floor. When I would ask what happened, he would reply, "Blaze did it." Blaze also emptied closets, flushed things down toilets, hid items, and did a great many other things that would generally require opposable thumbs — a fact I once pointed out to my son. It was explained to me that Blaze's thumbs only appeared in front of my son and promptly disappeared when I entered the room. I wasn't buying Blaze being the culprit this time either.

"No seriously, hon. My friend was really freaked out yesterday. I'm trying to figure out what she may have heard."

"She heard Blaze, Mom. He walks around saying 'Mama' and looking for you when you aren't home. He does it all the time. Sometimes, he does it when I rub his belly, too. I'll show you." And off my son went to get Blaze, the wonder cat.

After returning with the cat, my son sat down on the floor with Blaze between his legs and started playing with him, rubbing his belly and tickling his paws. Blaze was playing right along. It wasn't long before Blaze grew tired of the play, and that's when he said it... "Mama."

"See?" my son asked. "I told you he could talk."

I couldn't believe my ears. Blaze could talk, and he did sound like a doll. I called my friend and told her about Blaze the wonder cat. She calmed down and agreed to stay on speaking terms with me. We both had a great laugh about the whole thing.

A few weeks later when I was on the couch watching an old movie, the entire house was dark, and I heard it... "Mama." I responded by calling out to Blaze, he called for me, and we continued until he jumped up on the couch and curled up with me for the remainder of the movie. I have to admit that it was pretty freaky hearing that doll-like "Mama" in a dark house.

My beloved Blaze continued to call me "Mama" until I lost him three years later, but I was never granted the privilege of seeing his magical, opposable thumbs.

— Donna L. Marsh —

34

If Only...

To bathe a cat takes brute force, perseverance, courage
of conviction — and a cat. The last ingredient is
usually hardest to come by.
~Stephen Baker

ometimes, there are way too many "ifs" to a story. *If* that little kid had not heard a faint meowing in a campground Dumpster and alerted a nearby adult, a helpless animal might have died. *If* that adult had not called me (the local patsy for animals in need), I would not have jumped in my car and raced to the rescue. *If* my vet did not love a challenge and had not figured out how to help the starving, sickly creature, I might have saved a few hundred bucks in veterinary care.

My part in this adventure started with a Dumpster dive to find the source of the weak meowing. I pulled out a small, bony and matted mess with huge blue eyes looking up at me. I could almost hear a little voice saying, "Please, help me." I took what I assumed was a kitten to my vet, who said it was not a kitten but an adult cat close to starvation. I will never know (nor do I want to) the cruel person who tossed this animal into the Dumpster, but I had already committed to either saving it or having my vet do the kindly thing.

Months later, thanks to excellent care, nutrition and a bundle of bucks, the cat officially joined our family. By this time, we knew she was a purebred Himalayan. She reached a healthy weight, and her coat not only grew out but almost touched the floor. We named her B.K. for Beautiful Kitty, and we loved her in spite of her skittish personality. Sometimes, it seemed she was waiting for another human to abuse her again.

If she did not have an overabundance of fur, maybe she would not have attracted fleas. Until B.K., no flea had ever been interested in our two dogs and one ordinary housecat. It never occurred to me to have B.K. professionally flea-dipped and bathed. I'm a do-it-yourself pet person, and the cat had already cost me a fortune. I bought a bottle of flea shampoo for cats and chose a day when I would have the house to myself. I took B.K. and a stack of towels into a small downstairs bathroom with an oversized sink. Since it's always cool on the Oregon coast, I turned on the wall heater ahead of time. Heaven forbid this cat (in that amazing fur coat) might get a chill. I should mention that our house, built in the 1950s, was dated in every way, especially that basement bathroom. We meant to update, but never got around to it. The shower stall was tiny, with an ugly shower curtain. The oversized sink sat on a cabinet with several oversized drawers, which were way too close to the inward-opening bathroom door. This is important information so you can picture the drama that was about to happen.

I've always considered cat bathing one of the major martial arts, and bathing B.K. was no exception. But I'm bigger and stronger than a cat, and all was going reasonably well. However, it was so warm in that bathroom I was forced to strip off my clothes — not a pretty picture. Just as I was about to towel her off, I heard the jangling noise of the telephone. If the noisy phone had not startled the cat, she would not have leaped out of my arms and gone airborne through the shower curtain. If I hadn't quickly exited the bathroom, closing the door behind me, the cat would not have frantically found the strength to get that bottom drawer out, thereby blocking the bathroom door from opening. If it hadn't been so hot from the wall heater, I would not have taken off my clothes. And if my husband hadn't gone to a meeting, he would have been home to help.

I debated calling the fire department, but decided that was a dumb idea. Luckily, we had a neighbor who worked at home. I called him, but not before throwing on jeans and a sweatshirt. Ten minutes later, my neighbor arrived with a toolbox and figured out how to open the bathroom door. It was no surprise to either of us when a ball of wet fur streaked past.

My neighbor will never know about my own naked streaking to answer the phone — and, by the way, it was a wrong number.

— Bobbie Jensen Lippman —

Stalker of Shadows

To a cat, "No" means "Not while I'm looking."
~Author Unknown

In the silence of my steamy club,
I stood serenely showering in my tub,
When I heard a shuffle.
A quaint, distinctly faint,
Softly padded shuffle,
On my brick-red rug and linoleum floor.
Then again a sound,
Muted and muffled,
Akin to crickets creeping close to a lion's roar.
To wit I peeked out and found,
That young cat I so adore,
Patroclus, playfully pounding back out the door.
Back to the ritual of rub and rinse,
When yet still his coy presence I could sense,
Stalking the shadows of my showering chore.
Quietly creeping,
Slowly sweeping across my bathroom floor.
And just as before
His playful plot again commenced.
For I was sure I heard the soft storm
Of padded paws pouncing upon porcelain form.
And from closed, soapy eyes I did imagine,

My Very Good, Very Bad Cat | 113

A tiny, dark and furry feline dragon,
Proudly perched atop that ivory throne,
Whose use this was not intended for.
From amidst the mist of foam,
That image twisted my lips into silent smirking,
That predator force so quietly lurking,
Searching for his perfect score.
Then gently came a scratching,
As if Nugent's fever ever was catching,
Latching upon my shower curtain tail.
And lifting it, as if certain to prevail,
He did not stall, he did not pause,
Nor did he fail,
Ears laid back and outstretched claws,
Did that cat sail,
And through the veil he was cast,
Crashing with a sorry splash,
Lashing out a loathsome wail.
Tables turned from hunter to prey,
This game he suddenly did not want to play.
His feet comically fought for gripping,
Slipping in the shower head spray,
Nearly tripping me in his angst to get away.
Finding purchase he so desperately needed,
In his escape he finally succeeded,
And fled the soggy scene
For the comfort of a cozy towel,
Where he licked himself dry and clean.
No longer the proud predator on prowl,
He looked upon me with wounded scowl.

— Kenneth A. White —

The Traveling Cat

As every cat owner knows, nobody owns a cat.
~Ellen Perry Berkeley

Having recently divorced, I moved from my comfortable home to a small apartment two miles away. I owned two loving cats. I packed them up with their belongings (bowls, beds, toys and scratching posts) and brought them with me.

My cats were used to going outside to exercise, but in my new apartment on the second floor, they were not afforded that freedom. For safety reasons, I intended to keep them inside. Alley Cat was content just looking out the window at anything that moved, and enjoyed countless hours of sleeping on the couch. Stripes, on the other hand, wasn't happy being cooped up and cried incessantly at the door, driving me a little batty. It was difficult for him to go outside because I had to walk down a flight of stairs to let him out. After two days, I gave in to his meowing and opened the door. He walked around the tiny yard, which seemed to satisfy his curiosity, and then scratched at the door and waited to be let in.

The next time Stripes ventured out, he went missing for three days. I searched up and down the neighborhood, calling out, "Stripes, come home."

When I returned home from work on the third day, the phone was ringing off the hook. It was the lady who had purchased my house. She informed me that Stripes was in her yard meowing, probably missing his home and looking for me.

My Very Good, Very Bad Cat | 115

Stripes had to cross many busy streets and a small park, and walk past a high school and over a set of railroad tracks to reach his destination. He was fortunate to have survived without injury. I wonder how many lives he used up in the process.

"I'll be right there!" I said. I jumped in the car and headed for my old house. Stripes was as happy to see me as I was to see him. He started purring and rubbing his head against my legs. I picked him up, kissed him, placed him on my lap, and drove home. The next day, just like *Groundhog Day*, the event repeated itself—again and again and again. By now, he had probably found a shortcut to get back home after walking the route multiple times.

Stripes made it perfectly clear that he refused to stay in my new apartment on a busy city street, opting for his old house with a yard full of trees and birds.

The new owners were intrigued by this stalker cat and even began feeding him. I felt guilty being caught in the middle of this odd situation. I bought a bag of Stripes' favorite food and left it at the house. I was called regularly with reports on my cat.

At first, Stripes slept in a cardboard box in the yard, but he was invited in eventually. I became jealous. Where was Stripes' loyalty to me after the past seven years of my undivided love and companionship? Being rejected by a cat is downright embarrassing.

The new owners offered to make Stripes an official member of their family when I had exhausted all attempts to keep my cat and failed. It was the perfect outcome. I've heard the expression, "If you love something, let it go." Reluctantly, I did. At least I had visitation rights.

— Irene Maran —

Cat Burglar

*Most of us rather like our cats to have a streak of
wickedness. I should not feel quite easy in the company
of any cat that walked about the house with
a saintly expression.*
~Beverly Nichols

When my husband and I were first married, my brother-in-law needed a place to stay. Of course, we opened our doors to him. Unfortunately, after a few months, I noticed things missing from my purse and even from the dresser in my bedroom. I told my husband I thought his brother was stealing from us, but what was missing was so small that we let it go.

A few months went by, and things kept going missing, specifically money. I never carried a lot of cash, so the money that was being taken wasn't enough to go accusing someone. I just let it go and started bringing my purse with me into the bedroom at night. Money still went missing. I was furious and about ready to kick my brother-in-law out of the house and write him off completely. After all, we had opened our doors to him. Was this how he repaid us?

One night, I couldn't sleep, so I went downstairs to get something to drink. Once I got to the bottom of the stairs, I heard something. I thought I was going to catch my brother-in-law in the act of stealing from me. This was going to be it!

I sneaked around the corner, and what did I see? My cat! He was digging in my purse, which I had forgotten to take upstairs that night.

My Very Good, Very Bad Cat | 117

I waited quietly to see what he was doing. He pulled out money and took off to the basement. I sneaked down the stairs to watch him. He came out from behind the stairs with nothing in his mouth. He headed back upstairs, and I went under the stairs to see that he had just put my money in his cat carrier. I also saw all the cash that had disappeared during my months of complaining to my husband, being angry at my brother-in-law, and being paranoid. My cat had $127 and months of receipts hidden in that cat carrier!

I learned a couple of important lessons from this: Never assume anything, and keep your cash in a wallet instead of just stuffing it into your purse!

— Shelley Faulhaber —

Salad Days

It's really the cat's house — we just pay the mortgage.
~Author Unknown

When you have a long-term illness, even simple things like laughter can fall by the wayside. That was the case for me. My painful autoimmune disorder proved to be almost impossible to treat, leaving me housebound and frustrated most days. But I had a secret weapon against unhappiness: Lucy. Lu was the queen of my house — a beautiful, if somewhat elderly, little tortoiseshell kitty who enjoyed a benevolent reign from her armchair throne. If there was anything Lu brought me, it was the simple joy of being her subject.

Though, to be honest, she was a very strange sovereign.

One night, when I was suffering from more than my usual pain, I fed Lu and then went into the kitchen to make my own meal. I had planned to make a chef's salad, but the pain made preparation difficult. I had to bend at the waist to chop up all of the ingredients, shifting from foot to foot to relieve the agony in my belly. By the end, I was almost in tears, but I managed to finish the salad. The diced bell peppers, julienned carrots, shredded cheese and crisp romaine lettuce looked delicious, and I knew I would enjoy every bite. Limping into the sitting room with the salad bowl in one hand, I grabbed a novel from a nearby shelf and sat down in Lucy's chair, just under the reading lamp.

Even after sitting, the pain remained sharp — so sharp that it killed my appetite. I had intended to eat while reading, but I realized with regret that it would be better to leave dinner until I could fully appreciate it. Feeling somewhat defeated, I placed the salad bowl in my lap and propped my feet up on the footstool, hoping the book I had chosen would help me wait out the worst of the discomfort. The story proved engrossing, and I quickly lost all awareness of my surroundings, including the fact that my cat was sitting nearby.

It was unusual for me to bring my dinner with me when I sat in Lucy's chair. Normally, I would only visit her chair in the morning with a mug of tea and a good book. Together, we would read for over an hour; sometimes, I would even read aloud to her. It was our special bonding time, and Lucy loved it. That night, however, she could tell something fundamental in the routine had changed, which left her uncertain as to how to respond. She stared at me hard, taking in the dinner in my lap, the book in my hand, and my evident intention of remaining in her chair for a while.

After many minutes of contemplation, the sight of her favourite person sitting on her throne proved to be too much for her. On some deep, instinctual feline level, she knew she was supposed to be sitting in my lap, even though there was something already in it. Deeply engrossed in my book, I didn't notice her wiggling bottom until it was too late. With a huge effort, Lucy launched her arthritic self up off the floor and onto the chair's arm. Then, so swiftly I couldn't stop her, she turned and sat down in my salad.

I froze, too shocked to move, but Lucy wasn't bothered in the least. With no indication that she felt anything out of place, Lucy worked her furry bottom into the salad bowl, trying to find the most comfortable position among the lettuce leaves.

We sat like that for one brief moment — me with my mouth open in disbelief and Lucy looking quite pleased with herself for regaining her rightful place — and then I burst out laughing.

Lu was annoyed when I lifted her out of my dinner. As I shook with laughter and headed toward the bathroom, she began to grumble and lash her tail, sending Parmesan cheese flying in all directions.

She flattened her ears. I was laughing so hard I had to lean against the bathroom wall. I turned on the faucet in the tub. But when I began to shampoo the Italian salad dressing off her bottom, she gave voice to her displeasure and yowled. As I soaped and giggled, Lucy continued to howl, making absolutely sure that I knew she was angry.

Never one to bite or scratch, Lucy would wail wholeheartedly when upset, and being quite deaf she wasn't entirely confident that I could hear her because she couldn't hear herself. When it came time to rinse, she stepped up her efforts, singing her annoyance in a pure, high tenor. By the time I had lifted her from the tub and finished working on her back end with the hair dryer, I was certain the neighbors would bang on the door, demanding to know just what I was doing. And I couldn't blame them if they did. Lucy was wailing like all of her nine lives were flashing in front of her eyes.

Once we left the bathroom, Lucy stopped her caterwauling immediately and resorted to cleaning herself, her outrage painfully obvious. When I spoke to her, she didn't respond, and when I reached out to scratch her ears, she shook them as though an insect had crawled across her head.

"All right, all right," I said, and left her to her sulking.

Still smiling, I limped back to the sitting room to remove the hairy remains of my dinner from the chair. As I bent to clean the upholstery with a wet cloth, I realized that though the pain was still intense, it didn't upset me quite so much. There was pain, but there was also my silly little Lu.

Later that night, Lucy found me on the sofa and climbed up into my lap to settle down, her dark face raised for a customary kiss. Her bottom was still slightly wet, but she seemed to have forgiven me. When I dropped a peck just over her eye, she burst into purrs and pushed her nose gently against my hand.

"You're a big weirdo, Lucy," I whispered, and meant it.

She looked up at me, her features as regal and patient as any member of the royal family. There was a rebuke in the look, and I realized my mistake.

"You're a big weirdo, your majesty," I said, correcting myself.

Placated, Lucy turned, pushed her damp little bottom against my shirt, and fell asleep.

— Alex Lester —

39

Crank Caller

It is impossible to keep a straight face in the presence
of one or more kittens.
~Cynthia E. Varnado

About three years ago, at approximately 2:45 a.m., I was awakened abruptly by the phone ringing. My heart started racing. No one calls that late unless it is an emergency or bad news. Then I noticed the number that was calling: my best friend Deb's cell phone.

I grabbed the receiver, but by then the call had disconnected. Panic set in. Was she hurt? Did her car break down on some back road leaving her alone and frightened? A dozen scenarios — none of them good — came to mind. I tried to call back immediately, but all it did was ring.

I woke up my husband because now I was frantic. He calmed me down enough to reason that the next step was to call her home telephone. No one answered. Needless to say, that only upped my level of panic.

I had no sooner jumped out of bed in rescue mode when my phone rang once more. Deb again. This time, I got a real person. She sounded distraught. "What is wrong? Why did you call? What happened?" she blurted out.

I started to answer, but then it dawned on me what she had said. "What? You called me and got me out of bed," I mumbled back, confused. She then said something along the line of my getting *her* out of bed and my calling *her* in the middle of the night, scaring her half to death. I sat down, trying to figure out this riddle. "But if you are home, why did you call me from your cell phone?" I asked. She answered that she hadn't used her cell phone.

I was ready to jump into another round of "Yes, you did!" and "What are you talking about?" when I stopped. At this point, I didn't know if I should be confused, angry, relieved or simply amused by the situation. Then she told me to hold on.

When she finally got back on the line, she was half-giggling. Rigel, one of her not-so-ferocious felines, appeared to have confiscated her cell phone, turned it on, and dialed me. Then when I called back the cat pushed the right button to answer, but then quickly pushed the disconnect button.

Now that we were no longer concerned about each other's wellbeing, we laughed about the cat chaos that had woken up both of us. Rigel would be known forevermore as the crank-call cat. But there was a little lesson in there for us as well—to not jump to negative conclusions before we asked a whole lot of questions.

— Pastor Wanda Christy-Shaner —

40

Nurturing Ninja

Kittens can happen to anyone.
~Paul Gallico

The door swung shut behind me as I entered the house, and my pulse quickened. I grinned. "Where is he? *What* is he?" I asked. My purse thumped to the floor.

"He's in the bathtub, but Sha..." Before he could finish my name, I skidded down the narrow hall and threw open the bathroom door.

His eyes weren't even open yet. Unable to get traction on the porcelain, his paws splayed out to the sides.

"Oooooohhhhh." My voice slid up the scale as I scooped up the tiny, black-and-white fluffball.

"Careful, Shan. His claws are sharp. Here, give him this."

Greg handed me a syringe, warm with milk. The kitten suckled it, all rumbling thunder and kneading paws.

"Where did he come from?"

I cuddled the kitten as Greg relayed the story. Our Australian Shepherd, Romeo, had suddenly taken off down the train tracks by our house. Greg noticed something in his mouth, so he chased the dog until he was able to tackle him. When he did, a ball of fur tumbled out, spitting attitude. Greg clutched him by the scruff, and a whisper of a hiss escaped him. But all that changed once Greg offered him the syringe.

"He's got quite a motor," I cooed. I tilted my ear toward him, wanting to feel his purr on my cheek. When I did, he released the syringe and sniffed, his breath and whiskers tickling my ear. Suddenly, he sucked my earlobe into his mouth.

Rumble, rumble, rumble.

"Greg," I whispered. "He's trying to nurse from my ear. Look. He's suckling!"

Greg peeked under my red locks and started laughing.

I caught the smile in his eyes. We both knew it. The kitten was home.

Ninja. We decided on the name because he protected his meals with so much feistiness that he'd stomp on the bowl, scattering his food everywhere in the process. But between mealtimes, he was pure sugar.

Sugar with a love of suckling.

He continued to go after earlobes, but he also suckled fingertips. And noses. Several times, I'd wake to a sharp pain in my eye, as he tried to suckle my eyelid. But the funniest suckling event, by far, was reserved for my husband.

Ninja bonded immediately with Greg. Perhaps it was because he gave Ninja his first syringe of milk. Perhaps Ninja saw Greg as the hero who rescued him from the dog. Or perhaps it was just because he thought Greg was his mother.

It was a Saturday. I was folding laundry in the bedroom, humming along to the radio. Greg had been napping on the futon all morning, and it was time for lunch. I rolled the final pair of socks and strolled into the living room, where I stopped short at the scene in front of me.

Greg gently snored, one arm raised above his head. And there, kneading on his chest, was Ninja.

Suckling Greg's nipple.

In 2001, there were no cameras on cell phones. Oh, how I wish there had been. But we did have an old camcorder. I ran into the spare room to load a tape, but being relatively technically inept, I couldn't make it work. I had no choice. I had to wake Greg.

"Wha? Shan, leave me… ouch! What the heck?"

"Shhhh! Don't move! You'll scare him away!"

Greg's eyes widened, his face contorting in half-shock, half-horror.

"This hurts, Shan!"

"Shhhh! How do I work this thing?" I turned the camcorder so he could see the buttons. Greg stared at me, slack-jawed.

"Are you kidding me?"

I giggled. "Do I look like I'm kidding you?" I started pushing buttons.

"Shannon, you're gonna break it. Ouch! This hurts!"

"Would you please whisper? Come on, baby... Can you not see the humor in this?"

Greg and I turned, simultaneously, toward his chest. Red dots circled Greg's nipple where Ninja's claws had pierced his skin. Oblivious to us, Ninja suckled and kneaded away.

Greg closed his eyes, trying to force away the smile. When he opened them again, my face was inches from his, and we both spit air, laughing silently.

Our kitten was trying to nurse.

From my husband.

"I can't believe I'm doing this." Greg took the camcorder from me and hit a few buttons. A blinking green light appeared. "Okay, it's recording."

"Now, can you just lean a little more that way so I can get a better view?"

"Don't push it, Shan." But he was laughing as he said it. He rolled a little, and Ninja released his grip.

"No! Get him to do it again," I said.

"I don't want him to do it again! It hurts!"

"Well, use the other one."

Greg raised his eyebrows at me.

"Come on... be a good sport. This is funny. You know this is funny."

For the next ten minutes, Greg obliged as I shot footage. Then he disengaged the kitten and stood up, shaking his head. "I can't believe that just happened."

I nuzzled Ninja. "You're a funny kitty, you know that? You want a treat?"

The next morning, I heard Greg shriek from the shower. I jumped out of bed and threw open the bathroom door. "Are you okay?" I asked.

Greg pulled back the curtain and glared at me.

"My nipples are raw!"

I put my hand over my mouth, stifling a laugh.

When he got out of the shower, he wrapped a towel around himself and immediately went to the phone.

"Who are you calling?" I asked.

Greg ignored me and dialed.

"Mom?"

Pause.

"Okay, you're going to think I'm crazy, but I just wanted to tell you I have a whole new respect for you."

Pause.

"Well, I think I know what it must've felt like to nurse children."

Pause.

"No, I haven't been drinking. Do you have a minute to hear a story?"

— Shannon Stocker —

Knock, Knock!

The cat is, above all things, a dramatist.
~Margaret Benson

It happened at the same time three nights in a row. At roughly 3:15, I was awakened by a strange noise, like the sound of a set of keys being jangled next to my ear. Each time, I snapped on my bedside table lamp and scanned the room. Everything seemed as it should be. The only sound I could hear was the soft hum of the refrigerator downstairs. My husband was away on a business trip, so I couldn't even blame him.

On the fourth night, I awoke at 3:13 a.m. I grumbled to myself, pulled the covers to my chin, closed my eyes and tried to get back to sleep. That's when I heard it — a gentle *pit-pat* down the hallway. *It's just Ringo,* I thought. Ringo was our family pet — a six-year-old, short-haired gray cat. With a white patch on his chest and matching white paws, he looked like he was wearing a permanent tuxedo. The *pit-pat* stopped just outside my open bedroom door. I squinted through one eye just a little bit, and by the light of the moon I could see Ringo watching me. I faked a light snore. Then, very slowly, he crept forward until he stood beside the head of my bed and in front of my bedside table.

Ringo turned his head and gave me one more quick glance before he, ever so slowly, lifted his right paw. Just as he was about to box the knocker-style knob on my bedside table like a punching bag, I sat up and yelled triumphantly, "Aha! It's you!" Ringo shot out of the room, skidded around the corner down the hall and took to the stairs as if his life depended on it. He never boxed my drawer pull in the middle of the night again — at least not when I was around.

A few years later, in our new home in British Columbia, I started noticing closet doors were being left open. I was, admittedly, annoyed by this, but instead of saying anything to my family, I just closed the bifold doors when I noticed they were open.

I was drifting off to sleep one night when I heard the bifold closet door in the hallway creak open slowly. Was there someone else in the house? It wasn't my husband. He was travelling again, and I knew it wasn't my daughter because she was at a friend's house. I heard the closet in her room open slowly with the same eerie creak.

I fumbled for the leftover length of closet rod from under my bed, which was quite heavy and an excellent substitute for a baseball bat. I ventured out into the hall with it and headed to my daughter's room. I flipped on every light switch I passed and searched the wide-open closets. Nothing. I checked my daughter's room, and then every other room, every corner, every cranny, even the garage. Still nothing. Just as I returned to my bedroom, sleepy and bewildered, my own closet door creaked open. There, sticking out from behind the door was three inches of gray tail. Ringo had figured out that all he had to do to open the closets was to put his paw underneath, jiggle and pull.

Sadly, Ringo, the nocturnal mischief-maker, is no longer with us. He lived to a ripe old age, and I am absolutely sure that he passed on his closet-opening techniques to his housemate and younger feline companion, Victoria. She has opened at least one closet door every night since he's been gone.

For a while after he passed, every time I heard a creak in the night, I couldn't help but fondly remember our dear, mischievous, tuxedoed prankster. Along with his protégé Victoria, he has inspired me to oil our closet-door hinges so that now I can get a good night's sleep.

— Carol L. MacKay —

Chapter 5

A Natural Therapist

Bella and Me

When a cat chooses to be friendly, it's a big deal
because a cat is picky.
~Mike Deupree

Bella had a bed at the back of the clinic where her food and water bowl were kept. She had another under the receptionist's desk, but we could usually find her curled up in a ball, sleeping on one of the chairs in the lobby.

I had a habit of patting Bella on the head, which I think she hated. I've always been more of a dog person. Perhaps Bella sensed that, which is why she didn't like me. The few times I petted her with nice, long strokes along her back, she turned and swatted at me. And I'm almost positive she had her claws out.

We often stared at each other, with her looking away first, and I wondered what it was about my touch that was different from the other girls. Jo Anne could sit at the front desk on a phone call, and Bella would jump up next to her, snuggling into Jo Anne's long brown hair and rubbing noses with her. Amanda would pick her up and carry her face-to-face like a baby, putting Bella's arms over her shoulders as she stroked her back. Bella would wrap her arms tightly around Amanda's neck, literally hugging her while she looked lovingly into her face.

Bella made a pest of herself at lunch and often circled the lunch table with no shame, occasionally meowing loudly in an effort to demand a bit of this or that be shared with her. Once I found her sitting on the floor next to my chair, staring up at me expectantly. Looking to improve our relationship, I broke off a tiny piece of my tuna sandwich and put it on the floor next to her, expecting her to gobble it up as she did other lunch offerings. Instead, she stared at it as if it were garbage, and then shifted her eyes back up at me with a look of abhorrence.

"That's tuna, ya know," I called after her as she stalked off without looking back.

Bella and I coexisted over the years. We would never be each other's favorites, but there was one thing that fascinated and impressed me about Bella: She always knew when euthanasia appointments were happening.

They were the part of my job that I dreaded, but there was no way around them. I was to receive the grieving family and their sick pet, explain the process to them, get their pet as comfortable as possible, handle the paperwork and let the doctor know when the family had finished saying goodbye.

Clients would ask me, "How do you do that part of your job? How do you handle it?" The truth was, after years of working at the clinic, euthanasia appointments never got any easier. Each one meant the loss of a family member. Whether it was an accident or a terminal illness, it was a loss as strong as a human loss for many. It was never an easy day, and it was always hard to know what to say. To me, the important thing was to offer comfort to the family members.

Bella knew this, and that's exactly what she offered. She couldn't read an appointment book, didn't know the words the doctor was saying, and didn't know what ailments each animal had. But when the saddest days came, and a euthanasia appointment walked through the front door, that tabby cat knew.

Those were the mornings we wouldn't find her curled up in a ball, napping on one of the chairs in the lobby. Those were the days she wasn't circling the lunch table. She would position herself somewhere near the front door and wait, and then watch intently as the family entered. If they sat in the lobby, she would jump up in the closest chair. If they wanted to pet her, she'd respond by rubbing her head against their hands.

Sometimes, she waited stoically outside the exam-room door

A Natural Therapist |

while the sounds of sobbing went on behind it. I remember an older gentleman coming out of an exam room shaking with grief. He made no sound; he just kept wiping away the tears. He went to the water cooler for a drink, his hands shaking the whole time. Bella was already waiting for him. When he sat down in the lobby, she followed him. She jumped up on his lap, and he hugged her and cried. She stayed with him, and the tenderness she displayed was one of the most touching things I had ever seen.

Bella would continue to get in my way at work, and I would continue to pat her on the head like a dog. And while we never snuggled together, I learned from her that not everyone in this life will like us, but there are still things we can appreciate about them.

— Beth Rice —

43

Chicken Soup
for the Soul.

Cat's Choice

Arguments are often like melodramas. They have a
predictable beginning, middle, and end.
~Gay Hendricks

As we planned our wedding and all the details of setting up a home together, we knew money was tight. We agreed that the wedding should be small. My fiancé worked hard to renovate an old house that would be our first home. Weekends and evenings after work, he hammered, drilled, and nailed while I tried to help but really did very little.

It was clear to me that this home was the gift he was bringing to the marriage. It would keep us comfortable and shelter the nucleus of what might become a small family. I didn't know how to sew cushions and curtains as many women did back then, nor did I have the talent to design fabulous interior décor. And almost all the money I had saved had gone toward the wedding. What gift could I possibly bring to the marriage?

Our wedding day drew closer, and the marriage gift became a larger and more impossible problem in my mind. I couldn't afford to buy anything first-rate. I was too fumble-fingered to make anything beautiful, so the prospect looked bleak.

A week before the wedding, one of the women I worked with mentioned that her Siamese cat had given birth to four kittens. A Siamese kitten! Could this become my special gift? Could I even afford such a special cat?

I had always wanted a pet, but owning one had never been possible. My fiancé had often told me stories of the fluffy white cat that had been the family pet when he was a boy. I was sure we would both love one of these truly special kittens, if only I could afford one. Holding my breath, I asked how much one of the kittens would cost.

"That much?!"

She must have seen the look on my face because she offered me a huge discount if I would work her weekend shifts for the next month.

"Done!"

This creamy-soft kitten with the dark-tipped nose turned out to be the perfect gift. We picked her up right after our three-day honeymoon and named her Tico. Promptly, she set to work helping with the renovations. She chased paintbrushes along the wall, tested the quality of the paint, and curled up on partly installed shelves. Her reward was often the charred remains of the meals I was learning to cook.

From her first day with us, she tried to share her time equally between us. For each time she stood on my husband's shoulder as he painted, she would also spend time by my feet as I ironed or on my lap as I darned socks. If my husband was late getting home from work, she would wait patiently beside the kitchen door. If I took too long in the bathroom, she sat by the door meowing impatiently.

But as newly married people do, we had arguments. My husband, raised in a large family, saw arguments as simply part of life — no big thing. Everyone would get over them soon enough. I was raised as an only child, and to me every small disagreement felt like the end of the marriage. Every little argument left me heartbroken, unable to see any possibility of reconciliation. Besides, I was right. I was *always* right. Of course, mine was the right opinion or course of action. Why did he so stubbornly hang on to a different point of view?

Then I noticed that each time we argued, Tico would sit hunched up on the floor halfway between us. If I spoke, she looked at me. If he spoke, she looked at him. Back and forth we went until we ran out of points to make or insults to hurl.

When a lull in the dispute occurred and there was a painful silence, Tico would get up and go sit beside one of us. It was as if she had judged the matter carefully and come to a reasoned decision. In her considered opinion, this person had the better case. Sometimes, it was me. Sometimes, it was my husband. Who she chose did not seem important — the choice itself seemed more important than clever words or being right.

To our relief, the problem had been solved, and the issue was settled. Whatever had been said was water under the bridge. The cat logic that had been applied ended the argument conclusively. I would have to accept that sometimes I might not be right — the cat had decreed it. There was nothing left to do but make up.

Making up seemed like Tico's favorite part. No longer was she forced to make a choice between two separate laps. The two laps were so close together that she could spread out over both of us.

— Valerie Fletcher Adolph —

44

The Cat Who Groomed Me

I have felt cats rubbing their faces against mine and
touching my cheek with claws carefully sheathed.
These things, to me, are expressions of love.
~James Herriot

I was still grieving a kitten I'd lost when I dreamed of another cat. This one had a black-and-white face and looked like the grown version of little Cleo. A few days after the dream, I perused the animals-for-adoption section of the local paper and saw a cat that looked like the one in my dream. A sudden certainty came over me.

I raced down to the shelter, newspaper clipping in hand, and walked through rows of cages. It was hard to ignore the mewling kittens and sad-eyed cats, but I was adamant. I had to find the cat with the black-and-white face. When I questioned the attendant, she took me to a line of cages where they housed sick animals. She assured me that Bosco only had a cold and was taking antibiotics.

"Do you want to hold him?" she asked.

Of course I did, and when she pulled that huge cat out of the cage and placed him in my arms, I knew he was the new addition to the family.

Bosco's physique reminded me of a little prizefighter, with his short legs, massive chest, and well-developed muscles. He was about six years old and weighed eighteen pounds. Wrestling him into a cat carrier was not easy. I had never encountered a cat with such strength in his legs, but the attendant and I persevered. Finally, he was inside, howling his displeasure at the top of his voice.

The drive home was only ten minutes, which was a blessing. The howling stopped when I released him in the living room where Sweetie Pie, my adult female cat, and Buddy the dog waited to see who was responsible for the caterwauling.

Bosco was twice Sweetie's size. She ran and hid. Buddy is part Border Collie. With herding in mind, he bounded up to Bosco, who arched and hissed, and then demonstrated he could hold his own with a dog who towered over him. Poor Buddy had his nose clawed. After that, he kept a respectful distance.

When he grew accustomed to the house, Bosco took to sitting on my bed, which was Sweetie's territory. They never fought, but circled each other cautiously. One night, I woke to find both cats sitting on the bed, one on each side, their backs to each other. That was the first step. Before long, Bosco and Sweetie were best friends. Bosco made friends with Buddy, too. He never clawed him again, and eventually they napped together on Buddy's dog bed.

Bosco and Sweetie often groomed each other. One night while Bosco sat on the pillow next to mine, he showed his affection by licking my hand. I reciprocated with scratches on his neck. The next day, he upped his game and groomed my hair. I don't think he liked the taste because he made coughing sounds as if human hair was not as appetizing as Sweetie's fur. It wasn't my favorite activity either, but I appreciated his efforts and distracted him with belly rubs.

What I did love was how he patted my face with his huge white paws. He never released his claws, which were impressively curved and strong enough to hoist his big body over a fence. He always touched me gently, so it felt like a furry feather touching my cheek.

When I learned I had breast cancer, my world took a sharp turn toward the dark side. The nightmare of premature death loomed, not to mention the challenges of living alone and caring for my animals during treatment. Since my prognosis was not great, I agreed to a chemo regimen more vigorous than the normal protocol. It would take six months, followed by six weeks of radiation.

All the animals were a great comfort during that year. After my diagnosis, Bosco slept beside me every night. He still licked my hand and rubbed my face, and sometimes he also groomed my rapidly thinning, increasingly dry locks.

I knew I would lose my hair, and one day I decided to shave off what was left.

On the night he found no hair on my head, Bosco's rough tongue scraped over my skin. I watched him cock his head. My transformation seemed to puzzle him. He tried again. I swear his broad face wrinkled into a kitty frown. He considered what to do next. Then he stroked my head with that big white paw, as if consoling me for my loss.

It was a relief to be home where I could wear only a simple cotton turban. The animals didn't care what I looked like. When I was out, I was embarrassed and self-conscious, even while wearing a wig or one of the hat and scarf combinations I came up with.

At night, feeling that big, soft paw rubbing across my scalp was a comfort. All through my treatment, Sweetie watched over me, Bosco petted me, and Buddy trailed me from room to room, placing his face on my knees whenever I sat down.

When my hair started growing back, Bosco noticed before I did. He licked my head quite vigorously one night, which prompted me to feel my scalp. Those first little tendrils of baby fuzz under my palm were a cause for celebration.

I got through that year with the help of family and friends, a great medical team, and my loving animals. While my hair grew back, Bosco continued his grooming. I was still not convinced he liked it, but it was his way of expressing his love.

For many years after that, Bosco graced my life. He was an elderly cat the last time he jumped up on my bed late at night. He settled on the pillow and purred. His soft white paw stroked my cheek. I petted him and scratched his ears, and then he jumped down.

A few minutes later, he screamed in pain. A blood clot had broken off and traveled to his heart. All the way to the vet that night, I sang to him, held him and told him how much he was loved — just as he did for me all those years before.

My sweet, gentle boy who stalked around my house like a feline prizefighter will always live in my heart.

— Carol March —

45

Chicken Soup for the Soul

Recovery Cat

*When I am feeling low all I have to do is watch my cat
and my courage returns.*
~Charles Bukowski

The year was 1998. I was drinking every day, and always to excess. I was in danger of losing my job, and if that happened, I knew it wouldn't be long before I lost my house as well.

Homeless? Me? As a "professional" female with several college degrees, I didn't fit the stereotypical picture of a bag lady, but what could I do?

What I did was quit drinking. Cold turkey. And that kicked off a depression so deep and debilitating that on weekends I didn't even bother to get out of bed, other than to eat and use the bathroom.

A trusted colleague suggested I get some counseling. I thought that meant I'd be prescribed some drugs to make me miss the alcohol a little less, but I was mistaken.

At the first session, the counselor gave me a list of things to do, including exercise, 12-Step Meetings, and vitamin supplements. She ended by telling me I needed to get a cat.

A cat? Are you kidding me? What in the world do I need a cat for? But my counselor explained that, living as a single woman, I had no one to care for, no one who needed me, and no one for whom I was responsible. She suggested if I had a cat, at least I would get my bum

out of bed on weekends because the cat would need to be fed. Well, okay. Maybe. At least a cat wasn't as demanding as a dog.

My goal was to avoid inpatient treatment. And to avoid that, I would do almost anything. But I didn't want a cat. I really, truly, without wavering, did. not. want. a. cat!

Nevertheless, I marched down to the Humane Society a few days later and entered The Cat Room begrudgingly. The rescued felines were put there after they'd been medically cleared. In that room, prospective adopters could interact with them and observe a little of their personalities and social skills.

I knew before I went into the room that I didn't want any of them. I could see that through the observation window. Some had hair too long, and I was sure I was allergic to long-haired cats. Some paid me no attention at all and continued napping without so much as looking in my direction. Conversely, a few wanted all of my attention, and worked feverishly to rub against my legs and head-butt against my hip when I sat on one of the chairs.

One bullseye black-and-gray tabby positioned himself in my lap, and alternated between dozing, and nosing other cats away from my lap. He wasn't aggressive or unkind; he just wanted to make sure he was the one I'd be taking home.

I didn't want a cat. But for the next nine years — the first nine years of my ongoing sobriety — this quietly supportive and attentive feline gave me a reason to hurry home after work and not stop at the bar for "just one," which could have led to nearly a dozen drinks.

We ate breakfast and dinner together every day. At night, we sat together on the couch and watched TV. I learned to work in my home office with a cat bed on the desk where a drink had been in the past. I told him all about my day at work, and he listened to my stories without judgment.

In other words, we became best friends. Who knew that a cat would be the final answer to both my loneliness and alcohol abuse? That first cat has been gone more than a decade, but I continue to have cats — now in multiples — in my home at all times. After all, if one could change my life for the better, there is no limit to what two or three rescues can accomplish!

—Sylvia A.—

46

Nurse Wolfy

The cat could very well be man's best friend but would
never stoop to admitting it.
~Doug Larson

When my daughter added Wolfy to the family, we knew he'd come from tough circumstances. Dana adopted the striking orange tabby with amber eyes from a shelter. She was told he'd been lost or abandoned and had been living on the streets. For nearly a month after she brought him to her Boston apartment, the tiny guy hid under the bed in her room, emerging only to eat and use the litter box.

Hoping for a warm companion, Dana worried she'd made a mistake by rescuing the ginger kitty that was wary of everyone and everything. I remember the day, weeks into becoming a pet-parent, when she texted a photo of Wolfy sitting on her bed by her side. Relief. Joy. Progress. The two bonded slowly from there, and by summer Wolfy had ventured into the rest of the apartment and learned to trust Dana and her two roommates.

Several months later, Dana had a two-week trip planned and didn't want to ask her roommates to care for Wolfy. I was excited to host my grandcat, but first we had to get to know each other. Dana brought Wolfy over a few times and left him with me for short periods. He hid under an upstairs bed or behind a massive living-room chair most of the time. I gave him space, spoke softly, and watched him acclimate to things like where I put his food and litter box. He kept his distance, rarely showing himself. When he did, he'd sit a room's length away and not allow physical contact.

Dana dropped off Wolfy and his gear and left for her trip. Within minutes of arriving, Wolfy claimed his hiding place behind the living-room chair. It was going to be a long two weeks.

As the days passed, Wolfy began to find new secure places to settle himself, and I noticed him choosing spots far from me but close enough that he could see and hear me. If I was at the kitchen table, he was around the corner under the dining-room credenza. If I was reading in our enclosed porch, he was under the ottoman in the adjacent sitting room. If I was in the basement doing laundry, he was crouched behind the big, wooden tool cabinet in the opposite corner. He moved with me, but never toward me. He was close, but always apart.

Then I got sick. When the first pains shot through my abdomen, I knew it was diverticulitis because I'd had it before. I adjusted my diet and tried to manage my symptoms, but I knew I wouldn't kick it without treatment. After the third day of pain that had me crying and doubled over, I resolved to take myself to the hospital the next day while I could still drive. I collapsed onto the living-room couch. Too riddled with fever and pain to make the trip upstairs to the bedroom for the night, I lay there in my clothes, moaning and sweating, moving in and out of semi-sleep. I prayed for morning to come quickly.

After an hour or so, I heard a noise, a tiny yip. I opened my eyes to find Wolfy on the rug next to the couch, his face eight inches from mine. I reached out, and he pushed his wet nose against the back of my hand, nuzzling me. I wasn't alone in my pain anymore.

Wolfy never left me during that difficult night. Whenever pain or chills broke my sleep and I opened my eyes, he was there, atop the piano, standing guard. Under the coffee table, looking straight into my eyes. Sitting erect on the rug within a foot of my face, staring at me. And, by morning, up on the couch with me, nestled in the space behind my knees, watching me intently.

As I made my way to the front door in the morning to leave for the hospital, he followed me. I patted and thanked him, and told him everything would be okay. He passed his body across the bottom of my legs to let me know he'd be there waiting when I came home.

— Lori Hein —

47

The Communal Cat

Some people have cats and go on to lead normal lives.
~Author Unknown

We've all heard stories of how companion animals can reduce blood pressure, calm prison inmates and give people the will to live. I read these articles through the years with a lukewarm reaction until I saw the effects of one plump cat on my mother.

When my father became ill, I flew quickly from the West Coast back to my prairie home. My stay would be lengthy, so I decided to bring along Farfinu — Farfy, for short — the calico cat. Mom welcomed her with warmth and affection, the same way she welcomed any of her grandchildren.

"She's a lot easier than a grandchild," Mom whispered, and then winked. "The only off-limits places are the tables," she added. "I don't like cats up on tables or countertops."

"Sure, Mom, whatever you say." Why mention that none of this would be my decision? Establishing house rules was up to our much-pampered nine-year-old cat. Besides, she's an indoor cat, and I often reminded my husband, Paul, that she's probably cleaner than him.

"You mean cleaner than *us*," he corrected.

"Sure, honey, whatever you say."

After my father's funeral, I hated the idea of leaving my mother alone in our family home of four decades. I also saw how happily the cat settled into her new routine. Mom assured me that kitty was welcome for as long as I wanted. "And wouldn't kitty rather stay with me?" she said. After all, Farfy went from a compact highrise with a mountain view (inspiring for humans, not cats) to the run of a spacious house with picture windows and perfect cat ledges. I was relieved to hear Mom's generous offer, even though Farfy kept roaming the counters.

Mom's generosity continued with a $500 cat enclosure for the back yard. And why not? It was Farfy's tenth birthday.

"Mom, you've never spent $500 on my birthday!" I said, watching my husband shake his head when I covered the phone to tell him the news.

"Don't take it personally, dear. I've never spent $500 on *anyone's* birthday. Until kitty."

Our cat isn't hurting in the dining department, either. Mom makes special treks to a pet-food store where she purchases brand-name foods. When it comes to Farfy, only the best will do. Mom cashed the first few checks I mailed for the Farfy Food Fund, but soon insisted that I stop sending them.

"I'll just rip them up. I'm the one getting pleasure from her, so why should you pay for her food?"

I argued with her several times, but I couldn't prevail against an eighty-year-old with a stubborn, kind heart. Same drill for vet vaccinations and check-ups. My mother refuses to accept any money for kitty's care.

Mom smiled during Farfy's recent check-up. The vet reminded my mother to ask for the seniors' discount.

"For who, me or the cat?" Mom asked.

"Take your pick," the doctor laughed.

Although it is bottomless, Mom's heart is unhealthy. For two decades, she's suffered from debilitating bouts of angina. One April day, she drove herself to the emergency room. Within a week, she had endured quadruple bypass surgery. Again, I flew home and stayed with Farfy while Mom spent a month in hospital. Despite feeling weak, Mom was anxious to return home and sleep in her own bed.

Cherry blossoms lined the neighborhood streets when my brother and I brought her home from the hospital. After helping Mom up the front steps and onto the living-room couch, Farfy trotted out to greet us. After one glimpse at the stretching cat, my mother began to cry. They were the only tears I witnessed during a difficult struggle to regain her health. And she admits that no number of needles, throat tubes, pain or anxiety had made the tears flow — until the sight of our communal cat.

This was the moment when I realized how precious Farfy has become. This was also the moment when I realized that Farfy might never live with us again, unless my mother is unable to look after the cat.

My mother is nowhere near that point. When I ask how kitty is doing during my phone calls home, Mom answers invariably, "She's a dear, wee soul, and I don't know what I'd do without her."

The cat is undeniably dear, but the description of wee is a downright misnomer. Weighing just under sixteen pounds on her last vet visit, she looks more raccoon than feline. If Farfy were a boxer, she'd be in the heavyweight division.

And at some unknown juncture, she also gained free run of all tabletops. During one of my visits home, I found Farfy stretched across an open newspaper on the kitchen table as Mom craned her neck to read around her. Later, I watched our cat snooze contentedly next to a flower-filled vase on the dining-room table.

"Leave her be, she's not dirty," Mom called out when I started to take Farfy off the fur-coated tablecloth. "She loves smelling the flowers. And when guests come over, I put on a fresh cloth."

As for those articles on how companion animals are good for people's physical and mental health, now I read them with gusto. If anything, I don't require more evidence; I have all the proof I need when I look at my mother and our communal cat.

— Shannon Kernaghan —

Stretch

*Until one has loved an animal, a part of one's soul
remains unawakened.*
~Anatole France

I came out of the subway, and there he was. Every night, it was the
same. He'd be sitting on the ground. When he saw me, he'd rise
and stretch against the brick wall. On rainy nights, he sat at the
bottom of the subway stairs, shielded from the weather.

He didn't frighten me. He was kind of scruffy but attractive. It
was obvious that he was homeless, and the street was his "yard." This
broke my heart. I felt sorry for him, but I didn't want to get involved.

One night, as I came up those steps, our eyes met. Then he came
right up to me and stretched into a kitty version of a downward-facing-
dog position. Call me a crazy cat-lady, but I found this endearing. I
don't know what got into me, but I gave him a pat on his mangled
head and said, "We've got to stop meeting like this." Then I picked
him up and said, "Okay, Stretch. We're going home."

He purred.

I took him home and placed us both in front of a mirror.

"Look at us! What a twosome!"

He was a mess, and so was I. What had I been thinking, bringing
a cat home when I couldn't even take care of myself?

I had recently lost someone I loved very much. He had died way
too early. I was in a state of depression. I had given up on practically

everything. When I didn't have to work, inertia and sleep became my only escapes.

But now I had a cat I was responsible for. I took an old brush and brushed his fur halfheartedly, taking out the knots. There was some Maine Coon in him and who knows what else, so there were tangles on his belly, too. I had to trim those with scissors. He didn't mind. He seemed to relish the attention. What emerged from the brushing was a brand-new cat — a beauty with black-and-white, short-and-long fur. He rolled on his back and purred, stretching. Always stretching.

"I'll get you a litter box tomorrow, Stretch. For tonight, please use this plastic box." I lined it with torn-up newspaper.

I had half a chicken thigh left in the fridge. We split it. I promised to do better the next day.

It was time for us to go to sleep. I placed a folded blanket next to my bed and showed it to the cat. He sniffed it, stretched and jumped up on my bed.

"Well, okay, if that's what you want, Stretch. Tomorrow, I will have to teach you some rules."

Guess who taught whom?

We went to sleep. Or rather, I tried. The first night, he woke me at 5:00 a.m. He had slept on my feet, and started rolling around and stretching early. Then he walked up to my face and gently patted my head as if to say, "Get up."

"No! It's too early, Stretch. Leave me alone." I moaned.

I turned over and covered my face with the blanket. He wouldn't have any of it. He tugged at my blanket gently with his teeth. We argued, and he won. In a way, I loved it.

Every night, it was the same. He woke me at the crack of dawn. His shenanigans would not allow me to sleep. Once more, I questioned my decision to rescue the stray. "What did I need this for?" I asked myself.

He'd get on my chest and purr. I'd watch him stretch to twice his length. He seemed to be saying, "Watch this! You can do this, too."

So, one morning I took his advice — stretching before getting out of bed. I pulled my knees into my chest, releasing the tension in my lower back. My hamstrings loosened up with gentle legs-in-the-air exercises. By the time I got out of bed, my body felt more relaxed and supple.

Once he had me stretching, that wasn't enough. I began to observe his actions. He peeked into closets, tried opening drawers, and climbed high up on the refrigerator. When Christmas came, I had to borrow a ladder to get him off the top of the tree.

He was a fearless, playful cat. He wanted to get into everything. He wasn't timid. He was inquisitive and seemed to thrive with each new experience. There was no limit to expanding his horizons.

Surprisingly, my previously lonely apartment soon became my haven — *our* haven. I couldn't wait to get home to see what mischief Stretch (and I) would get into next. At first, he made me smile. Eventually, his antics had me laughing.

Observing his actions, it dawned on me that the cat was still teaching me — to grow, to develop, to be curious, to embrace life — in essence, to stretch. When I saw him stretching as he came out of his litter box, I wondered if this was another lesson meant for me — to stretch outside of the box.

The cat had not been wrong so far, so I tried it — stretching outside of the proverbial box. I started reading more books. I took a real-estate course. I bought a book to brush up on my French. I tried Thai food and liked it. I took up sewing and continued my ballet lessons, which I had abandoned years earlier. I went back to church.

I took up yoga, which taught me to stretch not just physically, but through meditation, mentally and emotionally.

Stretch wiped away my sadness. Living with him, my depression eased. Joy returned unexpectedly.

I opened my mind to new things. As I developed, I landed a more interesting job and made new friends.

When I finally ventured outside of my home to go out socially, I brought in a kitty to be a buddy for Stretch. He deserved the companionship. We both thrived.

My Stretch is gone now. He and I lived and stretched together harmoniously for more than a decade. It was a long, long time ago, but the lessons I learned from him continue to enrich me still.

A Natural Therapist | 153

Today, when I open my eyes in the morning, I still see him stretching at my feet, reminding me to do the same. I picture him in a kitty-version of downward-facing dog as I first found him at that subway station.

I never dreamed a mere cat from the streets could have the power to teach me such a simple but compelling lesson — to stretch.

Yes, we learn from our parents, from our friends and from experience. But the best advice I ever got was from this adventurous cat — to stretch physically, mentally and emotionally — to stretch for life.

These were life lessons I learned and never forgot from a cat named Stretch.

— Eva Carter —

New York, the Cat

Attitude is a little thing that makes a big difference.
~Winston Churchill

I was working in a Louisiana pet store when I first met New York. The Humane Society called him New York because he was originally from Brooklyn. His owner moved to Louisiana, fell on hard times and decided to give him up to a shelter. He was a large gray cat with strange black markings. If one looked very closely, they seemed to spell out words. He had fangs that were always exposed and very large feet. It didn't take a lot of research to discover that he was not a typical house cat. He was a cross between a house cat and a Bengal.

The store provided a space for local shelters to keep some of their cats for adoption so they could get exposure to more potential pet parents. They left New York in one of our stainless-steel kennels. To call him anti-social would be an understatement. He would hide behind his litter box anytime a potential adopter entered the room, but he seemed to be drawn to me. His kennel was shoulder-height to me, and when I called him, he would saunter up to me and place his front paws on my shoulder.

One day, I opened his kennel to show him to a potential pet parent and allowed the man to reach inside. In true New York form, the cat arched his back and hissed at the man, who quickly recoiled at the sight of the large, angry cat. I leaned in and scolded him for his behavior, and he strolled over and climbed on my shoulder. The man looked at me and said, "That's your cat. He chose you."

After two weeks, the Humane Society worker returned to the store to remove New York and replace him with a pair of small kittens. She said that they would have a better chance of being adopted. She returned New York to the shelter.

I thought about New York every time I entered the cat room. I worried about him and wondered what would become of the cat with the bad attitude. I had no intentions of adopting a cat. I already had one cat and four dogs at the time, but somehow this cat had left an impression on me. Was he really supposed to be my cat?

I was working late one night almost three months later when the Humane Society worker came by to check on the cats. We struck up a conversation, and I told her about my experience with New York. I could see the glint in her eye as I spoke about him, and she told me that he was living in her house. My heart broke when she told me he was still being kept in a cage.

She said that she took him home because he was considered to be not adoptable, and that the shelter might need to make the decision to put him down. Hearing this, I filled out the paperwork on the spot, and the worker delivered New York to me at the store the next day.

When I brought him home, he beat up my dogs! When he got excited, he ran four feet up the walls, flipped in the air and never missed a step. I am convinced that my other cat thinks he's crazy.

I learned the first time he got outside that New York had never seen grass. Grass was so traumatic, in fact, that he ran up a tree and onto my roof. I called him for hours, but he opted to settle down on top of the chimney and go to sleep. That was the first time I ever climbed on my roof. Thanks to New York, it wouldn't be the last.

For about six months, the dogs hid from my new cat. My kids avoided him, and I'm fairly certain my other cat was plotting against him — and possibly me. But every day when I got home from work, New York greeted me by climbing up my leg and perching on my shoulder. He would rub his face on mine and purr, then leap off and trot away to wreak havoc on the rest of the house.

When my family questioned my decision to bring home such a

bad cat, I told them that since we lived in the country, it would be nice to have a good mouser. The first time New York saw a mouse, however, he jumped on the table to hide from it and broke a crystal vase. New York finds mice quite terrifying. Betta fish, however, are delicious.

In the spring of 2016, my elderly father moved in with me. He was never a cat person, and I worried that he and New York would not get along. As time passed, I noticed that New York wasn't greeting me the way he used to. The dogs roamed freely through the house, and the other cat seemed to have forgiven me. One night, I watched as my father scooped up New York and took him to his room. I waited a bit and then went to check on them. They were lying in bed together watching television. I closed the door and let them be. Later, I realized that this had become a nightly ritual. My father had chosen New York, and New York had responded with patience and love. I was elated by their relationship because my father had just lost his companion of ten years, and he needed the kind of bond that only a pet can provide.

We have now lost my father, and New York is again terrorizing the other pets, running up the walls, and leaping on and off my shoulder. In my time of grief, he has shown me a little extra attention. I ask myself how he knew that he was needed and why he took on the role of support animal so readily, something that seemed so contradictory to his character. We had a strange bond when we met, and that bond was solidified by the compassion that he showed to my beloved father at the end of his life.

He may be the cat who chose me, but if the roles were reversed, I hope I would have chosen him. New York will spend the rest of his days in my good graces. If you stumble upon my home, pay attention to the "Beware of Cat" sign unless, of course, you're a mouse.

— Bonnie J. Taylor —

Dr. Bella Is In

*If there were to be a universal sound depicting peace,
I would surely vote for the purr.*
~Barbara L. Diamond

I t was a sad, strange time. We had quickly gone from three dogs to none at all. On top of that, one of our daughters was having issues that were making home life somewhat difficult. She kept hinting that she wanted a cat, but my husband and I weren't ready for a new pet. Our home life was stressful as it was, without adding the obligation of a new pet. Plus, our daughter had recently watched a cat die only days after rescuing the poor thing.

One day, in an attempt to find some sort of structure in the middle of emotional chaos, I decided to work in the front yard. I was sitting beneath one of our front windows, pulling desperately at the long blades of grass daring to grow up through the lantana, when this tabby kitten, probably about six months old, appeared at my side.

The kitten was sweet — friendly, yet in absolute control. She played the elusive card, rubbing up against me, and then dodging my hands when I tried to reach out and pet her. I managed to win the game once or twice before she finally ran off toward a truck parked beside the house and dove under it.

Fast-forward a couple of days later. One of our daughters opened the front door to go to the store. The tabby materialized out of nowhere and ran inside.

"No! Get out!" I yelled.

Crazy cat. Did she not understand that we didn't want any pets?

In hindsight, I should have known how things would play out that moment. Even the daughter who didn't like cats was fascinated by her (and kept letting her inside).

Still, I stuck to my guns. No pets. No messes. No thanks.

That lasted only a few days. This kitten had other ideas. She took over the house.

Time passed. Things were still tense with our daughter. But with Bella's arrival, something had changed. This independent, bossy, wide-eyed feline brought a serenity, an acceptance, a sounding board, to every member of our house. What had once been a feeling of "I'm all alone here" in matters concerning parenting, or trying to be a teenager, or being a sister, or simply wanting to fit in with the world, had now been tempered by an aloof tabby who loved us and allowed us to love her back (once in a while).

If someone had asked me during that tumultuous time if I thought bringing a sassy cat into the mix would have helped the family dynamic, I would have laughed. But that's exactly what happened. Bella filled a hole that only our one daughter knew needed to be filled. Bella was our therapist. Our sounding board. Our friend. A neutral tie to one another, a subject to talk about that didn't induce any strain.

I found out later that our daughter had actually prayed for a cat. And lo and behold, Bella was there soon after, insisting on being a part of our lives. She even became the adoptive mom to an emaciated kitten we rescued from our driveway a few months later, and then again to another cat that same daughter and my husband fell in love with six months after that. (Yes, we now have three cats.)

If you ask people who don't like pets the reason for that choice, they tend to give the same reasons. The fur makes a mess. The house might get destroyed. It's a total pain picking up their messes. Not to mention how much it costs to take care of them for their entire lives.

After losing our three dogs, that's how I felt. We had recently remodeled our kitchen, which meant new furniture and floors. There was no rational reason to bring an animal into all that.

But when a little ball of fur heals the invisible tear in a heart, things like occasional claw marks or having to vacuum up perpetual fur bunnies are well worth the price. Sure, finding a nick on my favorite couch is disappointing, but I will replace the couch eventually. I won't, however, be able to replace the way that little troublemaker helped mend our whole family.

Bella isn't an average rescue cat. We didn't rescue her — she rescued us.

— Esther Stevens —

51

A Cat's Mother

Motherhood: All love begins and ends there.
~Robert Browning

I'm a happy member of an eleven-person household. My parents have nine children, and I am one of them. While some people might see large families as overwhelming and stressful, there is nothing more unifying than when we welcome a new member into our home.

When there's a baby in the house, we all gather around in delight at the simplest things — watching him take a bath for the first time, laughing at her facial expressions with her first bite of baby food, or cheering him on as he takes his first steps. Maybe this is why my parents decided to have so many children — and they tried for more, but after the nine of us were born my mother had three miscarriages.

It's been six years since we've welcomed a baby into the house. Immediately after each loss, I asked myself tearfully, *How will God provide the much-needed glue? Who will my family gather around in delight and awe? And who will my mother cradle in her arms and rock in her chair every day?*

About two years ago, my dad and my brothers went on a camping trip. We own a property full of log cabins, lakes, and wide-open spaces. The night they were supposed to come home, my mom got a call from my dad. He had found an abandoned kitten in an old, rundown barn. My dad believed that with all the commotion of humans making camp at the usually quiet outdoor property, the mother cat had abandoned the kitten. It was very young and would freeze to death if it didn't have care.

We already had two cats and a dog. For a household already bursting with eleven people, my mom believed we'd be crazy to welcome any more pets — which is why I wasn't surprised by my mother's reaction to my father's phone call. But her protests didn't work. My dad is a shameless cat lover. The kitten was coming home.

While the men of the house were driving home with the kitten the women of the house tried to prepare for their guest. For my mother, the preparation wasn't much more than stomping around the house in frustration, muttering about how the house was already a mess, declaring that she would only allow the kitten to stay long enough to find another home, and making us all promise to do our part to care for it.

It was raining when the boys arrived, and the rush of cool, wet air that came into the house was accompanied by the heart-melting cries of one black kitten that hardly fit into the palm of a hand.

When the pitiful sobs of the kitten reached my mother's ears, all protests about the inconvenience of an additional animal ended. Maternal instinct took over, and within two seconds of entering the room, the kitten was wrapped in my mother's arms and being soothed in the same rocking chair that nine other children had been rocked and comforted in. Children gathered around, all wanting a chance to hold and feed the newcomer.

Needless to say, the kitten would not be transferring to a new home. She had found her family, and especially her new mother. In the months that followed, my family took turns waking up to the kitten's cries in the middle of the night to feed her from her bottle. We played with her, petted her, and held her when she got scared of the dog. We laughed when her first can of cat food left crumbs all over her whiskers. And we agreed unanimously to call her Ariel after the Disney mermaid when we gave her a bath and discovered she loved water.

Ariel is an adventure-seeker. She can be lovable but tends to be more playful and independent, always searching around the house for new experiences and curiosities. She tends to avoid the company of the kids because they can be too rough. Perhaps remembering that first day when my mother comforted her after the trauma of being left alone in the cold, Ariel always seeks out the company of my mother. Ariel cries when my mother's not home, follows her around the house, purrs on her lap while she's reading a book, and nestles around her head every night while she's sleeping.

I had worried about the gap left in my family when my mother discovered she would not be having any more children. But ever since Ariel arrived unexpectedly, she has been the glue that unites my family and the happy salve to my mother's sore heart.

— Elizabeth Citrowske —

Who's in Charge Here?

52

Mr. Nibbles

I have studied many philosophers and many cats.
The wisdom of cats is infinitely superior.
~Hippolyte Taine

I've owned my fair share of cats over the years, but Mr. Nibbles remains my all-time favorite. He was everything one could ask for in a cat. And if he seemed to entertain too high an opinion of himself sometimes (a character trait not uncommon in cats), he more than made up for it by being all-around good company.

I should precede this account by confessing that I was a teenager back when Mr. Nibbles was the resident cat. So perhaps, if fault were to be found, I should shoulder the lion's share of it. I could be as thoughtless and irresponsible as any other teenager. Between the two of us, Mr. Nibbles was certainly the more mature and, by far, the more dignified. He had a serenity of manner that rarely deserted him and bespoke a lifetime of acquired wisdom. It would be fair to say that I was, as it were, the pupil and Mr. Nibbles the instructor, a role he filled with considerable élan.

That brings me to the incident of the Slinky. We all remember the Slinky from our childhoods. It was more than just a toy. It was a gadget with unlimited potential and, it is hardly an exaggeration to say, ranks as one of the great innovations of the pre-computer era.

Naturally, one of the first things that occurred to me upon receiving it as a gift was to test the Slinky out on Mr. Nibbles. I knew just how to go about it, too. Curiosity has lured many a cat into trouble, if not into ruin—and so it was with Mr. Nibbles. He had to explore and investigate any novel phenomenon that crossed his path. He had to discover not only *what* it was, but *why* it was what it was. So when Mr. Nibbles first heard the Slinky making its way down the stairs, his initial instinct, impossible to resist, was to thoroughly investigate the matter.

Fortunately, he only arrived at the bottom of the stairs when the Slinky had already completed its descent. Mr. Nibbles stalked around the serpentine metal loops, now sprawled motionless upon the carpet. He was wary at first, properly so, unable to make out what he was dealing with and whether it represented any sort of threat.

"What do you make of that, Nibs?" I addressed him. "Pretty special, huh? I'm willing to bet you've never encountered anything like it before, right?"

Mr. Nibbles looked at me. He seemed to recognize that I was egging him on and appeared to suspect that my motives might be something less than pure. In spite of this, Mr. Nibbles, after making a thorough survey of the situation, approached the Slinky. He batted it with one paw. The Slinky didn't budge. It lay there inertly. After a few more swats with his paw, Mr. Nibbles threw a scornful look at me, as if to say, "That's the best that you got?"

I smiled at him, knowing that I had set this up perfectly. "Hold on, now," I cautioned. "Don't rush to judgment. You haven't seen anything yet." I grabbed the Slinky and bounded up the stairs two at a time. "Watch this!" I sent the Slinky on its way.

Anyone who remembers the characteristic sound and motion of a Slinky won't be surprised that Mr. Nibbles' eyes widened in astonishment. He arched his back and emitted a low hissing sound, warning the Slinky off in no uncertain terms. The Slinky didn't get the message. It continued its descent with chilling, inexorable determination. Mr. Nibbles held his ground a moment longer and then, concluding that discretion was the better part of valor, turned tail and bolted from the room.

I had a good laugh at Mr. Nibbles' expense over the whole affair. It wasn't often that I got the better of him. But, as things turned out, my sense of triumph was premature. Mr. Nibbles bided his time, allowing me to imagine that he had gotten over his mortification. Then he hit back — hard.

I made the mistake of leaving the Slinky out while no one was home and Mr. Nibbles had the run of the house. When I returned, I encountered a scene that will remain etched in my memory forever. The Slinky had been battered and mauled, wrapped around the legs of tables and chairs, and turned this way and that. It was hopelessly tangled and stretched. Mr. Nibbles had exacted a terrible revenge. I suspected that, all along, he had simply been waiting for an opportune moment to strike. My carelessness had given him that opportunity, and he had taken full advantage of it.

Despite my best efforts, I was unable to nurse the Slinky back to health. The damage proved irreparable. Never again would it be able to navigate its way down the stairs. Never again would it sow terror and inflict humiliation. I could do nothing but deposit the remains in the trash, an ignominious end to a brilliant career.

But the incident was not a total loss. I did learn not to act so rashly or with so little regard to the consequence for myself and others. It's a lesson that has stood me in good stead in all the years since, one that I have taken to heart. It must be said that Mr. Nibbles, though perhaps not conscious of doing so, showed me the way in other respects as well. It was through and by his example that I became versed in the finer points of napping, a talent I have put to good use consistently. One had only to observe Mr. Nibbles in his natural state to absorb lessons whose merits and worth were borne out again and again.

Mr. Nibbles holds a special place in my heart still. Growing up would not have been half so much fun without him. I could pay Mr. Nibbles no higher compliment than to refer to him as a true companion and friend. Though my current cat, Mirage, is a fine fellow in his own right, he is no Mr. Nibbles.

But then, what cat is?

— Thomas Canfield —

Snow Cat

Blessed are the curious for they shall have adventures.
~Lovelle Drachman

Everyone loved Auntie Joe's cat T. She got him at the end of April when he was just eight weeks old — a curious, friendly, fearless gray tiger. He was hilariously clumsy, too. When leaping onto a table, he'd usually collide headfirst with the edge and flip back onto the floor, paws clawing ineffectively at the air.

I lived next door to Auntie Joe and Uncle Pete and used to spend more time at their house than mine. Mama had just given birth to my baby brother, Albert, and I was glad to escape the seemingly endless diaper changing and wailing, as well as the flood of Mama's friends and relatives cooing over the baby as if they'd never seen an infant before. Mama was glad not to have me pouting underfoot. Joe and Pete had no children of their own, so they seemed happy with my company.

Summer was the best season. The warm days were endless. The watermelons were red and dripping with sweet juice. Some nights, I got to sleep outside on the back screened porch with T in my arms, counting the stars.

I spent most of the time playing with T. He was an explorer, and we spent hours hiding in the long grass by the oak tree, catching grasshoppers by day and fireflies at night.

Then winter came, blowing leaves off trees and covering the ground with snow. T went to the front door demanding to be let out. He stepped gingerly into the cold and then began digging down frantically, trying to find the warm, green earth. He stayed out as long as he could, and then raced back to Auntie's window, yowling pitifully. Once back inside, he searched for a new reality. He stumbled to the side door, crying for us to open it. He was shocked to discover snow there, too. Then he tried out back. Surely this white stuff couldn't be everywhere? Where had his sunny, verdant world gone? Surely if Auntie opened just the right door, it would be summer.

Every day after school that winter, T helped me with my homework, usually by sitting on it. And when the snow melted, I trained him to follow me down the street by dragging a string behind me.

On August 29th, T went out as usual, but he didn't come home that night. Joe and I were really worried. He'd never done that before. But Uncle Pete said we were worrywarts.

"It's normal for cats to stay out all night. They are nocturnal. That means they are 'creatures of the night,'" he said in a scary Dracula voice. "He's almost a year old, well past kittenhood. He's exploring. Just wait a day or two, and he'll come back."

But T didn't return. Auntie Joe and I walked the neighborhood, searching every street and alley. We knocked on doors and talked to neighbors. We made a flyer. We drove to a store and printed fifty copies, which we posted all over the neighborhood. I saw a dead opossum. But no one had seen T.

The next year, on April 12th — yes, I remember the date — I was helping Auntie Joe make cookies. They were chocolate chip, my favorite. We'd just dabbed them on the tray, licked the spoons and put them in the oven when we heard a high-pitched wailing at the back door.

Joe opened it, and T came bounding into the room. He rubbed his nose violently against Joe's shins and rolled on his back demanding belly rubs.

We opened a can of tuna, and he lapped up the juice happily. But true to form, he refused to touch the actual fish. He wasn't starving, or even hungry. In fact, T looked plump and well-groomed, not at all like a cat that had been lost in the wintry suburbs of Pennsylvania for eight months.

"Where have you been, T?" Joe asked, cradling him in her arms.

Who's in Charge Here? |

T just purred and blinked.

With T back, it was set to be the perfect summer, playing in Joe's sprinkler, selling lemonade, making cookies and hunting gopher snakes in the thick grass at the back of Auntie's yard. Sometimes, when Mama let me stay over, T would sit on my lap while we watched movies. Like me, he was outside all day, but he always came in by twilight.

When I dropped by Auntie's on August 29th, T didn't come yowling to the door for a nose rub, as he usually did.

"Where's T?" I asked.

"He ran outside yesterday at about 3:00 and didn't come home," Uncle Pete said.

"He didn't come back all night?" I asked.

"No," Pete said, "but don't worry. Cats often stay out all night. T probably knows that summer's ending, and he wants to make the most of the warm nights."

But T didn't come back that day or the next. Auntie and I searched and searched. We posted flyers and asked neighbors, but he'd vanished once again. It was even harder to get past it this time. I missed his little falsetto mew, the way he'd greet me at the door and follow me around the yard. I couldn't have any pets because my baby brother, Albert, was allergic to almost everything.

The school year passed slowly, as school years do, but summer came finally. I was at home when the phone rang. It was Auntie Joe.

"T's back," she said.

I looked at the calendar — April 12th — the exact same day he'd returned before. We didn't know what to make of it. It was a mystery for sure.

But things didn't get truly strange until the next year when T vanished once again on August 29th and returned once again on April 12th.

When August 29th came around, we were ready. Auntie Joe, Uncle Pete and I spent the day inside, playing *Monopoly* and watching T. Pete had just bought up all of Boardwalk and was looking to make a killing when T ran to the door and started digging at it and crying. Pete opened the door and T leapt over Pete's foot and bounded down the street as though he were late for an appointment. We raced after him, just managing to keep his tail in sight. Then he turned a corner and disappeared. We'd lost him. It was as though he'd vanished into another world. Maybe he'd return in eight months, or maybe we'd never see him again. Where had he gone and why? Didn't he love us? Didn't he love me?

As I was getting ready for the long wait, Auntie grabbed my arm and pointed across the street from where we were standing. There was a silver trailer parked in front of a neat brick house. On the steps leading into the interior stood a fit, elderly woman and a silver-haired man. But they were not what Auntie was pointing at. Auntie was pointing at T, who was sitting on the silver stairs licking his paw, as if he belonged there and it was his home.

"Is that your cat?" Joe called, walking toward the trailer.

T took one look at her and raced inside.

"Why, no," the woman said. She had a high, thin voice, sweet as a midsummer nightingale. "But isn't he the sweetest thing? He showed up just about, was it four years ago, dear?" she asked the silver-haired man. He nodded.

"Yes," she continued. "He just appeared right when we were leaving on our annual trip to Florida. We go there every winter. It's just too cold for our old bones here. And little Toby—that's what we named him—just wandered into our trailer, so we took him with us. Well, he was sweet as they come. But when we came back on August 29th, as we always do, he ran away. We looked for him a bit, but he'd just disappeared. The next year, he came back just as we were leaving, and he's joined us on every trip since."

Joe, Pete and I were silent. It seemed wrong to drag T from his trailer. He'd discovered a way to escape winter, and I think we all envied him.

"Well, have a nice trip," Joe said.

"Oh, you betcha," the woman said, mounting the stairs and turning to wave goodbye.

We walked home.

It wasn't until we got inside, all sitting at Auntie's table, that Pete started laughing.

"I'll be darned," he said. "I've heard of snowbirds, but this is the first time I've ever heard of a snow cat!"

—E.E. King—

54

Pumpkin's Drinking Problem

Cats do not have to be shown how to have a good time,
for they are unfailingly ingenious in that respect.
~James Mason

One would think my cat was born under a water sign. Pumpkin's obsession with water began at an early age. He started with sinks and worked his way up from there. That stream of running water captivated him in a way that only a cat could understand. And the love affair continues to this day. Like his counterparts in the wild, he seeks out fresh, running H2O. He will sit next to the sink and yell until I do his bidding. He not only likes to sip right from the faucet, but depending on his "cattitude" on any given day, he may prefer to simply sit and gaze at the cascading stream. When the mood strikes him, he performs the most complicated of his many sink scenarios, letting water run over his ear and the side of his furry face while he grooms his paw.

During the past few years, Pumpkin has elevated his hobby to the fine art of bathtub haunting. The tub in our house is wonderfully large and deep. He considers it his private cave and often sets up camp there. Time after time, I'll search the house for him, feeling a chill of terror: "Oh, no, he couldn't have gotten out!" At last, I peer over the edge of the tub to see him ensconced in his headquarters, staring back rebelliously, fixed in his sphinx pose. If I dare make eye contact, it's all over. He leaps up onto the edge like a crazed jack-in-the box and demands to have the water turned on. His favorite part of this routine is to stop and wait tensely like a wound-up spring until I am about to shut off the faucet. Then he swoops in to "catch" the water with his paw before it disappears. He has not yet succeeded at this, but he never tires of trying.

From time to time, Pumpkin steps up his fixation a level and ventures into the shower right after I have exited. Any continuing drip is something that must be studied at length.

I spent big bucks to get one of those pet water bowls that plug in to provide a constant stream of water day and night. After I set it up and presented it triumphantly to our tiny tyrant, he gave me a scathing look and trotted off to the sink.

On rare occasions, Pumpkin does condescend to drink out of his special fountain. This takes place only after I feed him hairball treats. Those sticky, little gems are lip-smacking good, leaving my kitty like a kid who just ate a mouthful of peanut butter. Even so, Pumpkin will visit the fountain only after verifying that no one is watching him. Heaven forbid he should be caught doing the very thing I want him to do. He's not a dog, after all. I pretend to busy myself in the kitchen until my nonchalant peek and his slurping sounds reveal that he is indeed using his designated water source.

A friend recently chided, "It's not really about water, is it? It's about control."

My reply: "What are cats for, if not to spoil shamelessly?"

— Kim Johnson McGuire —

55

Tattle Tale

Some people say that cats are sneaky, evil, and cruel.
True, and they have many other fine qualities as well.
~Missy Dizick

Grandpa had been smoking cigarettes, cigars, and an occasional pipe since his days in the military. But Grandma never approved. Not only was it a serious health risk, but it was also an expensive and dirty habit. So Grandpa promised he would stop smoking, and he tried to quit. But a nicotine addiction can be a struggle to overcome. Occasionally, Grandma would smell a whiff of cigarette smoke as she leaned in to give him a hug when he came home from work.

One day when the stress of his job had been too much to handle, Grandpa bought a pack of cigarettes and smoked one on his commute home.

When he got home, Grandma frowned and asked him sternly, "Have you been smoking again?"

Caught and embarrassed, Grandpa fibbed "no" to get out of the hot seat.

Shaking her head, Grandma sat down and looked at him calmly. Grandpa was hoping he could get to his coat pocket to dispose of the evidence before Grandma found it.

As Grandma started to ask him to come clean, their cat came strolling into the kitchen and hopped onto the table — with a new cigarette hanging out of his mouth in exactly the right position, as though he was just looking for a light.

Always appreciative of the humor in situations, neither Grandpa nor Grandma missed a beat.

"It's not me, it's him!" he blurted.

"I'm sorry I doubted you," Grandma replied, her eyebrows raised. "Clearly, it's the cat who's the smoker in this family."

Grandpa promised not to lie or smoke ever again. And this time, he managed to keep his promise.

As he told me the story decades later, he added, "If even the cat was worried about my health and conspiring to get me in trouble, I knew it was time to stop!"

— Teresa Murphy —

56

She Came with the House

*The power of finding beauty in the humblest things
makes home happy and life lovely.*
~Louisa May Alcott

The impeccably dressed woman was trying to dislodge a furry bundle from its perch on her shoulder. Like a baby, the furry bundle was voicing her displeasure at the attempted separation.

"Oh, my goodness, who is this?" I asked, abandoning my purse and coat at the door and walking over to the real estate agent. I scratched the small cat on the head, and she began to purr.

"This is Mouse," the woman answered, cradling the cat against her shoulder once more. "She thinks she's a baby."

"Mouse!" I was delighted, and continued to pet the seal point Siamese. Mouse had an overbite, her two small fangs protruded from the sides of her mouth, and her bright blue eyes were slightly crossed. My husband, Chris, cleared his throat, and I stepped away from the cat reluctantly to commence our tour of the house.

The ranch house sat on a quarter-acre, treed lot. It was tastefully decorated with gorgeous details that we both loved, including a floor-to-ceiling fieldstone fireplace, a kitchen nicer than any I had ever cooked in, and a four-season sunroom built onto the back of the house. I pictured our family sitting by the fire in the winter and eating together in the big dining room. I pictured myself writing in the sunroom, inspired by the quiet calm. I had never been in this house before, but it felt like home.

As we walked through the rooms, Mouse followed us. She jumped on and off the chairs in the sunroom and stayed at our heels as we inspected closets. She jumped onto a bench in the master bedroom and started meowing at us as we peeked into the small bathroom en suite. Chris smiled at her.

"I know," he said, moving to her and scratching her behind her big brown ears. "This is your home. We're just looking."

My husband was not usually one to fawn over animals, but it was hard not to be smitten with Mouse.

We were visiting my in-laws in my husband's hometown, three hours away from Toronto, where we had lived for ten years. Our two small girls were at their grandparents' house, splashing in the pool and eating watermelon, while Chris and I attended the open house. With every recent visit to my in-laws in their quiet, historic town, we had begun to talk about how much we were all enjoying our time there, allowing a "what if…" to creep into our conversations.

Our life in the city was becoming more stressful each month, stretching us beyond our means financially and emotionally. The company where I had worked for more than a dozen years was on the verge of a transformation I didn't feel able to make with them. I was also craving more time with our daughters, who were three and five years old. Chris was trying to shift his work schedule to accommodate our needs, and the constant worry for our future and wellbeing was taking a toll on all of us. We needed to make a change.

After spending more time in the house than we had anticipated, we spoke to the agent regarding a few of the home's details. After crouching to give Mouse one last pat, we left. We had barely made it to our car before I made an announcement.

"I want the house. And that cat too, please."

Chris laughed. "I liked the house, too. A lot. And I liked the cat, but I don't think she's part of the bargain."

We talked about the house the entire three-hour drive home and throughout the next two weeks until our conversation morphed from "What if?" to "Why not?"

My husband could work full-time from home. I could switch to being a freelance writer since the cost of living was so much cheaper outside of the city. The girls were so young they would adjust quickly. We could come back and visit Toronto whenever we wanted. It felt nearly perfect, although I wished that there had been a sign, a spark of providence that went beyond logistics and planning to show me that this was meant to be. *Don't be foolish,* I admonished myself silently. *You don't need a sign. You just need to make a choice.*

We drove back the next weekend and made an offer on the house. It was accepted. We were leaving Toronto for a small town and our dream life.

On our final tour of the house, we held Mouse as we measured rooms, discovered nooks and crannies, and began fantasizing about our future there.

"Oh, Mouse," I said. "I'm sorry you have to leave this place, but we'll take good care of it for you, and I know you'll love your new home, too."

But the real estate agent dropped a bombshell on us. "Oh, no," she said. "Mouse isn't going with the homeowners; they're moving to be closer to their family, and their granddaughter is allergic to cats. Mouse is going to the shelter."

My heart sunk at the thought of this beautiful, friendly cat going to a shelter, but then I realized something. I had my sign.

"She's staying here," I said definitively. "We'll adopt her. After all, it's her house."

A quick phone call with the sellers and the casual adoption was complete. When we moved in a few months later, there was a bit of a welcome package for us, and a lovely note about Mouse — her age (nine or ten), her health (perfect), her personality (easily gleaned, immediately loved). We settled in together.

Mouse became my first and most loyal friend in our new home. She was my comfort during those lonely early days and my constant companion as I eased into a routine that allowed family and work life to finally be balanced. She was also the best ambassador and co-host we could have hoped for. Her friendly demeanor won over everyone who visited. There was never a lap or shoulder Mouse did not want to perch upon, no scratch behind the ear or backrub she would deny a potential friend.

For the seven years we had her, our girls doted on Mouse, cuddling with her in bed or sprawling with her in front of the hearth, warmed by the fire and each other. If there was ever any moment of trouble adjusting to our new surroundings, Mouse, with her boundless affection, vocalizations and charm, helped rectify it immediately. It was impossible to be in a bad mood for long when Mouse jumped on our laps and began to purr.

"She came with the house," we proudly told anybody who made her acquaintance — a lucky, lovable sign that showed us we were exactly where we were meant to be.

— Karen Green —

The Littlest Art Critic

Perhaps it is because cats do not live by human patterns, do not fit themselves into prescribed behavior, that they are so united to creative people.

~Andre Norton

In our small town, the local galleries stay open late the first Friday of every month to share food and wine with locals and tourists. Guest artists are usually present to talk about their work. We were regular visitors at many of the galleries with our white Persian, Joshua, in tow. Always on a leash, Joshua looked forward to the gallery night when many of the galleries saved a shrimp or piece of cheese for our little art connoisseur.

One September evening, Joshua sported a little blue jacket and was enjoying a piece of shrimp against one wall when an artist prepared to speak. Unfortunately, the wall where Joshua was eating was the same wall where the artist's work was displayed. I pondered what to do as people lined up to hear the artist. How could I possibly move the cat while he savored his shrimp and the visitors were watching him? I stepped back and hoped no one would pay attention to the fluffy feline happily downing his treat. Just then, the gallery owner introduced the artist, and he stepped up, blocking any attempt to extract Joshua.

No worries. Joshua stopped eating, turned toward the artist and sat down. He listened intently as the artist talked about his work. I, however, remained uncomfortable. Joshua now commanded even more attention than the artist, who kept glancing down at the cat.

Who's in Charge Here? | 181

Embarrassed, I inched forward. I planned on removing Joshua as soon as the talk was over. However, the artist had other plans. Suddenly, he stopped talking about his art.

"Enough about me," he proclaimed. "I just love cats!" With that, he stopped speaking and moved toward Joshua, patting him on the head.

Seeming to know the talk was over, Joshua let the artist pet him and then started out of the gallery, heading toward his next treat.

It only goes to show that even cats have manners and pay attention when someone is talking. Maybe we could learn from Joshua.

— Carol L. Gandolfo —

Roo

Prowling his own quiet backyard or asleep by the fire,
he is still only a whisker away from the wilds.
~Jean Burden

She arrived by limousine on a Monday afternoon. I stood in the driveway with my two children as the uniformed driver ceremoniously opened the back door of the car and removed the tiny cat carrier. The driver had made the three-and-a-half-hour trip from Manhattan to my little town on the North Shore of Massachusetts to deliver a twelve-week-old Bengal kitten.

I wasn't looking for a cat when I'd spotted the ad on Craigslist a week before. My ten-year-old daughter, Coco, had recently been forced to give away her guinea pig after it was discovered that I was so allergic I couldn't even be in the same room with Mr. Nibbles without having an asthma attack. Cats, on the other hand, were fine. We already had Buster, a gentle, dignified, twenty-year-old tuxedo cat who we had rescued from a local animal shelter when he was eight. And then there was Coco Kitty, a shy tabby who happened to have the same name as my daughter. We'd agreed to adopt her when a good friend moved to an apartment that didn't allow pets.

Coco had squealed when the photo popped up after I clicked on the listing for a free Bengal kitten. Lying on her back as if to show off her leopard-spotted belly, the fuzzy, little creature was sleeping on a blanket next to a stuffed cat that was twice her size. In a second photo, she was posed with a miniature ukulele, one paw across the strings.

Who's in Charge Here? | 183

"It's sooooooo cute! Please, Mom, we've never had a kitten!"

"Very special Bengal kitten free to the right home," the ad read. "Please fill out and e-mail the attached application if interested."

Curious, I clicked on the link. The four-page document asked for a brief bio of each member of the potential adopter's household, including age, profession, and hobbies. There was a place to describe the house itself and whether it was located in a city, suburb or rural area. The application asked for a list of other pets in the house and a description of their personalities. There was a section for a short essay where the applicants were asked to make a case for why they would provide the best home for this cat. Intrigued, and with Coco's encouragement, I began to write.

When the response arrived in my inbox a couple of days later, I felt like I'd won a prize.

"We were picked!" I exclaimed as Coco peered over my shoulder to read the e-mail.

"After careful consideration of a number of applicants, I'm happy to inform you that I've selected your family for the kitten's forever home."

Eager to make arrangements for pickup, I replied, "Great! I can drive to your location or meet somewhere, whichever you prefer."

"I live in New York," the kitten's mysterious owner answered. "Let me know what day and time is good for you, and I'll send my car and driver."

"Oh, no!" I typed back, crestfallen. "I think there's been a misunderstanding. I live near Boston."

"I know," came the response. "That's not a problem. I think your family will provide the best home for this cat, and I'm willing to have her delivered at your convenience."

I turned to Coco. "This has to be some kind of a Craigslist scam. I can't figure it out, but there's no way someone is giving away a Bengal kitten *and* driving it here for free. I'm sorry, honey."

"Maybe it's just a nice person who wants to find a good home for their cat," my sweet, ten-year-old daughter suggested.

"I'm afraid that's not how the world works," I responded cynically.

"Can't we just say 'yes' and see if it's true?" she pleaded, hands

184 | Who's in Charge Here?

clasped together, big brown eyes open wide.

"Okay, but don't get your hopes up."

Three days later, Roo stepped out of her carrier and into our kitchen with all the confidence of a full-size leopard. With a squeaky meow, she strode right up to twenty-two-pound Buster, who regarded this four-pound ball of fur with suspicion. Coco Kitty trotted into the kitchen, tentatively approached the newest member of our family, and dashed into a closet to hide after an exchange of hisses.

In the days that followed, I would come to question my judgment. Despite her cute appearance, Roo was as wild as any cat prowling the African savannah. She soon made us aware of a mouse problem in our creaky old Victorian, depositing a dead rodent outside each of our bedroom doors three nights in a row. The gift-mice were intact, without a mark on them. It was obvious we were dealing with a stone-cold assassin.

With the mouse problem resolved, and in need of a new game, Roo entertained herself by taking things apart and hiding the pieces. One day, while I worked at my desk, she reached into a laser printer next to my computer and removed something, absconding with the small bit of plastic before I could stop her. The printer never worked again. Single earrings would disappear when a pair was left out on the bureau. A little Eiffel Tower statue vanished from the mantel. Legos, paper clips, and coins went missing. Q-tips, carried crosswise in her mouth like a tango dancer's rose, were added to a growing collection under the fridge. Our new cat wasn't interested in finding a sunny spot to nap in like Buster and Coco Kitty. She wanted a job to do.

Clearly, we weren't going to tame Roo, but we learned to adapt and appreciate her for the wild creature she was. The fish tank got a cover that clamped shut. The office, with its array of electronics, was off-limits. Plants were moved to a secure location. Battery-powered cat toys were utilized. Eventually, Buster and Coco Kitty made peace with this wild interloper, demonstrating proper grooming and litter-box etiquette, and playing with her on occasion.

The humans in the house came to love Roo both in spite of, and because of, her wildness. As we got to know her, we could see that she was a study in contradictions: fiercely independent but very social; ferocious, but also affectionate; strong-willed, yet eager to please. In time, she began to climb tentatively into an available lap for a snuggle, purring loudly.

Roo was a complex creature with her own unique needs and demands, but with a little patience and a lot of love, she came to accept us as her family.

—Janet Spicer—

Feline Feng Shui

Even if you have just destroyed a Ming vase, purr.
Usually, all will be forgiven.
~Lenny Rubenstein

Our house had seemed empty in the weeks since we'd said a sad goodbye to our fifteen-year-old kitty, Pumpkin. We were determined that our next pet would be a cuddly lap cat. So we bypassed the kittens at the shelter and headed for the adult cats, reasoning that we'd be able to see their fully formed personalities. When a black-and-white, one-year-old charmer settled himself in my husband's lap and began purring loudly, we knew we had found the one. We took him home and christened him Sam I Am.

It turned out our screening process for lap cats had gone awry. Unknown to the volunteers at the shelter, Sam was actually running a high fever — hence, his clingy, loving, subdued nature. When we got him home, he started to go downhill fast. Soon, he was lying around listlessly, refusing to eat.

After several stressful and pricey trips to the vet, Sammy was on the mend — and that's when the real Sam I Am emerged. We found ourselves humming the old Kenny Rogers tune, but with a twist — "You *re*decorated my life."

Now in the pink of health, Sam I Am began his project of modifying our home décor to suit his taste. As soon as he grew tall enough, he jumped onto the back of our furniture and started pawing at any painting within reach. Industrial-sized spray bottles did not deter him in the least. The treacherous teetering of these wall hangings was more than we could bear. What if something fell on him? Soon, all paintings were stripped from our walls except one lone fishing boat watercolor that rests just inches from the ceiling.

By the way, our innocent, little bundle with the "Who me?" eyes had not been aged correctly at the shelter. It turned out he was not full-grown when we adopted him. Within six months, he blossomed from eight pounds to a solid fifteen pounds — strong enough to knock over heavy objects and tall enough to reach anything formerly out of bounds. And faster than a speeding bullet.

We don't have a wall-mounted, flat-screen TV yet, but Sam may be forcing our hand. One of his favorite antics is to launch himself up behind electronic fixtures and wreak havoc with the tangle of cords I've so carefully taped together back there. Now we've closed the gaps at the sides of the wall units using paper grocery bags affixed with purple duct tape (for extra flair). Classy! But we've got to protect ourselves. After all, we spent hours hooking up point A to point B when we set up everything.

The beautiful trailing philodendron we had showcased on a plant stand nearly met its demise when Sam knocked it over on the carpet and inspected his handiwork proudly. That plant has been removed to the tip-top shelf of said wall units. The empty plant stand is now a cat launching pad.

Our lovely new shower curtain has also fallen victim to the cat. We live on the coast, and I had proudly selected a seaside theme with beautiful blue and green hues and famous sea-related sayings. Then the hide-and-seek games began. Sam I Am excels at jumping into the tub, spinning around like a Tasmanian devil, and then grabbing the shower curtain for a little hang-by-the-claws trick as he peeks out, looking criminally cute. After assessing the damage to curtain and liner, we concurred that we must keep them tucked up behind the nearby towel rack, thus exposing our shampoos, lotions and potions, and ruining the restroom feng shui for mere humans.

Other redecorating ideas abound. Vertical blinds have been gnawed on generously, but we try to turn a blind eye. There is only so much we can take. Stuffed animals appear mysteriously in the middle of the living-room floor with their fluffy innards strewn all around. Yesterday, we spied Sam toting a panda bear by the nape of its neck. Lamp shades? Several have been removed and sequestered to a high closet shelf because of kitty's nibbling needs. His scratching post sits squarely in the middle of the living room, lest he should decide he prefers it to the big easy chair.

We've stopped short of removing mirrors, simply wincing as Sam stands tall and does his wiggle-waggle dance, pawing at his reflection and knocking the glass crooked into a precarious angle.

Sometimes, we want to cry, but we laugh instead at Sam's crazy antics. What humor and joy he has brought to us with his mischief. When he pads into the kitchen and gently taps my leg with a soft paw to indicate he is ready to be fed, I look at this feline with the rabbity soft fur, saucer-like golden eyes, and black-spotted pattern and can't help but smile. Yes, he still spurns lap sitting, but wherever we are in the house, he appears magically nearby, sprawled out on the carpet with half-mast eyes keeping a close watch on his humans.

As long as Sam I Am is in our home, either zipping down the hall like his tail is on fire or stretched out sleek, beautiful and proud, our decor looks just about "purrfect."

And that feng shui suits us just fine.

— Kim Johnson McGuire —

My Cat Bed

A cat allows you to sleep on the bed. On the edge.
~Jenny de Vries

Once again, I found myself teetering precariously on the edge of my twin-size bed. My body was incredibly tense, and I feared I might tumble over the side and onto the unforgiving floor below if I so much as breathed. This wasn't too far outside the realm of possibility because I had done it many times before. I didn't want tonight to be a repeat of all those other nights.

It was only about a two-and-a-half-foot drop, but it might as well have been twenty feet. Regardless of the actual height of the bed, it still hurt when I fell. On top of the pain, the loud *thump* of my body hitting the floor usually alerted my parents downstairs that I had fallen out of the bed again. As I hung there on the edge, my body tense with anticipation of meeting the hard floor below, I felt those familiar paws pushing against my back. It was my cat, Smokey, who was currently taking up the entire bed while leaving just a small sliver of space for me.

I always started out in the middle of my bed, but somehow found myself being pushed toward the edge as the night progressed. The evening would start out innocently enough with my gray companion jumping up onto the bed to curl up beside me. All would be well for a few minutes, but then I would start to feel two small paws push up against my back and shoulder blades. Naturally, I assumed this gesture meant to scoot back a little, so I obliged happily and gave my furry friend some space so that he could sleep more comfortably. That way, he would have his space, and I would have mine.

Then I would feel those paws pushing up against my back again. Had I somehow shifted closer without knowing? Feeling like a terrible pet owner and friend, I inched closer to the edge of my bed so that my cat would have his space again. This process would repeat until one of two things happened — either I fell off the bed and hit the floor, or I got up and moved to the other side of the bed only to repeat the entire cycle.

I have no idea why I sacrificed my comfy bed to my cat so willingly. He slept all day anyway. I was the one who needed the rest. However, I was afraid that if I didn't please him, he would move on to one of my brothers' rooms. It wouldn't have been so easy for him to stage a hostile takeover with my brothers' beds. They wouldn't have yielded to those paws of his as easily as I did. He'd have to be content with curling up into a ball at their sides if he wanted to stay with one of them. Why do that when he could trick me and take the entire bed for himself?

I recall several nights when I just ended up sleeping on the floor and let him have the whole bed to himself.

Well, that was about to stop. No longer was I going to allow myself to be manipulated by my cat. I was bigger. I was superior! He was lucky he even got to lie in bed with me. I could have easily closed my door and left him to fend for himself.

I suddenly realized that maybe Smokey was trying to teach me something by doing this to me every night. Maybe he was trying to teach me to stand up for myself and not let others push me around. He certainly never let anyone push him around or tell him what to do. Perhaps that was why he chose to sleep with me every night. He did it to teach me this important life lesson so that I would be better prepared for the future. That had to be it! Well, I was certainly going to make this change right now. I was going to stand up for myself, starting with taking back my bed — *thump!*

—Jaiden Deubler—

The Sacred Role

When women support each other,
incredible things happen.
~Author Unknown

Opening the door, I was startled by a gray blur that ran through my legs and up the stairs, pausing only to beat up my Pomeranian, Junior.

A gray-striped tabby cat made herself at home on my sofa. She began cleaning herself casually. My new calico kitten, who'd joined our family only a week before, watched her cautiously from a distance.

Junior retreated to the bedroom.

"Who do you belong to?" I asked as I lifted her up. She purred as I stroked her head. Placing her in the bathroom, I returned with a dish of food and water. She didn't seem thin, but she tucked hungrily into her food.

I assumed she must be a neighbor's cat who had gotten out by accident. A few people allowed their cats to walk around outside where I lived, but I'd never seen this one before.

"Alright, time for you to go home," I informed her. I took her outside, intending to follow her home and knock on her owner's door. Cats always seemed to have a way of knowing where to go.

I sat her down, and she bolted back in, returning to my sofa. I knocked on the doors of my immediate neighbors while the cat rested in my living room.

The young girl several doors down from me explained, "I'm sure she's a stray. She's been hanging out down by the creek forever. I've fed her before, but I can never get her to come in."

I called my husband and he told me to put her in the bathroom, and he'd deal with her when he got home from work. "We just got Sabby Cat. We can't have two cats. I have to put my foot down."

My husband returned that night. What a pushover. Within minutes, the cat was named Stormy, and he belonged to her. Anyone who knows anything about cats knows one doesn't own cats; they own us.

Stormy was always my husband's cat. She'd perch on his desk when he'd leave for work and make a game of knocking items onto me if I tried to sit and use the computer.

Every night, she was the first to greet him when he'd return from work, and she took ownership of his lap whenever he sat.

As the days went on, we noticed that Stormy was growing round. She had an appointment at the vet for her shots, and they confirmed our worst fear. Stormy was expecting.

The day she delivered, it was a gray, quiet day. My son, husband, and I were lying on the bed, cuddling and watching football, when she walked up to me and showed me she'd begun to deliver.

"This is woman stuff. You take care of her." My husband took my son to the living room, closing us in the bedroom.

I placed Stormy carefully in her box. I'd taken the time to research and prepare exactly what she needed. I sat on the small sofa in the bedroom with my book. In three seconds, she was on my lap, purring and kneading my leg.

"Come on, girl. I made it nice for you." I tried putting her in the box again, and again she jumped up. It was obvious she was about to push. The kitten was protruding from her. I grabbed a throw blanket from my bed and laid it next to me. She lay down immediately and, as I stroked her, she gave birth to her first baby—a little gray male my son would name Chiefy.

We sat together all night on that little red sofa. I dozed next to her and her mewling kittens as they arrived one after another. As she tired, it became my job to wipe their faces and noses clean. Between kittens, she'd stand on my leg, kneading as I stroked her back. She was happy for the help. At 3:00 a.m. the next day, the last kitten was born.

A friend of mine once said, "Women need other women." I never understood what she meant until I was needed by Stormy.

Stormy may have been Daddy's girl, but it wasn't him she came to when it was time to give birth, and it wasn't him she relied on to clean up her kittens. I was the only one she trusted to handle her babies for several weeks. This was indeed a sacred experience in which females had supported each other through time eternal, including females of many species.

From that day forward, Stormy was known as Mommy Cat.

—Nicole Ann Rook McAlister—

The Unlikeliest of Friends

*Friendship is the hardest thing in the world to explain.
It's not something you learn in school. But if you
haven't learned the meaning of friendship, you really
haven't learned anything.*
~Muhammad Ali

One of our cats had passed away and left his brother, Red, wandering the property, yowling in loneliness. I knew the only solution would be to find a kitten to replace the feline that was missing. At a visit to a local Amish farm, I spied an orange-and-white kitten meandering around the outbuildings. Seeing her reminded me of my quest for a new cat, so I asked my friend if she had any new kittens available.

"You can take that one." She nodded to the marbled kitten. "Someone dropped her off, and we can't take another cat."

Without hesitation, I scooped her up, dubbing her Splash for the stroke of white colour that streaked across her orange back. On the way home, she purred and watched the passing fields from the van's front seat.

I was surprised by how tame she was. However, I had one concern with introducing a new cat to our collection of animals — especially one as friendly as her. Our Shepherd, Bee, had a distinct dislike of all things cat and had made her view clear to the stray felines that skirted the perimeter of our property. Our own cats were wise enough to keep their territory limited to the barn and fields. The house cat knew

Who's in Charge Here? | 195

where all the key hiding places were that a big dog couldn't fit into. Even in the house, she skirted Bee's pillow by a few yards, certain that if she got too close, those big teeth might make their mark. That left Bee to rule her canine domain with an iron paw. My concern was that the kitten didn't understand all of this and would become a victim of Bee's prey drive.

I took Splash to the barn where she and Red became instant friends. It didn't take long for her yellow eyes to catch a glimpse of the house and light up. I could see she knew there was a better life to be had there. She validated what I had suspected — she had been a house kitten. She had far more knowledge of house life than a wild-born barn cat and made a straight line for the door to the back kitchen.

Bee enjoyed the freedom of the porch and the house's surrounding land, so when the kitten meandered up the drive toward her, Bee came charging, all fire and fury. I sucked in a breath, knowing I would never be able to react fast enough and expecting the worst.

And then the kitten bristled like a porcupine on caffeine. She faced her opponent fearlessly and swiped at the approaching muzzle with a tiny paw. Bee pulled to an abrupt stop, confused by the reaction. I could see clearly that she yearned to have the kitten tuck tail and run so she could chase, but Splash wasn't made of that kind of stuff. She stood her ground — fluff and bravado — and took a second swipe. Bee stiffened and waited. I held my breath. The kitten relaxed and then began to coil around Bee's legs. And then the unexpected happened: Bee turned and slinked off to her mat by the back door.

Every day for the next few weeks, the kitten would find her way to the porch early in the morning, and Bee would charge out the back door to chase her away, only to find a persistent and unruffled nemesis. A month passed, and we began to notice that Bee was eager to go out in the morning and would wag her tail when Splash approached. Over the next few months, we watched an aggressive dislike turn into a playful friendship between the five-month-old kitten and the nine-year-old dog. They began to share the back-door mat and sometimes the treats that were set outside for the dog. And always, the kitten greeted the dog with a rubbing of the legs and her throaty purr.

Our most recent surprise came when we called Bee to her kennel. Splash trotted beside her. The two of them settled on their haunches and watched me latch the gate. While I sat on the porch with a friend, the two companions romped and played with the toys and each other. My friend and I chatted and chuckled over the strange relationship, and the thought struck me that this dog and cat weren't so different from the nations of this world.

We are all different in unique and interesting ways. Some of us have been raised to believe that aggression toward one another is the solution to our own existence. Some of us are like Bee, who charges in with the intention of dealing with an unwanted intrusion. Some of us are like Splash, just wanting someone to share life with and not really caring about past reputation or appearance.

I watched as an old dog and a young cat preached a sermon from which the world would benefit. It was a sermon of love.

The two became the best of pals. Bee still rules the place, and Splash still hunts mice, meows and purrs. They are two very different animals with instincts that should put them at odds. Yet they have come to a place where all differences are set aside, and they enjoy each other fully. Why can't we?

— Donna Fawcett —

Chapter 7

Making Better Humans

Anything Helps

*Somewhere along the way, we must learn that there is
nothing greater than to do something for others.*
~Martin Luther King, Jr.

The University Village Plaza is a short distance from my house. It has all the basic necessities a person needs, like a grocery store and pharmacy. I enjoy going there a few times a week for two main reasons. The first reason is that the grocery store has the best potato wedges I've ever had. The second and more important reason is Arthur.

Arthur is a big, striped orange tabby cat who hangs out in the plaza. He likes to sit outside the stores and greet all the plaza patrons with enthusiasm. It seems he's never met a human he didn't like. I've heard he lives in a house nearby and walks over to the plaza every morning when he's let out. He is clearly loved and cared for by his family. Around his neck hangs a collar with a heart-shaped tag that reads: "My name is Arthur. I have a home."

On a particularly cold and rainy winter afternoon, I got a craving for those delicious potato wedges and decided to brave the elements to get some. Upon arriving at the plaza, I noticed a young man sitting outside the grocery store. His clothes were dirty and ill-suited to the chilly wet weather, and he was shaking with cold. Next to him was a paper cup and a cardboard sign that read: "Poor, hungry, cold. Anything helps."

I felt the familiar pang of sadness that I always feel when I see someone in need. The man smiled at me, and I managed to return a half-smile before bowing my head to look at the ground as I walked past. I always feel so powerless and awkward in these situations. I never carry cash on me. And, besides, would a couple dollars really help anyway? I crossed to the coffee shop to get a green tea and took a seat by the window to drink it. It didn't taste as good as usual.

After I finished my tea, I walked back across the parking lot to the grocery store. I glanced over to where the young man had been sitting. What I saw made me pause. He was still there, and he was not alone. Nestled on his lap was Arthur, purring contentedly. The young man was leaning over him protectively, shielding his furry body from the rain. The man looked up at me and smiled as he had before and said, "This little guy is so awesome. He's keeping me warm while I keep him dry. We're helping each other out, you know?" Slowly, I returned his smile and nodded.

In that moment, I realized the significance of small things in a way I hadn't considered before. I had dismissed my own ability to help the young man because I felt like it wouldn't have been enough. I'd convinced myself that a couple of dollars, a coffee, or even some kind words from me couldn't fix the man's life, so I shouldn't bother trying. Arthur showed me why I should bother, and he did it without knowing the young man needed anything at all. When I got inside the store to get my potato wedges, I bought some for the man outside as well. After all, as Arthur had taught me, anything helps.

— Liz R. Sparkes —

A Sheep in Wolf's Clothing

Bravery is being the only one who knows you're afraid.
~Franklin P. Jones

We adopted Nicki and Vicki when they were just five weeks old. Their mother had been poisoned, and we had to rescue her litter of five kittens from where they had been left under our neighbor's porch.

We tried for days to coax the kittens out with little pieces of meat and saucers of milk. When we finally caught them, we found three healthy kittens and two scrawny ones, half the size of the others. My husband and I took the tiny ones. Though we questioned whether they would survive, they were two tiny spitfires, wild in every sense of the word. It took more than a month of patience and kindness before they decided to give domestication a try.

When we started our teaching careers, they travelled with us to the Ozarks and settled in as house kitties on Lickskillet Farm. Though they wanted to be outdoor cats, the landlord's huge German Shepherd, Lick, made going outside very dangerous for them. So Nicki and Vicki were confined in the house most of the time.

Even as adults, they remained tiny. Nicki, the smaller and friendlier of the two, often draped herself around my neck while I corrected papers in the evening while Vicki curled herself around my feet. They brought me comfort as I struggled to plan lessons for the big, rowdy farm boys in my classes who paid little attention to their quiet, 5'1" English teacher.

Making Better Humans | 201

From the very first week of school, the boys had ignored my requests for quiet and order. Instead, they chose to throw books and bully the younger students by knocking their books off their desks and shoving them from their chairs. I had thought that if I used the patience and kindness I had used to tame Nicki and Vicki, I might regain control of my classes, but that strategy didn't work. So I was worn out and frustrated at the end of each school day. Only Nicki and Vicki seemed to bring calm back into my life.

In late autumn, we realized that Nicki and Vicki were pregnant. We were very excited about the prospect of more cats since our drafty, old farm house, and the landlord's barns, attracted many mice. During their pregnancies, the sisters became enemies, and I feared for their kittens being born into a very nasty feud. So we kept them separated in the house — Nicki in the kitchen and Vicki in the bedroom. This saddened me considerably because I could no longer look forward to coming home to peace and quiet after struggling through days of chaos in class. Instead of soothing purrs, the house was filled with cats yowling as threats were hurled back and forth through the bedroom door.

Nicki had her six babies first, and we made sure the doors were always shut so that a jealous Vicki wouldn't harm the kittens. Two days later when Vicki delivered five kittens of her own, she was totally captivated by them. We hoped the feud was over. Still, we kept the two families apart... or so we thought.

A week later, we came home from school to find the box in the kitchen empty. Six kittens had just disappeared. I rushed into the other room and was amazed to find Vicki and eleven kittens sound asleep all together; Nicki was nowhere to be seen. A few hours later, all eleven kittens were in the box in the kitchen with Nicki, while Vicki took a break. The girls had apparently mended fences and joined forces.

When the kittens were about two months old, we moved the families to the enclosed back porch where they had fun climbing the screens. When they were three months old, they ventured into the back yard for the first time.

During that first foray into the "wild," something amazing happened. While the kittens played by the steps, the landlord's big Shepherd dashed into the yard and headed straight toward them, barking and snarling. I thought they were goners!

Suddenly, a shriek and fierce battle cry split the air. Little Nicki, who had been on babysitting duty, flew off the porch and leaped directly onto Lick's head, screaming and growling! She bit and scratched… and the fur flew. She ran up over Lick's head and down his back just as Vicki rounded the corner of the house and followed her sister's path. Lick was so shocked by the attack that he tucked in his tail and fled. I was astounded! Those two tiny cats found the courage to face down a fierce dog. Though Lick could have destroyed them easily, their ferocity confused him, and the bully backed down. For the rest of our time on Lickskillet Farm, anytime either Nicki or Vicki appeared outside, Lick ran for the barn.

As I thought about what had happened, I couldn't help but wonder about their tactic of meeting the bully head-on, even though they were tiny. Maybe it might work on the big boys who wreaked havoc in my classes. Perhaps meeting their belligerence with ferocity instead of trying to reason with them might be the key to gaining control. The next day, I changed my demeanor and, remarkably, my classroom's dynamics.

From then on, at the beginning of each year, I entered my classroom with a show of sureness and strength instead of the shyness and timidity that I truly felt. For the next thirty-five years, until I retired, I never had another problem with discipline. I started each year remembering Nicki and Vicki's courage and no one ever dared to call my bluff.

— Sue Bonebrake —

Who Wants a Cat Named Feral?

You and I do not see things as they are.
We see things as we are.
~Herb Cohen

I heard the little girl ask her mother if they could adopt the cat that was named Feral. The mother explained that "feral" was not the cat's name, but was a warning on the sign on the cage. She said, "It means the cat is wild and mean. I don't think this is a good cat for you... Let's keep looking."

The little girl moved on in search of the perfect kitty, but my curiosity was piqued. Peering in at what I expected would be a wild, savage cat, my eyes met the lifeless blue ones of a small, frail white cat. She lay cowering in the back of the cage. I noticed a string hanging loosely around her neck. The shelter volunteer informed me it was used to catch her, and she would not let anyone get close enough to remove it.

Apparently, five months in the tiny cage had taken the wildness from her. While all the cats around her meowed and pawed through their cages to woo me, the unwanted feral cat lay still. This was not my perfect kitty, so just like the little girl and her mother, I moved on. I left the shelter disappointed about not finding my perfect cat, which for me was a Siamese.

Several weeks passed, and I found myself returning to the animal

Making Better Humans

shelter. This time, I was not looking for a Siamese; instead, I wondered if "Feral" was still there.

The string that hung loosely around her neck had pulled on my heart strings, and I decided that if she was still there, she would leave with me. I was not a stranger to the damage that labels can do — I was ready to take a risk.

Feral was indeed waiting there. As I reached into her cage and lifted her out, she offered little resistance. Gently, I removed the string — marking the end of her captivity.

It was no surprise that she found sanctuary under my bed once we got home. For several weeks, she received her food, water and litter box there. I knew the feral label and five months in the cage had immobilized her, making it impossible for her to be all she was meant to be. It would take time for her to trust me.

I named her Pooka after Jimmy Stewart's imaginary friend in the movie *Harvey*. She was not a six-foot rabbit, but she was my imaginary friend. While she lived under my bed, only I knew of her existence. I would sit on the floor softly calling her name and assuring her of her safety. I gave her time.

Several weeks passed. Little by little, the distance between Pooka and me shortened until she emerged one day, never to go into hiding again. Today, she awakens from a nap on top of my bed — not under it. Pooka purrs softly as her paw touches my face to awaken me from the nap she encouraged me to take. Together, we bask in the sunlight, and I am thankful a label did not deter me from finding my "perfect cat."

— Nancy King Barnes —

If Cat Can Change...

Motivation is what gets you started.
Habit is what keeps you going.
~Jim Rohn

E very cat we've ever known has had its food preferences. Angelina, or Gina for short, had a strange obsession with those black, brittle seaweed sheets called nori that are used to make sushi. Whenever I would take some out of the package, Gina would bolt into the kitchen and claw at me for a few sheets. To watch her chew with crazed relish made me wonder if there were components of catnip in Nori.

Pumpkin loved seafood, whether it was fresh, canned or dried in a lovely seafood variety with both chewy and crunchy bits. All the pet food brands were acceptable as long as they tasted of seafood. We tried to trick her with her favorite brand in chicken flavor, but Pumpkin turned up her nose and went on a hunger strike until the menu included "ocean fish."

So, when a stray cat decided to adopt us, we presented a generous bowl of seafood cat food, thinking that this would be a treat for the thin, starving waif. Imagine our surprise to find that this cat, named Cat (long story for this unimaginative name), had standards that did not include seafood. Cat preferred beef. And, we learned later, Cool Ranch Doritos.

I wondered if perhaps Cat's street life had exposed her to trash bins filled with junk-food leftovers. When we put out healthy and nutritious cat food, she nibbled and upchucked whatever she got down. She showed more preference and tolerance for canned cat food, yet it was clear her tastes ran more to chips and fast food.

We knew when her meals were unsatisfactory because she would harass us with loud meows, head bumps, and sit-ins on our laptop keyboards. If we tried to ignore her and go about our business, she would run in a zigzag pattern between our legs in order to trip us. And trip us she did. Putting her outside did little good. Who could resist her forlorn face staring at us through the window? Or her pawing to come indoors like a banished, abused child? Sheepishly, we'd let her back in and cave to her cravings within a few hours.

French fries, hamburgers, taco meat and cheese, sugar cookies, chicken nuggets and fish sandwiches were her particular favorites. She ate like a college freshman with an unlimited meal budget. Animal advocates, like parenting experts, would be horrified at our weakness in giving in to a cat. Humans, of course, should know better. We were shortening her lifespan and setting her up for serious health problems. We felt guilty.

In our defense, we not only tried but insisted on putting out the good stuff for her and refrained from offering junk food for as long as we could. We justified this by saying that we were afraid she'd run away and become a street cat again so that she could revert to her Dumpster delicacies. Besides, it's a habit of loving cat owners to give in to their picky loves. Everyone knows that we humans exist only to cater to the whims of our cats.

Plus, her adopted humans were not such great role models. After all, we ate chips and fast food, which is how we learned she had a penchant for it, too. Her clean-eating meals of lean chicken and fresh fish would last as long as our resolve to eat fish and salads, which was about three days at a stretch. We felt trapped by our taste buds that had been trained to prefer saturated fats, starches, and sugars.

But as we contemplated Cat's diet — and ours — we realized it was time for a change. We steeled ourselves to resist her pitiful complaints.

At first, she went on a food strike. We held firm, pointing to her canned and dry food bowls. When she complained too long, we put her outside with her bowls and went on with our day. One morning, she nibbled at her food dish and then finished it off with a lick. At the dinner table, she would sit in a chair to await her portion, but we simply put a bit of her canned food on a tiny plate, so she assumed we were all eating the same food. Soon, she began to look forward to her healthier offerings. I decided to offer healthier meals to the family and ignore their complaints, too.

"If you don't like it, you can make yourself a peanut butter sandwich or pour a bowl of cereal," I'd say, knowing that they would be too lazy to get in the car to fetch fast food. It took a little while for our human taste buds to adapt to fast-food-free meals, but eventually it became easier for all of us to opt for salads with lean proteins over chips and burgers. Cat would get a little handout of lean chicken breast once in a while, but she learned that our plates were filled mostly with vegetables now.

"Sorry, Cat," my son would say, holding out a piece of cooked carrot. "This is what we're having." Cat would sniff at the steamed vegetable and then eat it. "Hey! She ate a carrot!"

"If Cat can change her taste buds, so can we," I said. "We're all creatures of habit, but habits can change."

Everyone agreed that this new healthier eating lifestyle was better for all of us. "It's funny how we care more about the health of our cat than ourselves," I remarked to the family.

"Maybe that's why she came into our lives," my husband said. "To teach us a thing or two about being more careful with what we put into our bodies."

As time went on, we all felt better. Cat's coat looked healthier and she seemed to have more energy, although only when she felt like it. "She seems to have more energy," my son said one day, trying to get her to play as she lazed in the sunny patio chair. Cat flicked her tail and squinted her eyes as though in a deep sun meditation. She was still a cat, after all, and would play when she felt like it and not because we wanted her to. Cat showed us that habits can change, though, and we were all the better for it.

— Lori Phillips —

Make Room for Charlie

*It always gives me a shiver when I see a cat seeing
what I can't see.*
~Eleanor Farjeon

Bits of gravel cut into my knees, and vehicles zipped past me. I prayed they would stay in their lanes and avoid the highway shoulder where I was kneeling on the asphalt, reaching into the long grass. I closed my eyes as a semitruck roared past; a rush of hot air and dirt blew across me. This wasn't the smartest thing I'd done all day, and I thought of the words my husband shouted as I jumped from the car and ran into traffic. "You'd better hope it's not a skunk!"

We were driving down Highway 16 when I spotted a tiny animal alongside the road. I've been known to escort everything from turtles to horses back to safety, so when I shouted, "Turn around!" LaMonte slowed instinctively and made a U-turn.

"What is it?" he asked.

"I think it's a kitty." It was dusk, and I had barely caught a glimpse of it against the dark asphalt. "Hurry, honey. I don't want it to get run over."

I feared the kitten would dart into the road before I got to it. As we slowed to a stop, I jumped out and ran across the highway, holding my hand up to an oncoming pickup driver who swerved and cursed me as he sped by.

"Hey, little guy," I said softly as I reached into the grass. When

I stroked his fur, he hissed so softly that it sounded like a whisper. Hoping I wasn't about to cradle a feral animal, I scooped him up and hurried back across the highway to the car.

"Well," LaMonte said, "I guess we have a cat now."

"Oh, no, we don't," I said. "I'll find it a home."

He grinned and shook his head, as if he'd just seen into my future. The next morning, he tried to convince me to keep the kitten. I insisted we were much too busy to take on another pet, especially one with a disability. As it turned out, the cat I'd rescued the night before was blind.

So I was quick to argue with LaMonte, and before we'd even had coffee, I listed a dozen reasons why we couldn't possibly keep the blind kitten. I used words like "special care" and "time commitment." But what I meant was: "Having a blind cat is going to be a huge inconvenience, and I'm not willing to make room in my world for any disruptions." My life revolved around a brutal work schedule that took up much of my time and attention. I couldn't imagine focusing on anything else.

He smiled and patted the kitten on the head. "Do what you want, but I think you should keep him. Besides, you gave him a name. He's yours now."

For two weeks, I tried to find a new residence for Charlie, but no amount of social-media posts or phone calls produced an adoption. My friends knew what I didn't: Charlie was already home.

It's been four years since I rescued a scared kitten from the highway, and I can't imagine life without him. Charlie may be blind, but looking back, I realize I was the one who couldn't see. I prejudged and assumed his disability would be a burden on our busy household. In reality, he has been my saving grace.

His companionship has been a buffer for the anxiety and chaos that life throws at me. He's been a welcome reminder that pets have the ability to heal hearts, lift spirits and provide comfort. Every nuzzle and purr reminds me to slow down, relax and enjoy the moment. His unconditional love was especially welcome when I lost that dreadful job.

And here's the coolest thing about Charlie: He has no idea he's blind! Not once have I had to provide him with "special care." He possesses more poise and finesse than any sighted cat I've encountered. He's been an endless source of affection, and we're amazed daily by his antics — like endless games of chase — whether he's chasing his tail, the dog, or a pesky housefly.

Recently, a friend said to me, "Charlie sure is lucky to have you." Maybe so, but this is what I believe: I'm lucky to have him.

— Ann Morrow —

68

Downward-Facing Cat

Cats never strike a pose that isn't photogenic.
~Lillian Jackson Braun

Previously, we had been living in Italy, where the mild climate encouraged a large feral-cat population to thrive. There, we usually had several cats lounging in our yard, since we always fed the visiting strays in our pleasant, cat-friendly neighborhood. But now, since we'd moved to the cooler climate in Germany, we were down to one older cat, and she was staying home more than ever. She was a smart cat who learned to play soccer as a kitten to pass the time by herself. She even trained us to play fetch with her, retrieving a kitty toy and plopping it back in our laps to throw for her again. But she seemed lonely and bored now, and began following us around the house more often than usual, looking for something interesting to do.

About this time, I was getting back into yoga after several years off. While going through my routine at home, Squeakers watched me closely. Before I knew it, she could perform an excellent version of the downward-facing-dog pose, followed by an upward-facing-dog stretch. It was uncanny how quickly she learned and copied the moves.

In the meantime, we had been checking animal shelters for a young companion for Squeakers. We were informed that a motherless litter was coming in, badly in need of a home. We thought we could manage to take on a couple kittens and that Squeakers would be thrilled at having new companions. When we met the litter, we were unable to pick just one or two kittens; we brought all five of them home, to Squeaker's abject horror. Within hours, everyone had cozied in except Squeakers, who protested adamantly from her hiding spot under the couch.

Because we lived on the edge of the Black Forest, we thought it prudent to get leashes for our little brood until they could handle themselves independently in the great outdoors. Foxes often lurked in the bushes, and hawks soaring overhead would make short work of a kitten. So every day we hitched them up individually and took the group for walks in the woods, as much for our benefit as theirs.

We did a little stretching beforehand to warm up, preparing for our excursions, cuing an eager Squeakers to start her stylized yoga routine. The next thing we knew, to our amazement, all our kittens began copying their big sister, doing what we now affectionately call the downward-facing cat. It was ridiculously cute to see a litter of kittens doing yoga stretches before their walk in the woods.

We became the talk of our village. When everyone took their dogs out for exercise, we took our brood of cats. Soon, we were letting the kittens go off their leashes as they learned to navigate their environment and stay with the pack. When we encountered other walkers on the trails who had never seen us before, they were enthralled by the image of a gaggle of cats following us through the forest.

As the kittens grew, they became faster and more agile, encouraging us to step up the pace. Before we knew it, we were getting back into shape after years of a sedentary lifestyle, forced to keep up with our furry personal trainers.

While our old cat Squeakers had taught them some new tricks, the kittens, in turn, taught us to appreciate the simple pleasure of a jaunt through the woods.

—Donna L. Roberts—

69

My Canine Cat

A cat is a puzzle for which there is no solution.
~Hazel Nicholson

I stepped into the animal shelter that afternoon with more than a little trepidation. It had barely been a week since my husband Bill and I lost our beloved Marlo after a brief illness. We had always adopted older or special-needs cats, but this time my husband suggested a change. So here we were, standing in the middle of the kitten room, as glowing sets of eyes peered out at us through the bars of their cages.

"Any kittens strike your fancy?" asked Millie, the adoption specialist.

I looked at her and back at all the kittens. I didn't know where to start.

Not missing a beat, Millie reached into a nearby cage and cupped a small, orange tabby into her hands. "This one's very sweet," she said. "He was just released to us from his foster mom today."

She held him toward me, and I cradled the ball of orange fur to my bosom. He began to purr. I began to fall in love. I looked up at my husband and said, "He's the one." And, without further hesitation, the kitten we named Samson became a member of our family.

It soon became apparent that Mille was right: Samson was sweet and attentive, not aloof or standoffish like many of the other cats that had shared our home through the years. He trained quickly. He came running when we called his name. He even played like a puppy, enjoying his own versions of fetch where he would either head-butt a ball or carry a toy back to us in his mouth. Afterward, when he tired of games, Samson would curl up at my feet as I read the newspaper in my favorite chair, only waking to stand on his hind legs and beg for a treat.

"Your Samson sounds more like a dog than a cat," remarked my friend Janie after hearing about my new pet. I assured her he was tabby through and through. Yet when I caught him chewing on a pair of my bedroom slippers, he again reminded me of a dog.

Janie's words only served to make me more aware of Samson's atypical feline behavior. Maybe it was time for me to admit it: Samson was confused. He was living like a dog in a cat suit. So, on his next wellness visit, I mentioned this anomaly to our vet, Dr. Andrew.

"Samson thinks he's a dog. He rolls over, plays fetch, begs and chews on my slippers. He'd probably ride in the car with his head out the window if I'd let him," I joked.

Dr. Andrew watched quietly until I finished my tirade. Then he said, "So what if he thinks he's a dog? It sounds like you've got the best of both worlds here with this little guy."

Hmm. I had to admit I agreed with Dr. Andrew's assessment. Having Samson in our home was like having the best of both worlds — a kitten and a puppy all wrapped up in one. He was fun and lovable, loyal and cuddly. Besides, who defines proper behavior in this world? It was right for Samson, and he was right for us.

Sometimes, we hold so tightly to our conventional expectations that we can't look past them to the blessing. I'm glad Dr. Andrew got through to me. Samson can act like a dog if he wants — or a cat. Whatever works for him.

— Monica A. Andermann —

70

One-Eyed Jack

People who love cats have some of the
biggest hearts around.
~Susan Easterly

I have always been a dog lover, so when I signed up to volunteer at the shelter, I envisioned myself working with dogs. Much to my surprise, I was assigned to the cat room on my first day there.

The "cat condos" were inhabited by cats of every size, color and temperament. My job was to unlock the condo if a potential adopting parent wanted to hold a cat. It was a simple task, but to be frank, I was afraid. Cats had always struck me as unpredictable and ready to scratch on a whim. I attribute this fear to a cat I had growing up. Josie was the "alley cat" variety — large, tough and vicious to the core!

On my first day, I unlocked many condos, and gradually I became a little more comfortable. But just as I was feeling more confident, I caught sight of the biggest, most awe-inspiring cat in the room: One-Eyed Jack.

A mammoth-sized, charcoal-gray fellow, One-Eyed Jack was housed in one of the top rows of condos. Perched on his ledge, he revealed one beautiful, jade-green eye and one gaping, empty socket. Initially, I was taken aback by his appearance, but once the newness wore off, I began to wonder about old One-Eyed Jack. Where had he come from? And how did he lose that eye? A fight? An accident? In a room with dozens of beautiful creatures, I wondered who in their right mind would want an awful-looking cat like Jack.

I thought about Jack a lot during the subsequent days. The next time I volunteered, he was still there, high in his penthouse condo. But I quickly noticed a petite, gray-haired lady facing him, maybe even talking to him. As I approached, she turned to face me, and I realized it was Mrs. Wexler, a delightful woman from my church.

I asked her, "Do you know this cat?"

"Yes," Mrs. Wexler told me. "I've seen One-Eyed Jack several times."

"I doubt many people give him much attention," I commented.

"Probably not. But he seems like such a nice cat."

I was glad to see that someone in the community saw something agreeable about this plainly unattractive feline. It gave me a little peace of mind that day. And much to my surprise, the next time I came in to volunteer, One-Eyed Jack was gone! I made a beeline for the front desk and asked where he was. The man on staff told me that he had been adopted. I was dumbfounded.

The next Sunday I was at church, I saw Mrs. Wexler in the hallway ahead of me. I hurried to catch up with her. "Have you been to the shelter recently? One-Eyed Jack was adopted."

"I know!" she smiled. "I brought him home on Friday."

"You adopted that cat?" I must have sounded surprised.

"Yes. I got him as a companion for the three-legged cat we already had at home. You know, some animals need us more than others."

I felt very small and embarrassed hearing her say that; that wasn't how I had looked at Jack at all. I had spent all of my time at the shelter gawking at him. I realized it takes a special person with a very large heart to look past an animal's physical appearance and make it part of her family. Now, when I do my volunteer work, I try to channel Mrs. Wexler's loving spirit for all animals—the nurtured and the needy alike. One-Eyed Jack was lucky that Mrs. Wexler came along, and so am I.

— Rebecca Edmisten —

71

A Mother's Soul

There are two lasting bequests we can give our
children. One is roots. The other is wings.
~Hodding Carter, Jr.

My husband and I made the long trip to Boston with our teen-aged son hoping that a pediatric neurosurgeon at Boston Children's Hospital would remove a brain tumor deemed inoperable by the local surgeon in Nebraska. Just finding the surgeon and being in Boston was a miracle in itself, but if she could save our son, it would be more than I could dare dream of. I had prayed so hard and so often for my son's life that it had become a way of life.

When they took our son to the operating room, we settled in for a long wait. We were both silent as we waited and watched for any sign of the surgeon coming to talk to us. Meanwhile, our oldest son called and announced that a stray cat had given birth to a litter of kittens in our garage. My husband told our son to bring her and the kittens inside from the cold and make them a bed in our bathtub. This same cat had given birth on our property several times before. Sadly, none of her kittens had ever survived, so we wanted to try and help her as much as we could.

I sat silently for a few minutes after the phone call and thought of how symbolic this litter of stray kittens was to me. This momma cat had tried time after time to keep her babies alive, and I had too. My son was on his third reoccurrence and in surgery fighting for his life.

I felt helpless. Momma cat must have felt the same with every litter that didn't make it. Quietly, I said a little prayer for her, too.

A couple of hours passed, and we finally got the news we had spent the last few years hoping for: The cancer had been entirely removed. It felt surreal, and I was afraid to believe it. But that quickly washed away when I saw my son smiling and talking. We called home to give the good news to our other children, and our oldest son told us that all but one of the kittens had died. Our son had named him Lucky.

We returned home after a week and got to meet this feisty, little yellow fur ball. He was so tiny and fragile that I wondered how something so delicate would make it in such a big world. Momma cat was not afraid of us like a normal stray cat, and she seemed content with her new bathtub home. We decided to keep them and care for them both as part of the family. After all, we had been handed a miracle in our son's recovery, and it only seemed right to help another mother fighting for her son.

The days turned into weeks, and Lucky got bigger, fluffier and cuter. He seemed stronger and loved to play almost as much as he wanted to be held. Momma cat was never too far away, making sure her precious baby was okay. I couldn't blame her; she had gone through so much to get this one kitten. I felt the same way. If our other kids had a cold or a headache, we would watch and make sure they were okay. But when our son got a cold, we would rush to the doctor with an uncontrollable fear that his cancer was back.

In a few months, Lucky was almost fully grown and taking care of himself. Momma cat was still around, but I noticed that her behavior began to change. She would disappear for hours at a time, leaving Lucky in the house. Sometimes, I would see her lounging around in the peaceful serenity of the garage. At first, I thought she just needed some "me time," but I began to suspect it was much more. It was clear that Lucky was healthy and strong now, and it was time for momma cat to let go. She was starting to pull herself away, allowing her kitten to explore and learn on his own.

I realized I needed to do the same. The cancer was gone, and it was time I allowed my son to be a kid. My desire to protect him was, in fact, keeping him from learning, exploring, and having fun on his own. It was time to trust he was well again and let him be the kid he was before his diagnosis.

One afternoon a few months later, I happened to look up and noticed that momma cat was peeking in the window from the corner. It was evident she was trying not to be noticed but was checking in on Lucky. As she watched him play with his toys, I could see how much she loved him. In a few short years, I would be doing the same thing as my children left home and started their own lives. Watching from the outside will be so hard; I just hope I do it with as much grace as momma cat. She looked up, and our eyes met for a lingering moment. Then she was gone. It would seem a mother's love is the same, no matter the language.

— Michelle Bruce —

Sister Act

*Siblings are the people we practice on, the people who
teach us about fairness and cooperation and kindness
and caring — quite often the hard way.*
~Pamela Dugdale

I'm a sucker for a pretty face — and, apparently, for tuxedo cats. Nine years ago, I received an e-mail from a friend trying to find homes for a litter of stray kittens. I made the mistake of clicking on the attached photo. An adorable black-and-white kitten that looked a lot like my beloved Mittsy, who had died a few years prior, filled my screen. I hadn't been looking to adopt another cat, but I went to see the kitten anyway a few days later.

Sitting on my friend's floor with a lapful of kitties, I fell in love. My friend had named the tuxedo kitten Misty — so similar to "Mittsy" that I took it as a sign we were meant to be together. I told my friend I would take her. But as we played, I noticed that Misty and one of her littermates were inseparable. That's when I made my second mistake. They were so cute together that I said I'd take both of them. It seemed heartless to split them up.

The sisters looked nothing alike. While Misty was black and white with symmetrical markings that made her look like she was wearing a tuxedo, Stormy was a long-limbed tortoiseshell with random splotches of orange among her mottled brown-and-tan fur. I soon discovered that their personalities couldn't be any more different, either. Misty was sociable, loved to eat, and was quite the talker; quiet Stormy was a picky eater who'd run and hide anytime someone came to the door.

After about a year of living with them, I realized they had tricked me. The formerly sweet, inseparable darlings had developed a serious case of sibling rivalry. They'd fight over who got to sit on my lap. Misty would steal Stormy's food. Stormy would stalk Misty, jump on her back and bite her. Much hissing would ensue. Misty frequently sported a scratch on her pretty white nose, a clear sign she had been sticking it somewhere it didn't belong.

I'd scold the instigator and often the provoker, too — trying (unsuccessfully) to reason with them.

"Misty, stop staring at Stormy's food while she's eating. You know it makes her uncomfortable."

"Stormy, stop chasing your sister. She's not in the mood to play."

And finally, in exasperation, "Why can't you two just get along? You're sisters!"

Then it hit me: I sounded just like my mother.

Like my kitties, I also had a sister. Not only are we physically very different, but our personalities developed into polar opposites as we got older. We rarely see eye to eye on any subject, a source of much frustration and miscommunication between us.

I began to notice the similarities between our relationship and personalities and those of my cats. My sister's chronic complaining reminded me of Misty's nonstop whining. The way I distanced myself from her paralleled Stormy's avoidance of Misty. My sister and I would push each other's buttons until the other lashed out in anger — but in words, never with a scratch to the nose! I began to examine our exchanges and compare them to how the cats fought. It was clear to me that when my cats were fighting, it was rarely one-sided. If Stormy swatted Misty, it was because she was following Stormy around too much and making a pest of herself. When Misty hissed at Stormy it was in response to Stormy's overly aggressive behavior. This insight highlighted the fact that, like them, I probably played a role in my sister's objectionable behavior.

I thought back to the last time I had snapped at my sister. She had said or done one thing after another that annoyed me and, like

Stormy, I ignored them until I reached my breaking point. Then I responded in anger. If I had set some boundaries sooner, as I often encouraged Stormy to do when Misty was ogling her food bowl, she might have backed off before it got to the boiling point. In other words, a well-timed growl earlier on might have prevented a claw to the nose, metaphorically speaking.

I began heeding some of the advice I had been doling out:

"She's just playing." (That's her way of engaging with me.)

"Give her some space."

"She didn't mean it."

"Don't let her steal your food." (Let her know when she's crossing a boundary.)

And especially, "What did you do to deserve it?"

I also noticed that, for all their faults, my kitties brought positive qualities to their sisterly relationship, too. Misty, like my own sister, was usually the one to initiate a rapprochement after a spat. Stormy, like me, deferred to her sister's wishes most of the time, letting Misty have her way.

While I can't say I now enjoy a perfectly harmonious relationship with my sister, adopting these two siblings has showcased the dynamics of antagonistic personalities for me. I'm reminded daily that it takes two to have an argument, and that lashing out is usually in response to an intrusion of some kind. And when I feel ready to write my sister off, I hear myself saying, "Why can't you two just get along? You're sisters."

— Susan Yanguas —

Chapter 8

Smart Cat

73

A Rare Jewel

A cat is the only domestic animal I know who toilet
trains itself and does a damned impressive job of it.
~Joseph Epstein

The tiny kitten appeared in my back yard one day. She was so small that she could curl up in the palm of my hand. I will never know where she came from, but she braved the dog, standing her ground against a huge white Husky whose snout was bigger than her whole body.

Little did I know that once I brought her inside, she would never leave my heart. She was soft as a bunny and snow-white all over except for the tips of her paws and her muzzle. These were a light shade of lavender. She had huge blue eyes, which I thought were because of her young age, but it turned out they would always remain blue. I took her to the vet to make sure she didn't have anything wrong with her, and he told me she was a Lavender Point Siamese.

The lavender reminded me of an amethyst, so I named her Jewel. From that day forward, she never ceased to amaze me with her unbelievable intelligence and talents. Immediately, she made my Husky-mix, Lady-Bear, her "bed" when the dog was in the house. She would climb on top of Lady and snuggle up in her fur, purring. If Lady decided to go munch some kibble in the kitchen or get a drink of water, the tiny cat would ride on her back. She rode the dog everywhere, and Lady was always careful not to roll over on her little passenger.

When she was old enough, I took Jewel to be spayed, but I

never let her go outside again. She was so delicate and precious; I was afraid someone would steal her, or she might get hurt. I bought her a collar that had little crystals in it the color of amethysts. She became the princess of our house, and all the other animals catered to her, especially Lady-Bear.

Jewel had a magic way with the other cats in the house and with any human who visited us. Everyone loved her. There was something mystical and highly intelligent in those large, blue eyes. She would follow me around as I did my housework and try to help. If I was sweeping a floor, she would dig out a "dust bunny" from under a table or behind the stove and present it to me proudly. If I was folding clothes and dropped a sock, she would fetch it for me like a dog.

I had to keep her out of my office because the computer fascinated her, and she wanted to be on my lap and tap the keyboard. I made the mistake of letting her do so, and she was overjoyed with it. She seemed to understand that touching a key made something appear on the screen. Obviously, I couldn't have that going on when trying to work. But I did let her play with the keyboard once in a while when I wasn't working. The rest of the time, the office door was closed to all cats.

Jewel watched everything and learned. After watching me wash dishes a few times, she would paw at the faucet when I put dishes in the sink. When I sat on the couch, she would paw at the side table drawer where I kept the remote for the television. But the most amazing thing she did was teach herself to use the toilet.

I've had many cats and dogs who tried to drink out of the toilet and made a mess, so I keep bathroom doors closed. But one morning when I was brushing my teeth, I'd left the door open, and Jewel came into the bathroom and checked out the commode. With a mouthful of toothpaste, I was in no position to shoo her out and close the door. But since she was so small, I was more worried that she'd fall in and drown, rather than make a mess. So I kept a close eye on her while I finished my morning grooming.

I noticed that she was not looking into the bowl like the other cats did. She was sitting on it, looking at me, with her backside over the edge of the seat. Then I heard it: She was relieving herself. When she was done, she turned around and started pawing at the toilet seat, as if trying to "bury" her deposit as she would in a litter box.

She didn't jump down and run off. She waited until I finished and then delicately padded to the other side of the toilet seat and pawed at the lever. She came back and pawed at me, and then went back and did it again. I reached over and pushed the handle, flushing the toilet. She watched the water swirl and then jumped up on the sink counter, stood up and put her front paws on me in a "good-girl pat," thanking me for being intelligent enough to know what she wanted me to do.

From that day on, she never used a litter box again. I didn't want to leave the master bathroom wide open for all cats and dogs to carouse in, but I have a smaller guest bathroom on the other end of the house, which I started leaving open for her. She learned that it belonged to her and would come and let me know when she needed her toilet flushed. I thought that the other cats might watch and mimic her, but none ever did.

Jewel has long since passed away. People who knew her still tell me stories they remember about her. She left an impression on everyone she met. When she passed, she took a part of my heart with her, and I doubt I will ever meet another magical cat like her in my lifetime. I was blessed to share my life with her.

—Joyce Laird—

74

Chicken Soup for the Soul

Cat Practitioner

I have lived with several Zen masters —
all of them cats.
~Eckhart Tolle

Our gray Russian-Blue cat was always loving with us, but she had caused problems at the local cat-sitting agency. We didn't know why, but this sudden change in behavior was cause for concern. Therefore, we had chosen this particular vet carefully based on recommendations from some other pet parents.

"Dr. Amsberry is an animal whisperer," they told us. "The minute he walks in the room, any pet — even a gerbil or tortoise — just seems to know that he is a gentle soul, and he soothes them immediately."

We sat in the cat room, stroking Ember's head while we waited. Ember was tense. We could feel the muscles in her shoulders hunch up and see her green eyes go to slits when Penny, the assistant, walked in. When she tried to weigh her, Ember hissed, whirling around with raking claws. Penny exited the room quickly, and I could hear her talking to Dr. Amsberry just outside the door.

Now Ember's tail looked like cotton candy. It began whipping back and forth as the door opened and Dr. Amsberry slid into the room with a confident smile. He talked to us for a few minutes while his eyes took in Ember's plumed tail and her flattened ears. When he finally reached out to rub her head, she screeched. Hissing, she went for his hand and then his face. He backed away.

"Sometimes," he said, "we have to wrap nervous animals in a

blanket. We roll them up like a taco, and then we can get our business done." If only that had been true. After the blanket had been shredded, she escaped to jump from shelf to shelf until she wound up, still hissing, on the top shelf.

Dr. Amsberry referred us to a vet who did home care.

Dr. Rogers came to the house expecting the worst, and he got it. "Something at the cat sitter traumatized her," he theorized as we pulled her, screeching, from under the bed. I feared we would not be able to keep Ember, as it seemed impossible to get her rabies shots or other vaccinations. They were important as we lived in an area teeming with wildlife, and she had insisted on periodically escaping the safety of our home from the moment she was adopted.

But then, I came down with sleep apnea, and Ember assumed a new role in my life. People with sleep apnea quit breathing while they are asleep. For most people, a CPAP machine is the solution. However, I have central sleep apnea, which means that not only do I not breathe, but I cannot remember *how* to breathe. Since I cannot breathe at all, if my husband wakes and pleads, "Tell me what to do," I can't answer him. Breathing and talking are linked.

Ember, being the dominant cat of three in our household, has chosen our bed for her nighttime slumbers. At first, she watched me gasping for breath from the end of the bed. But one night, when I had yet another incident, she became an active member of my medical team. As I lay sleeping, not yet aware that I had quit breathing, I felt her wiggle past my arms to where my head was half-buried in my pillow. I heard her crying. Perhaps it is our training as a mother that any cry, animal or human, makes us respond. I turned over, realized I was not breathing, and again could not remember how to take a breath.

That was when Ember became a feline paramedic. She crawled up my chest, put her furred paws against my throat and patted fiercely. For reasons yet unknown, it startled me into taking a breath. When my pounding heart slowed to normal, she laid her head against my neck and began to purr. She stayed there until I fell asleep again.

It has been a few years now, and Ember has perfected her medical techniques. Sometimes, she will curl up next to me immediately, her body warm and her paws resting on my throat. Inevitably, I will have an apnea episode, and she is there, ready. Lately, when I begin breathing again, she sometimes stands on my chest, with my head against her chest and her feet planted firmly by my ears. She is not purring yet; she is listening. Finally, she will stand down, put her mouth next to my ear and purr me back to sleep again.

One night, my husband asked me, "Do you remember what Ember did when Pierot was dying?" Pierot was a tiny, white kitten with a black mask across his face and a deformed heart. When we adopted him from the shelter, we vowed to nurse him as long as he was not in pain. However, he was often ill, shaking with the fevers that eventually claimed his life. Ember would curl around him on the sofa, surrounding his tiny body with her bigger one. She kept him warm, licked his ears, and seemed to love him unconditionally. With every other living animal and human, she operated differently, always letting them know who could approach her and who could not. "She was a healer," he reminded me, "even many years ago."

Ember still attacks the vet if he comes to the house. She still hisses at people who invade her space uninvited. But, for the most part, she is a well-groomed, intelligent cat who likes things done her way, loves whom she loves, and — in one of her nine lives — apparently earned a medical degree.

— Susan A. Shumway —

75

Hunter?

The phrase "domestic cat" is an oxymoron.
~George Will

"**D**oes your cat hunt?" a guest asked, motioning toward a table at the end of the couch. Boots, our black cat with a white nose and paws, lay under the end table as we conversed. We had no air conditioning—it was rarely hot enough to need it in our home in the woods of northwestern Montana. But that day the heat seared our area and, seeking a breeze, we had opened every window and door, including the back door, which had no screen.

Stopping to think, I wrinkled my forehead. "I don't know," I said finally. "She's outside a lot, but comes in some, too." I scratched my head. "I don't think I've ever seen her with a catch."

I pondered a moment longer. Boots's everyday calmness and purring provided lessons on contentment. She gave my husband and me a lot of love and humor. What did she do when she went outside?

"Given our country acreage," I added, "we hired her to keep the vermin from becoming pests. I don't know if she's doing her job or not."

Boots stood up, walked out from under the table, and disappeared out the back door.

"Cats are curious creatures," I added. "Sometimes, I think Boots is trying to talk. She's a barrel of fun, but we never know quite what to expect."

Among our three guest families and ourselves, the conversation wandered amiably. A short time later, another guest asked, "What does your cat have?" He gazed at a spot under the same end table.

Everyone looked. I turned, too.

Boots sat in the same spot she'd just left, but something small and brown lay between her front paws. I stared, and then moved closer. My mouth dropped open. The small, brown addition was a dead mouse. "I-I-I do believe… she hunts," I stammered. "And… understands human language."

Was that a grin on her face? As soon as I acknowledged her prowess, Boots raised her head with an air of pride. She stood, picked up the mouse in her teeth, and walked out the back door, never bringing us such an offering again. She didn't need to — she'd made her point.

— Helen Heavirland —

76

Tricky Tiger

A cat will do what it wants when it wants,
and there's not a thing you can do about it.
~Frank Perkins

"What's the matter with you now?" I yelled from the kitchen. Quickly, I ran my hands under the faucet and shook off the excess water while I rushed to the front door. This was the third time Tiger had asked to be let out in the last hour. My lasagna wasn't getting made.

My orange tabby was standing in front of the door. I met his reproachful stare with my aggravated own.

"What? Not moving fast enough for you?" I said as I opened the screen door to let him out. He ignored the question and strode out with a touch of affectionate contempt in his swishing tail.

"Yeah, fine, enjoy your stroll. I'll just be in the kitchen waiting for you to summon me," I said with as much sarcasm as I could muster. He never even looked back.

I let go of the non-latching screen door, viciously hoping against hope that the bang from its warped frame against the door jamb would startle him, but he just kept on going with nary a glance back. That cat was on to my tricks, and he couldn't have been any less concerned.

He'd always been a bit of a trickster. The day my daughter and I brought him home—a furry, orange ball no more than six weeks old—he remained completely silent on the long car ride, no matter our enticements. We decided finally that he was mute. The thought filled me with so much love and compassion that I became determined to make his life as easy as possible.

That night, after everyone went to bed, he started meowing at the top of his lungs and hasn't stopped yet. Everything was an occasion for him to express himself, and he wasn't shy about it.

I went back to the kitchen feeling enslaved to the ungrateful cat, and as resentful as ever.

Forty minutes later, I put the lasagna in the oven, and decided to reward myself with a well-deserved cup of coffee and a few minutes with my book. I sat at the breakfast nook, from which I had an unobstructed view of the living room and the open front door. The coffee tasted wonderful, the kitchen smelled great, and I still hadn't figured out the identity of the beautiful young lady's murderer, even though I had read over half of the story. Life was good.

A scratching sound interrupted my reading. My mouth dropped open in amazement as I watched Tiger daintily reach a leg in the small gap between the screen door and the front door frame, widen the space with the familiar ease of long practice, and let himself in silently. He seemed quite pleased with himself. He walked over to the couch, curled up in his favorite spot, and closed his eyes.

He hadn't noticed me sitting in the breakfast nook, watching him with visions of vengeance burning in my eyes. This conniving beast had known how to open the door on his own all along, yet he meowed, screeched, and otherwise yelled at me to do it for him twenty times a day. Without any hint of guilt.

I was fuming!

I thought of the hundreds of interruptions he had inflicted upon me over the last few years, of his continued disregard and obvious contempt for the importance of my activities. I recalled the time I ran out of the bathroom naked and soapy, shampoo stinging my eyes, because he was screaming so loudly I thought he had hurt himself. Instead, I found him sitting calmly by the door, waiting for me to open it. I remembered his unrelenting scratching of the doorframe, which drove me to distraction, and the chiding eyes staring at me unblinkingly when I took too long to get to him.

That cat had never once allowed me to sleep in. Oh, I had been such a dupe!

As I sat my coffee cup on the table, he opened his eyes suddenly and looked at me. I looked back. Seconds became a minute. I knew he knew I knew! It was obvious he was considering his options. A moment later, he got to his feet, yawned, stretched, and jumped from the couch, and strolled casually over to the kitchen nook. Ignoring my fury, he began to rub against my legs, purring softly.

"Come on, girl," I think he said. "It was all in good fun. And I did you a favor, you know. You do need the exercise." His purring grew louder.

As I reached down to swat, or perhaps pet him — I hadn't made up my mind yet — he gave me a last half-sardonic, half-affectionate look, walked to the door and let himself out with no hesitation. He never again asked me to open the door for him.

Years later, when my youngest girl, a first-grader, told me that she didn't need to learn to read since I read to her every day, I remembered the incident. "Darling," I said, "let me tell you about Old Tiger. Tiger was a smart and cunning cat who shared my house years ago. Tiger couldn't see any good reason to do for himself what I always did for him." She giggled as I recounted the events of that long-ago spring day. She not only enjoyed the tale but saw herself in my old friend.

"Smart cat, wasn't he?" I said. "So, I am sure you understand why you'll be reading to me from now on instead of the other way around." She frowned, and after a moment, she smirked.

"He was a great teacher, your Tiger," she said.

"Yes," I laughed, "he was. Sure prepared me for you, didn't he, baby?"

— Michele Roch —

77

The Queen Who Served

Intelligence in the cat is underrated.
~Louis Wain

While searching among the cages at a local animal shelter, my dad spotted a tiny, gray kitten who extended her little paw as if to say, "Please take me home with you." In that moment, she claimed my dad's heart. With my help, he took her home and named her Penelope after his favorite character in Greek mythology.

Weeks before, I had finally talked my dad into adopting a kitten. Having just turned eighty-five, he seemed lonely after his second wife died of cancer, and I thought he would benefit from the companionship of an easy-care pet.

Little Penelope adapted to my dad's home by knocking objects off his counters, tables and shelves. After pawing a newfound treasure onto the carpeted floor, she would bat it around for hours. Although my dad scolded Penelope gently for her antics, he forgave her quickly. That kitty truly had my dad wrapped around her little paw.

When Penelope sauntered into the living room, my dad's face lit up with joy as he called her name repeatedly. Being a kitty, she played hard-to-get, which only added to her allure. On monumental occasions, she allowed him to pet her.

In no time, my dad dubbed Penelope "Queen of the Manor." Her every whim and wish became his command—nothing but the best food, treats, litter and toys for Queen Penelope. In return, she "allowed" my dad to reside in his home.

When Queen Penelope deemed the cleanliness of her litter box to be short of her royal standards, she alerted my dad by pooping on the rug in his basement. Always the dutiful servant, my dad cleaned up her mess cheerfully.

Queen Penelope's arrival coincided with Dad's renewed interest in chess. A retired engineer, my dad quickly grew bored of merely playing the game. Instead, he set up a chessboard with black and gray pieces to study the board layout and calculate statistical probabilities of various moves.

One Sunday when I visited my dad at his home, Queen Penelope was batting a small object on the floor. I took a closer look. It was a chess piece — the gray queen. Out of the thirty-two chess pieces on the board, Penelope had somehow chosen the one piece that resembled her most. Even more amazing was my dad's report that she consistently chose only that chess piece to bat around the floor.

"Queen Penelope wouldn't bother with a lowly rook or pawn," he joked.

Although his mood brightened with Penelope as his daily companion, my dad's physical stamina deteriorated, which made living alone more difficult. He refused my invitations to live with me, and stubbornly refused to wear a medic-alert button in case he fell. He grumbled as I connected cordless phones in each room of his home and insisted that he purchase a cell phone to place in his shirt pocket.

Although not ideal, I satisfied my concerns by calling and visiting frequently, and securing his next-door neighbor's assistance with periodic check-ins.

Penelope continued to be the apple of my dad's eye, but I recognized that caring for a kitty placed a strain on him. So I started cleaning the litter box and filling her food and water dishes.

This went on for a while, and I hoped the situation would be sustainable. Then, one Saturday evening, I called my dad at our usual time. Sounding tired, he reported that he had run errands and completed several household chores. I promised to visit the next day with the warning that I planned to bring paperwork for purchasing a medic-alert button. Of course, he scoffed at the idea as he watched little Penelope batting the queen chess piece on the floor.

The next morning, I called Dad, but there was no answer. I called his neighbor, but there was no answer there either. Then I called the hospital where his doctor was affiliated. The staff member refused to give any information, citing privacy laws. I slammed down the phone in frustration.

I called another hospital and learned my father had been admitted to the emergency room an hour before.

When I arrived at the emergency room, my dad looked bruised and exhausted. Shortly after our phone call the previous night, he'd started to fix dinner when he fell. Unable to get up, he tried to use his cell phone, but it wouldn't work. He crawled across the kitchen floor to the cordless phone, but it was dead. Over the next ten hours, he slowly inched his way to the other cordless phone in the living room and was finally able to call 911.

Tears streamed down my face as I heard him recount how Penelope remained at his side throughout his painful ordeal. Once a queen, Penelope now proved to be a loyal servant to my dad in his hours of desperate need. After a long day in the hospital, I went to my dad's home to check in on little Penelope. She was too scared to approach me.

In the kitchen, I saw severely burned pans on the stove and phones scattered on the floor. Dad's cell phone couldn't dial 911 because it had been programmed with a different area code than his home location. I also noticed that the kitchen cordless phone was not properly plugged in to the receptacle. I imagined my dad's struggle, with Penelope by his side.

The next day, the hospital doctor reported, "Your father has terminal cancer." As those horrible words reeled in my mind, I took Penelope home with me. She hid under my bed all night.

Ten days later, my dad died. During our last conversation, he thanked me for convincing him to adopt Penelope. Although a queen, she had served him well in his moments of joy and pain.

Honoring my dad's last request, I paid a royal tribute to Queen Penelope at his memorial service and placed the gray queen chess piece in his pocket so she could accompany him in spirit.

Happily, my own kitty welcomed Penelope into our home. Every time I look at "The Queen Who Served," I remember my father and the joy she brought him.

—Jessica Loftus—

78

Thermometer Cat

*Animals know more than we think and think
a great deal more than we know.*
~Irene Pepperberg

Some years ago, my wife Debbie and I lived in a small town in the hills east of San Francisco Bay. We had an older female tabby cat named Gina who had been with us for many years and had moved with us several times. One evening, during a walk around our neighborhood, another female tabby befriended us and followed us home. She had a collar but no tag and looked to be underfed. This was in the days before the implanting of microchips to identify stray animals. After making inquiries and trying to determine whether she already had a home, we resigned ourselves to the fact that she had just adopted us, to the delight of our daughter.

The two cats were at odds initially, but eventually got along after the younger one tired of taunting the older one. We named the new cat Mouser due to her prolific hunting ability. Eventually, we shortened it to "Mau," which also seemed appropriate because of her frequent forlorn cries.

After a few years, Gina passed on and Mau became our only pet. As she aged, she began to hunt less and spent most of her days lounging around the house. Our climate was fairly temperate, but winter temperatures were often quite cool in the shadow of the East Bay Hills, and she always seemed to find a cozy spot in the sun or near the fireplace. It was always out of the areas of foot traffic, so she would not be disturbed.

One morning, we noticed Mau was lying on the carpet in the family room, directly in the walkway to the kitchen. For the next several days, Mau spent most of her time in this new spot as we continued to walk around or step over her. We wondered if something was wrong with her, but her behavior was otherwise normal — no loss of appetite or other worrisome signs. At about the same time, Debbie noticed that the water pressure at the kitchen sink seemed to be a bit low. It wasn't a drastic change, but she did mention it to me.

After a few days, Debbie bent down to check on Mau and pet her as she lay in her new favorite spot. She noticed immediately that the carpet around the cat felt quite warm, and not just from the cat sleeping there. Feeling around with her hand, Debbie found that the section of flooring around the entire area where the cat had chosen to lounge was noticeably warm. Leave it to a cat to find the warmest spot in the house to sleep, but why was the floor so warm there?

When I got home, we discussed the situation and decided to peel back the carpet around the cat's new lounging area. When we found traces of moisture on the surface of the underlying concrete slab, we called our insurance agent, who sent out a contractor to investigate. The eventual conclusion was that a hot-water pipe — the one that supplied the kitchen sink — had broken and been leaking for some time. Hundreds of gallons of hot water had probably escaped and were eating away at the soil beneath our home's foundation.

Soon, workers arrived to begin demolition of the family room, removing the furniture and carpet, and digging out a large section of concrete with a jackhammer so the leaky pipe could be isolated and replaced. After a week of messy excavation, repair, and reconstruction at the cost of many thousands of dollars, the problem was finally fixed and the room put back in order. Thankfully, our homeowner's insurance covered the bulk of the repair bill.

The early detection of the problem, thanks to Mau, undoubtedly prevented further loss of water and energy, and perhaps an even costlier repair bill. The moral of the story is that cats are very attuned to their environment, and sometimes we need to pay attention to what they are trying to tell us. Do not always let sleeping cats lie!

We decided to reward the good kitty for her vigilance and compensate her for the inconvenience of being displaced during the repairs. She got a new bed that we placed in a warm corner near the fireplace, and since then we have paid a little more attention to our cat's sleeping habits.

— Don Patton —

79

Chicken Soup for the Soul.

Opera Singer

I think that cats are spirits incarnated on Earth.
A cat, I am sure, could walk on a cloud
without falling through it.
~Jules Verne

Colossal is the perfect way to describe Skitty. From the day we adopted him, he was a big boy. He wasn't overweight; he was just a large, orange tabby. If I didn't know better, I'd have thought he was part lion. But his meow was far from a roar! It was quite comical to hear such a large cat with the most quiet, gentle voice, especially since he was extremely verbal.

Skitty wanted to be heard. He would let us know his excitement when we gave him his favorite treats, or his displeasure when we couldn't get the can of cat food opened quickly. That's when we discovered he sounded like a soprano opera singer.

Skitty would often sit on one of the stools in our kitchen, looking lovingly toward the top of the refrigerator where his kitty treats were stored in a tin can. He would constantly "sing" until he got a treat. The funniest part was that he looked like he was on stage singing an aria at the opera. I have to admit that sometimes I took my time getting the treats just so I could hear his singing voice a little longer.

His talent was too great not to share with our friends. My kids would often bring their friends around to hear Skitty sing. My sons, Alex and Spencer, had a few friends over to play video games one afternoon. Before they started, my boys insisted that everyone sit for an opera performance by Skitty. All the boys gathered around as Spencer placed Skitty on the stool. Alex jiggled the tin container of treats, which got Skitty's attention instantly, and he performed on cue. All the boys roared with laughter. Spencer stood in front of the refrigerator and waved his hands, pretending to be the maestro conducting the singer. The more attention Skitty got, the more he performed.

Skitty wasn't shy about voicing his opinion or showing off his singing talents to impress. Usually, there was an ulterior motive behind his performances that involved food. One morning, my friend dropped by for an unexpected visit. "I come bearing bagels and lox!" she said, smiling as she handed me the bag. Little did my friend know that lox was one of Skitty's special treats, reserved for special occasions. I placed the bag on the kitchen table and got the coffee brewing. Skitty stood on the chair, right next to the table by the bag of bagels and lox. He made us aware that he knew there was something mighty good in that bag, and he wanted some of what we were having.

Out came Skitty's rendition of Luciano Pavarotti's "O Sole Mio." Mouth wide open, he sang with determination for a few minutes until we caved in and gave him some bits of lox as a reward for a job well done.

Singing for food wasn't the only time Skitty was verbal. One Saturday morning, we decided to sleep in a little longer and I had a dream about strolling on the beach. I heard a cat meowing — a soft meow, just like Skitty's. Suddenly, my dream changed. Now, I was walking in a garden, looking behind bushes to see where the sound was coming from. "Where are you, kitty?" I said as I walked from bush to bush looking for a cat. I felt the cat was calling out to me for help. I was upset because I couldn't find him.

In my dream, I was looking frantically for the cat when I felt a big thump on my chest. I woke up, startled from such a realistic dream, to see Skitty sitting on my chest, meowing frantically. This was so out of character for him. Immediately, I knew that something wasn't right. "What's the matter, boy? What's wrong?" I asked him as he continued to get more vocal. His meow was now the loudest and deepest I'd ever heard.

I woke my husband Harold and told him something was amiss. "Show me what's wrong, Skitty," I said as Harold and I followed him down the hall toward the kitchen. Before we got there, I heard a clicking sound and smelled the distinct odor of gas.

Two burners on the stove were turned on. The back burner had a flame. The front burner was clicking to indicate it was trying to light, but it wasn't working and thus the gas was flowing out without being burned off. The odor of gas was unbearably strong. Quickly, we turned off the burners and opened the windows. If Skitty hadn't alerted us, Harold said we could have had an explosion from all the gas that was hanging in the air right over the lit burner. Since our whole family was sleeping at the time, we will never know how the burners were turned on. We are guessing that one of our dogs spied cookies that had been left on top of the stove. They were just too enticing for the dogs to resist, and one of them probably tried to jump up and get the cookies. In the process, the knobs were turned on accidentally.

After everything settled down, I bent down, gave Skitty a hug and thanked him for being a tattletale on one of his furry siblings. I wanted to do something special for Skitty, so I made a trip to the local deli where I bought bagels and lox. My plan was to give Skitty a little extra lox as a way to show our appreciation. This was certainly a special occasion, and he deserved his special treat.

My family gathered around the kitchen table for breakfast while Skitty sat motionless, eyeing every movement I made when I took his beloved lox out of the bag. As I unwrapped his delicacy, he began to serenade us with the sweetest aria he had ever sung.

— Dorann Weber —

80

The Cat Who Lost Her Meow

How you behave toward cats here below determines
your status in Heaven.
~Robert A. Heinlein

She opened her mouth, but only a small, squeaky sound came out. She tried again, but no sound came out this time. My normally chatty cat was perplexed by the sudden loss of her ability to communicate verbally with me.

I stooped down, patted her head, and scratched behind her ears. Sydney always loved having her chin stroked, but I knew that the area near her neck and mouth would still be sore after surgery. While she risked losing her voice with the surgery, it was necessary to remove some growths.

But how does one explain this to a cat?

Working from home, I always loved listening to Sydney's vocalizations throughout the day. She would sit by the window and chirp at the birds. She chattered at the neighbors who walked their dogs. I always felt like we were having lively conversations.

Sydney would make a "meep" sound when she saw me go into the kitchen, as if to ask, "Is it lunchtime yet?" When I returned home from errands, she would greet me at the door with a chipper "meow" as if to say, "Good to see you!" And when she wanted more food, a demanding howl would emerge as she guided me toward her bowl.

Those sounds filled my days, and I felt a sense of deep loss to never hear them again.

Smart Cat | 247

Sydney was struggling, too. "I'm sorry," I whispered to her. "We'll figure out another way." But how?

Over the next few weeks, I would hear the patter of Sydney's paws on the hardwood floors and then... silence. But not total silence exactly. I learned to listen to Sydney in a different way.

I listened to the sound of her paws in a way I never noticed before. I could tell when she was walking with determination to find a new spot by the window by the quick-paced *pat, pat, pat* sound. I learned that the *pat, pat* pause *pat, pat* when Sydney was walking in a circle near me meant she wanted me to give her some cuddles. When Sydney came into the office and raced back and forth across the room as if in a game of tag by herself, I knew she needed me to play with her, and I reached for her toys.

Sydney also learned how to communicate with me in a new way. One day, I looked down as she dropped a gray, fuzzy ball on my toes. She had never done that before, and she looked at me and tilted her head as if to say, "Wanna play fetch?"

Sydney also learned how to use her paw-steps to grab my attention. While only ten pounds, my little tortoiseshell kitty learned how to use the weight of her body to make louder steps, especially if she wanted to eat! She sounded like she was marching in and out, in and out of the office, until I couldn't ignore her. I knew I was getting my marching orders to feed her!

Over the next few months, we learned a new language. The rhythm of Sydney's paws, the tempo of her pace, and tone of each step became music to my ears.

Sydney taught me to find new ways to do things. When I thought that I had to accept that our special communications were a thing of the past, Sydney taught me to keep an open mind and to listen. She taught me to really hear the many things I had overlooked in how she was communicating. We both learned to adapt and we continued to grow together. What a relief that was!

— Angela Cleveland —

Cranky Cat Saves the Day

*We often take for granted the very things that most
deserve our gratitude.*
~Cynthia Ozick

When I was a teenager, my father took a job in Saudi Arabia. My mom, brother and I moved in with my grandmother while my mom searched for a new place for us to live. My grandmother was a widow and lived alone, with the exception of her two cats, Patches and Smokey.

Patches was a playful, friendly, little calico cat, while Smokey was a huge, gray shorthair that had the disposition of the Terminator. The only person Smokey liked or even tolerated was my grandmother, to whom she was a constant and loving companion. Smokey would let people know she didn't like them by either giving them a cold stare or growling at them, or both. Anybody who came to Grandmother's door was subject to Smokey's evil stare and growls.

Smokey was also naughty. She'd jump on the table during meals and try to steal the food from our plates. My grandmother would laugh and then scoop up her naughty cat and reward her with tidbits.

My grandmother had a habit of staying up every night to watch *The Late Show*, often falling asleep on the sofa and not waking up until the next morning. Since her living room was drafty, she'd use an electric blanket to stay warm and would cuddle up with Smokey under the blanket. Late one night, my mother and I were awakened by a loud crash and meowing. We jumped out of bed and ran to the living room. We found Smokey smacking my grandmother in the face and nipping her on the ear while smoke spiraled up from the sofa.

Quickly seeing that the electric blanket was on fire, my mother yanked her mother off the sofa. Then she pulled the cord for the blanket out of the wall while I ran to get a pan of water and open the front door to let in some fresh air. My mother and I put out the smoldering fire on the sofa and then checked my grandmother, who was miraculously unharmed.

My mother determined quickly that the electric blanket had gotten folded under my grandmother and overheated. Because my grandmother had enjoyed a drink of sherry and was a heavy sleeper, she hadn't smelled or felt anything. She would have been badly burned if not for the quick thinking of Smokey. Apparently, Smokey had knocked over a very large and heavy ceramic lamp. Its breaking sound woke my mother and me. And when my grandmother slept through that, Smokey nipped and smacked my grandmother's face until she awakened.

If not for Smokey's quick thinking, there might have been a catastrophe. After that night, Smokey could do no wrong in my grandmother's eyes. Smokey ate dinner with us every night while seated on the dinner table in a place of honor.

— Leslee W. Kahler —

Seeing Double

A catless writer is almost inconceivable.
~Barbara Holland

My friends Jonathan and Zoe left Taiwan to return to the States in the summer of 1969. They asked if we would take their two cats as they weren't sure where they would be for the next several weeks. We agreed at once. Billy and Peaches had been raised together and were very close. They spent most of the day together, took their naps together, and groomed each other.

Billy was a gray-and-black-striped cat, and Peaches was, well, just peachy. One day, Billy hurt his right front paw on something, gashing the pad of his foot. We took him to our vet, Dr. Chinn, who sterilized his wound and gave him some antibiotics. It healed neatly.

One day, Billy disappeared. We weren't too worried about him as we thought he'd be back for dinner, but days went by. No one had seen him in our neighborhood. About a month later, I was riding in a taxi on the outskirts of Taipei and saw a dead cat on the road with the same fur colors as Billy. I yelled at the taxi driver to stop. I got out and examined the poor cat's right front paw, and there was Billy's scar. I was heartbroken. The taxi driver took me to Dr. Chinn, who came back with me, putting the cat tenderly into a box.

Later that week, the cat's cremated remains were interred in a Buddhist pet cemetery, a reverent restful place for beloved pets, with eternal flames, incense, and chanted prayers. Our whole family wept. I put Billy's picture on the mantel and thought about him whenever I looked at it. Peaches seemed listless.

A couple of months went by.

Looking out the front window one day, I saw Peaches licking a stray cat very tenderly. He was a bedraggled fellow, very skinny, with matted fur. We brought him in, fed him and cleaned him up as best we could. And then it struck us that Peaches knew this cat, recognized him in spite of his appearance. We looked at his right front paw and, yes, there was the scar from the old injury.

Billy had come home.

—Judy Rebbeck Watten—

Chapter 9

Learning to Love the Cat

83

If I Name You Shakespeare

Cats are endless opportunities for revelation.
~Leslie Kapp

A chorus of caterwauls filled the cat room. As I scanned each of the cages, a silver tabby joined the hopeless song. "Maw... oooooow." I unlatched his cage, and he climbed into my arms, telling me stories I could only imagine. "Maw... oooooow."

"I'm taking you to live with my dad," I told the cat. "He's eighty years old and cranky, and he does *not* like cats!"

Though we'd had many cats while I was growing up, Dad had ignored each and every one. He had always been a self-proclaimed dog lover. Since there was no way I could help him take care of the needs of a dog, I began filling out paperwork to adopt the six-month-old tabby. I knew Dad would be mad at me, but he had been lonely and blue since Mom passed away, so he needed this cat as much as this cat needed him. He would forgive me eventually, wouldn't he?

"My dad lives all alone and needs someone to talk to," I explained to the cat as we left the shelter. "He spends his time reading and writing, and his favorite writer is William Shakespeare. So you see, if I name you Shakespeare, he might like you."

Dad's apartment smelled like old books and lead pencils. He smiled at me, sporting a toothless grin, his scruffy white hair curling over his ears. "Dad, look what I brought you," I said in my jolliest voice. "This is Shakespeare."

"Shakespeare?" Dad grumbled. "What kind of name is that for a cat? You can't dump a cat on me!"

"Oh, Dad! He's been living in a cage at the animal shelter. Just take care of him for a few weeks. See how it goes. I brought everything you need: food, bowls, a litter box and kitty litter. And I'll stop by every day to help take care of him." After a great deal of complaining, he agreed to keep the cat.

"What's in a name?" Dad muttered, looking into Shakespeare's curious eyes. "That which we call a rose, by any other word would smell as sweet." I smiled, wondering if Dad was going to spend his days spouting Shakespearean lines at the cat. When I left, he was leaning on his cane, scowling at Shakespeare who was exploring the small apartment. "What am I supposed to do with him until you come back?"

"Just talk to him," I replied. "I'll stop by tomorrow. Call me if you need anything."

When I arrived the next day, Dad was moving books off his window ledge. "It's all yours," he said to Shakespeare. "A cat should have a place to admire nature." We all gazed out the window at the bright fall day.

"All the world's a stage," Dad said, scratching Shakespeare between his ears. "And all the men and women merely players. They have their exits and their entrances, and one man in his time plays many parts. My current part appears to be humoring my daughter as a cat sitter!" Dad chuckled as he sat in his recliner. "Come hither, young Shakespeare," he invited, patting his lap. "It is time you learn the language of your namesake, William Shakespeare." The cat settled gingerly into Dad's lap. "Reading Shakespeare is like sipping a cup of hot tea," Dad said. "One must do it very slowly." Then he opened a tattered copy of *Macbeth* and began reading.

I visited often, bringing books, butter toffee, and home-cooked dinners. I drove Dad to the grocery store, where he carefully selected Shakespeare's meals and bought him catnip toys and fresh grasses. He read to his cat frequently. Sometimes, I sat on the sofa and listened, too. On one of these occasions, Dad tipped the book sideways to grin at Shakespeare. "You're a nice, little creature to have around," he said. "But don't tell my daughter I said so." Then he winked at me.

Sometimes, I brought fresh catnip from my garden. When I tossed it into the air, Shakespeare leapt after it, wrestling it to the ground. His antics always made Dad laugh, which made me happy. One day, he asked me what would happen to his cat when he died. "Oh, Dad! You don't need to worry about that," I said. "If something happens to you, Shakespeare will come live with me and Bill."

"There will come a time, my friend," Dad told his cat, "that you will chase a real bird, and you will climb a tree. And you will feel the wind in your whiskers."

Ten years passed, and Dad grew frail. He began reading less and watching TV more. He also slept more. A nurse visited twice a week, and a helper came in three days a week. But Dad remained happy and content in his little apartment with his cat.

Sometime in Dad's eighty-ninth year, he was reading Shakespeare's sonnets. "Like as the waves make towards the pebbled shore," he mumbled. "So do our minutes hasten to their end; each changing place with that which goes before." He stroked Shakespeare's head softly. "You've been a good cat. To me, fair friend, you never can be old."

Not long after that day, Dad passed away. I buried my face in Shakespeare's neck. "Now, my father's little companion, you will live with me and Bill. We have two cats and a dog who will be happy to meet you."

When I introduced Shakespeare to our cats, one hissed at him, and the other swatted him on the head. But our dog wagged his tail and sniffed him gently. When I fed our new clan of three cats, they gobbled up their food, and then they stared at each other. Through the cold, wintry months, the cats tolerated each other, but by spring, they were chummy friends.

It was a sunny day in early May, and the breeze was warm and gentle. Birds sang and bullfrogs croaked in our neighbor's pond. Shakespeare was watching through the window as the other two cats sunned themselves luxuriously on our patio. "Would you like to join them?" I offered, holding the door wide-open. Sniffing the sweet scent of spring and freshly cut grass, Shakespeare crept over the threshold, poking his nose into the outside world for the first time. A bird flew over his head into a tree. The breeze tickled his whiskers. He ran toward the tree. Up he went. Up. Up. Up. When he stopped, he gazed at the world below.

"Maw... ooooow."

And then I remembered. "There will come a time, my friend, that you will chase a real bird, and you will climb a tree. And you will feel the wind in your whiskers."

—Susan Trewhella—

84

I Married Her Whole Family

*One reason we admire cats is for their proficiency in
one-upmanship. They always seem to come out on top,
no matter what they are doing, or pretend they do.*
~Barbara Webster

When one marries a girl, one marries her whole family. I had been told this many times in life, but what I didn't anticipate was learning to live with a pair of cats — especially a grumpy one.

Yes, there are a lot of adjustments to be made when transitioning from singlehood to married life. I was in love and willing to do anything for the love of my life — even if it meant living with cats. But I knew I'd need patience, and I hoped the cats would be patient with me after the honeymoon.

My first few nights were spent fighting for my spot in the bed. I let my wife pick the side she wanted, knowing this was one of those lifetime decisions. I know of no couple who has switched sides of the bed, except for medical necessity. What I didn't know was that my bride had already been on her side of the bed long before she met me.

Her cats, Renoir ("Renny") and Monet, had their own side of the bed, and they weren't backing down.

Renny and I began to coexist quickly. He liked being petted, and I didn't mind giving a few positive strokes here and there. After I filled his food and water dish a few times, he lightened up quite a bit.

Monet, on the other paw, didn't like consuming the same oxygen as me. He didn't even like me cleaning the litter box. I'm sure there's a right way and a wrong way to do just about anything, but I was glad I didn't have to rely on Monet for long-term employment.

That first night, I could feel cats walking up and down the bed all night long, between my wife and me, maintaining a demilitarized zone. I honestly believe they were trying to figure out how to attack me without her finding out.

I stayed patient.

The next night, the furry duo contained me by marching around the top half of my body, nipping occasionally at my bare feet. One cat, probably Monet (who never conceded anything to me), decided I had too many toes.

And I stayed patient.

After a few weeks, I began feeling a nocturnal nip at my ear that didn't come with a warm, loving embrace. Instead, it made me flinch and check to see if I now had an unwanted piercing.

Still patient.

Then there was the morning I woke up feeling like I was wearing a Daniel Boone cap, but one that was alive. Then I noticed the flip of a cat's tail across my forehead. Slowly, I opened my eyes to find Monet's "other end" far closer to my nose than anyone would ever want.

This time, I'll confess, I was less patient than before.

But I recovered quickly because I love my wife, and she loves her cats.

Eventually, Monet and I figured out how to tolerate each other. I wish I could report we got along, but that isn't really accurate. Every time I entered a room, he sneered and left. But it seemed to work as long as necessary. His needs were met, and life moved along.

After about three years of marriage, the time came to show the ultimate mercy to Monet. I stood at my wife's side as she said her final goodbye, and I cried right with her. I even petted Monet, who seemed to at least tolerate my gesture.

The house seemed empty without him, and it was hard to watch

Renny search the house for his buddy.

This is the first time I've admitted I miss him. But Monet was a part of my married life. For better or for worse.

— Mark A. Howe —

85

Marching to a Different Drummer

Cats are only human, they have their faults.
~Kingsley Amis

Two days after settling Mama Cat and her four newborn kittens on my screened porch, my daughter Chelsea headed to Seattle for a new job, leaving me to foster the kittens until they were ready for adoption.

The three calico sisters blossomed, and I was proud of my skill as a foster mom. But my ego deflated whenever I studied the emerald-eyed, tawny guy I began to call Miz — short for Miz-fit, Miz-creant or just plain Miz-ery.

His sisters ignored him and Mama Cat often walked away from him while he was nursing. His yowls annoyed us all, but he wouldn't allow me to comfort him. Something was amiss with this tiny, golden guy.

I quizzed my friends who knew about cats.

"He's introverted?" Marti guessed.

"His social skills are delayed?" Connie looked baffled.

When I pointed out his very unkitten-like behavior of sleeping alone in the corner of a cardboard box he'd found, they rolled their eyes. "Call us when he's off to military school!"

But it wasn't funny to me. He was missing the critical eight-week socialization window that ensured he'd fit into his future human family. And with Chelsea graduated and gone, I was not going to be Miz's family. I had an empty nest and big plans.

At the hospital where I worked, I queried my colleagues. "A prenatal wiring error?"

The nurses shot side-glances at each other and hurried away from my obsessive discussions of this problem kitten. "Off to do rounds! Catch you later!"

At home, when I sought reassurance by phone, friends with caller ID refused to pick up. Solving the puzzle of Miz appeared to be my problem.

But where to start? Might deafness be the problem? I devised a not-so-scientific test: sneaking up behind him and banging together pot lids. Miz soared a foot in the air and fled to his cardboard box. Hearing: normal.

I checked Internet veterinary sites in vain. Autism doesn't exist in cats. Bipolar was unlikely—and, by the way, owners should stop sharing their Prozac.

Defeated, I crept off to bed. If the little guy needed to march to his own drummer, so be it. As long as he was gaining weight, I'd allow him his space.

A week later, after putting Mama and the calicos to bed, I turned and saw Miz curled forlornly in his tattered box. I felt a pang of guilt for neglecting him in favor of his sweet sisters.

Without thinking, I lifted Miz from a sound sleep.

"Yow! Pfft!" He escaped my grasp like a miniature Houdini and scrambled over my shoulder right into the hood of my sweatshirt! There he fell asleep. And began to purr!

I was giddy. For the next hour, I sat on the floor, humming every lullaby I'd sung to Chelsea.

Brrrriiing! Damn phone!

Miz awoke in a frenzy, needle-tipped claws plowing furrows down the back of my neck as he dashed for the safety of his box.

The kittens' two-month birthday arrived. The calico sisters' new owners were picking them up as soon as they had their immunizations.

"What a terrific foster mom you are," the vet said after inspecting the sisters. "These kittens are perfect!" He beamed, unaware I'd made a separate appointment for Miz two days later.

"Wonderful kittens!" The cheery receptionist smiled as I paid.

"Beautiful coats!" added a lady in the waiting room. I bowed my head in humility as if I'd birthed those kittens myself, conveniently forgetting they'd see the real me when I brought in Miz.

Miz's appointment came all too soon.

"This might go well," I reasoned. "Miz could surprise me." Still, opting for safety, I held him down with my knee while I buckled him into a harness and leash. But as if he lived to fulfill my worst expectations, Miz refused his carrier, exploded out of my hands and disappeared under the sofa. Hauling on his leash, I reeled him out as he squealed and spat. I crammed him into the carrier, and then made a brief detour to the bathroom to daub my wounds before heading to the vet.

Iodine tattoos on display, I hugged Miz's jolting, hissing carrier to my chest as I entered the vet's office. Raised eyebrows greeted me. Realizing it was too late to feign normalcy, I slunk to a seat and waited to be ushered into the inner sanctum of inoculations. By the time it was our turn, Miz was vibrating like an exposed 220-volt wire.

Before I could explain Miz's somewhat unusual personality, Dr. Carter opened the carrier, reached in and got a handful of kitten. Miz responded by turning into a two-pound tornado.

I watched in horror as the startled vet juggled my hissing, spitting kitten. "Holy sh-- cow!" he said, trying to shake off Miz as the little kitten wrapped himself around Dr. Carter's forearm and brutally bunny kicked the dumbfounded vet.

"So sorry!" I apologized as I peeled off Miz, praying those jagged scratches didn't need stitches.

Once his arm was liberated, the vet backed away. "I'm running late. No time to work with your little guy today." He tossed me the towel he'd used to wipe his arm and indicated I should wrap my squirming bundle of fur for immediate departure. Miz and I were ushered out.

With his kitten shots postponed indefinitely, Miz rode home in his carrier wrapped like a burrito in the vet's towel.

"For pity's sake, Miz," I scolded as I drove, "now what do we do for a vet?"

"Yow!" said the burrito.

Chelsea came for Christmas and begged for Mama Cat.

"Mom, I miss her! Besides, you have Miz for company," she said, ignoring the fact that Miz as anyone's "companion" was a bit of a stretch.

And then it was just Miz and me in a house too big for the two of us, going neither forward nor backward. But one cold morning eight months later, everything changed.

Miz's piercing yowl from the kitchen informed me I'd forgotten his breakfast. He tracked me to the bedroom where I was huddled under my quilt, nursing a cold. When I didn't respond to his verbal entreaties, he startled me by hopping on the bed and tiptoeing over to stare into my eyes.

I risked a one-fingered stroke of his lush, golden coat, and for the first time he didn't shun my touch.

We live like this now — parallel souls in our daily dance. Some days, we waltz slowly, almost in step. Other days, we perform a discordant tango, each of us aloof and facing away, but always aware. I treasure the nights he glides into the bedroom and curls up behind my knees, though he's never there in the morning. On good days, I turn unexpectedly and find him behind me, as close and quiet as a shadow.

I understand my gorgeous guy will forever be a stranger in a strange land. But in learning to embrace his uniqueness, my heart is full. No longer needing to question his differences, I address him as Miz-ter Miz.

His whiskers quiver as if he's smiling.

— Ange Crawford —

86

Purrfect Love

If purring could be encapsulated, it'd be the
most powerful anti-depressant on the
pharmaceutical market.
~Alexis F. Hope

My husband Lou begged me for years to get a cat. But I'm a dog person. What would I do with a cat?

When my children were six and eight, I finally gave in so they would have the opportunity to grow up with a pet. I agreed with the provision that Lou would take most of the responsibility for the care of the new kitten.

Tabby wasn't too intrusive and was much easier to care for than a dog. True to his word, Lou fed the cat and cleaned the litter box faithfully. The children loved having a pet, but it was Lou who developed the strongest bond. Tabby would sleep on Lou's chest almost every night.

About two years later, my mother moved in with us. Like me, she was also a dog person and didn't pay much attention to Tabby.

Then a day came that changed my world forever. Lou told me he was not happy and would be moving out of the house within a few days. I was stunned. How could he leave his family? I felt like we were being abandoned with an additional act of betrayal — he was moving to an apartment that would not take animals. He was leaving the cat with me!

Tabby was lonely, and my already broken heart cracked a bit more to see her pad throughout the house looking for her friend. She was stuck with me and became my total responsibility, along with my two confused teenagers and my mother who was showing signs of Alzheimer's.

We all managed the best we could. To my surprise, Tabby became the constant in my life. The children went off to college. Suddenly, the house that held five people and a cat now contained two people and a cat.

I sold our house and bought a lovely duplex. Mom, Tabby, and I settled into our new home. It signaled a new beginning for the three of us. I went off to work each day, and my mother started staying home more and more. Amazingly, Tabby became her companion. Mom talked to her and held her on her lap. I was grateful for the comfort Tabby provided, and that Mom was getting extra attention that I couldn't provide.

During the day, twenty-seven active kindergartners were under my care. I loved my job, even though it was exhausting. Then I came home to a mother demonstrating progressive memory issues. I missed my children and was just getting by, both emotionally and financially. It was a relief that Tabby demanded nothing from me. She was literally my quiet in the storm.

Growing up, my mother would tell me, "Nothing is so bad that it couldn't get worse." Unfortunately, she was right. My mother developed lung cancer with a poor prognosis. Suddenly, I had no one to turn to but Tabby. She was the one I began to hold and tell how scared I was. I allowed her to sleep with me. Her warm body snuggled next to mine gave me a sense of comfort and security. At least I knew she wasn't going anywhere.

Those weeks were a blur of work, worry, and stress. In the midst of my struggle, I had a heart attack. Now the house contained a mother with dementia and cancer, and me, who was recuperating. Tabby was our faithful, loving presence.

On Christmas Eve, my mother died. For a few days, the house was filled with family. When they left, all that remained was a lonely and frightening quiet. Again, Tabby padded around the house looking for her friend. I went back to work, and Tabby would greet me at the door when I came home.

One evening, I realized there was no conversation in the house. Tabby probably missed the sound of voices. I got in the habit of talking to her. In the morning, I would say, "Goodbye. See you later. Have a nice day." Tabby would watch me close the door.

My attitude toward the cat had changed so much since her arrival so long ago. Back then, I could not anticipate that Tabby would become such a welcome and constant friend. Her behavior was like a loyal dog. She would follow me into every room. She sat at my feet when I worked on the computer or watched TV. I was glad to know she would be waiting for me at the end of the day.

When Tabby wanted me to wake up, she would knock her head against mine repeatedly. One morning after Tabby delivered her wake-up routine, I noticed there was blood on my bedspread. I gathered her in my arms and started to inspect her body. I saw a bloody bulge that was not evident before. I ran with Tabby to the vet. She had developed a fast-growing, painful tumor. I had not seen her acting uncomfortable and felt terrible that I was unaware of it. There had been no warning. The recommendation was to let her go because of the size of the tumor and the progressive pain associated with it.

I survived my divorce, selling and moving into a new home, my children going off to college, my mother's death, and my heart attack with strength and fortitude. The loss of Tabby was almost more than I could endure. My grief for her was stronger than any I had known. My heart ached, realizing how much this loving cat had watched over me and helped me endure my greatest sorrows.

I held Tabby in my arms, and I thanked her for the sixteen years we spent together as the vet released her. I came home, and then there was just me. The house was totally quiet, and I was truly alone. A few days later, I received a condolence card in the mail. I was so grateful that someone understood. I had lost a member of the family.

—Jean Ferratier—

What Tandy Knows

If we treated everyone we meet with the same affection
we bestow upon our favorite cat, they, too, would purr.
~Martin Buxbaum

We moved into our new home and discovered it was directly across the street from the neighborhood cat lady. We smiled and went to say "hello."

The cat lady's name was Claudette. She was sweet but spacey. She told me she was worried that she had Alzheimer's because her memory was so bad. She said, "It happened to my mom." It took her six months to learn my name, and she never knew what day of the week it was, but she also had moments of perfect clarity and quick wit. I liked Claudette a lot.

There were cats in Claudette's front yard and dogs in the back. Most of the dogs were rescues. The cats were strays, dumps, and offspring. When I discovered that the cats were not fixed, I arranged to get the girls spayed.

The night before their appointment, we rounded up Tandy, Rena, Callie, and Coonie. Tandy was a gorgeous, longhaired calico. Claudette said that she was the very first one, left behind by a neighbor at least ten years before. Claudette couldn't remember, but I was pretty sure the other three girls were Tandy's daughters, probably from the same litter.

I took them for surgery and kept them overnight for recovery. Coonie was sick, so she spent ten days on meds. When she was finally spayed, we asked Claudette if we could keep her. She agreed, and

Coonie became ours.

Months passed. Rena disappeared, and Callie did, too. Other cats came and went. Claudette was unaware of who was new and who was missing—she just fed and loved whoever was there.

The one constant was Tandy. She stayed close to home. But I adored her from afar because she almost never let me pet her.

About a year later, Claudette's mental health declined sharply. She turned the dogs loose and moved into her car. When I asked her why she didn't live in her house anymore, she replied, "I never really have." She didn't remember living in her house!

I grew concerned when Claudette slept in her car with the dogs, going inside her house only to feed the animals. Then Claudette stopped getting out of her car. She let out the dogs, but she stayed inside. The cats all came across the street to eat in our carport—even Tandy, who had never left her yard. I called Emergency Medical Services and Claudette went to the hospital and then into a nursing home.

The dogcatcher took the dogs, and I was left with the cats. Other than Tandy, they were living on our side of the street anyway. I hoped Tandy would transition on her own since Claudette was gone, but she continued to slip over to eat and then bolt if she saw us watching. I worried she would get hit by a car because she didn't look—she just ran.

After a week, I borrowed a trap to set up in Claudette's yard. I knew it might take awhile, with all the cats in the neighborhood, as well as raccoons and opossums. Mike was just hoping we didn't catch a skunk!

Surprisingly, we caught Tandy the very first night! That little girl was ready to surrender.

I moved her into my bedroom. She was warm, dry and safe. She cuddled. She purred. She loved being petted. She even snuggled with me at night. I could only imagine the relief she must have felt.

So I was floored a week later when I found her gone. It was a warm day, so I had opened the window. The metal mesh screen had a hole in it, and there was fluffy hair all around it. Tandy had gone home.

Of course, there was nobody there, so she had to come back across the street to eat, but she would still only do it when she thought we weren't looking. After a few days, I borrowed a trap again.

Then the games began. I knew we wouldn't catch Tandy until she was ready, but I really didn't expect her to send everyone else while she laughed in the shadows!

We caught Midnight. Three times. We caught Tigger three times. We caught Em. We caught an opossum twice. We caught a raccoon. And finally, after nearly a week, we caught Tandy. She was ready to try again.

But now I understood. It wasn't about comfort. It was about her comfort zone. It wasn't about "better." It was about what she knew. Being too cold or too hot, taking shelter under a trailer to stay out of the weather, waiting to be fed, never having fresh water… not a great life, but a familiar life.

It was like growing up in a dysfunctional family. Even when she was offered something better, she returned instinctively to what she knew because it was all she knew.

More than anything, my sweet, beautiful girl needed understanding. I could try to reprogram her, but first I had to accept her as she was.

I'd been trying to learn that lesson with humans for decades. It finally got through with a cat!

—Linda Sabourin—

Salesman Cat

*When you touch a cat with your spirit, in return they
touch your soul with their heart.*
~Author Unknown

he Sedona Humane Society decided to create its first dog and
cat calendars as a fundraiser. Pet owners could buy a page for
their dog or cat, first come first served. As an added bonus,
for every dollar raised for the dog or cat in that calendar, the
owner earned one point. The dog and the cat with the most points
would earn the cover photo on their respective calendars. Two of
my friends decided we would work together at raising money and
then split the money three ways for our cats. We made cookies and
headed uptown to sell them just outside Gifts Galore, a local shop
that catered to tourists.

Since Joshua was the only cat of the three who walked on a leash
and enjoyed going out into the community, we took him along to raise
money. It was a hot day, however, and the pavement was too hot for
his little paws. Since another friend owned Gifts Galore and Joshua
was a frequent visitor, he was allowed to sit on his favorite chair in
the back of the store.

While we humans sat outside trying to keep cool and sell cookies,
Joshua was allowed to remain in the store away from the hot pavement.
Both my husband and I kept an eye on the doors to the store to ensure
no one left with a white cat with large, green eyes. Every so often, we
would take turns going inside to check on Joshua, only to find him

sleeping peacefully on a leather chair in the clothing section.

When a family of four, with a boy and a girl, entered the shop and headed toward the back of the store, I went in and wandered toward Joshua. The girl, about twelve, petted him. Joshua was obviously enjoying her touch. Nearby, her brother, a boy of about nine or ten, shifted from one foot to another.

"You can pet him," I told him. I patted Joshua's head.

"I can't." The boy lowered his eyes. "I'm allergic to cats."

"He's hypoallergenic," I told the mother and father. Then I regaled them with the stories of many people who, over the years, were able to pet Joshua. I explained he had been a therapy cat in California and was somewhat famous in Sedona.

The son looked at his father with longing. "Can I, Dad?"

The father frowned, but nodded finally. The boy dropped to his knees and touched Joshua tentatively on the head. The cat responded with his normal head bump and looked into the boy's face. Soon, the boy was caressing the cat without a care in the world.

"I can pet him, Mom. Look, no reaction." He leaned in, and Joshua kissed his face. "Dad, can we get a cat like this?"

The father folded his arms, but watched both his children as they stroked the purring feline. The mother smiled and then turned to her husband. Her eyes widened, and she nodded toward the children.

"We'll see," the father said. "We'll talk about it when we get home."

"Okay, kids," the mother said as she put her arm around her daughter's shoulder. "We'd better get going."

The daughter stood and joined her parents. The son got up reluctantly and moved away from Joshua, and then looked back over his shoulder.

Then I saw something I never saw Joshua do. He put his two front feet on the back of the chair and reached out to the boy with his right paw. The boy sighed loudly, hurried back the five feet to Joshua and fell to his knees, putting his arms around the cat.

With tears in his eyes, the young boy looked up at his father. "Please, Dad, can we get a cat like this?"

Both the mother and daughter looked at the father expectantly.

The father took a deep breath and let out the air slowly. Then he took out his cell phone and looked over at me. "What breed did you say this cat is?"

I always knew Joshua was a gift to me, but now I saw he was a gift for others, too.

— Carol L. Gandolfo —

The Cat Reader

*There's always room for a story that can transport
people to another place.*
~J.K. Rowling

It had been a few years since I had last volunteered anywhere, and I was looking for a new assignment. But where? The answer was my local animal shelter. After printing off the application, I remember distinctly ticking off the "dog" box before I posted it.

A few weeks later, a lady called to ask if I were still interested. Then she told me they had an opening for a cat reader. My mind started to race. *What did she say? A cat reader? Did I hear her correctly?* "There has been a mistake," I explained. "I checked the dog box."

I was familiar with children reading to dogs to improve their reading skills — but why would I read to a cat? The woman explained that the cats were strays or rescues from abusive situations, and they needed socializing before they were deemed adoptable. Having a person read to them allowed them to share a space with someone who was non-threatening. They were free to roam the room and do as they liked while I read. I responded, "I have had two previous volunteer reading stints. As a volunteer, I am willing to do what is required of me. I will be there."

The first four weeks were uneventful. Most weeks, there was just one cat in the room. On one occasion, there were three, and another time two, but that was because they were found together. I did my thing, and the cats did theirs. Beyond saying "hi" when I entered, I made no effort to touch them. If they wanted my attention, I assumed they would let me know.

Then I met Selena. Selena was my "Velcro cat." The first time I entered the room, she rushed toward me. She sat on my lap. And when I read, she acted like she wanted to put her head in my mouth. Was she trying to guess what I had for breakfast? (Note to self: Do not eat tuna-salad sandwiches for breakfast on the day you are going to read to a cat.) Thinking she wanted my attention, I petted her. Suddenly, she lunged at my hand. I couldn't believe it. What had I done wrong? I have lymphedema in one arm and cannot afford to be bitten, clawed, or scratched.

When I arrived home after that first time with Selena, my neighbour, a cat owner, was outside gardening. After I explained what had happened, he lent me a book on cat behaviour. Then I searched the Internet and found some helpful videos, including "You're Petting Your Cat All Wrong!" by Jackson Galaxy, a well-known cat expert. That's when I learned the concept of overstimulation. Jackson demonstrated on his own cat. Three strokes, and the cat got up and walked away. He emphasised monitoring the tail. If it starts to twitch, there's a good chance the person will be bitten, so stop petting. Whether dealing with people or animals, one must always observe body language and take heed. But one must first learn the body language for that species, and the individuals within the species. We are all unique.

Armed with new knowledge, I went back the next week ready to read to Selena. It was amazing to me that she would want to be so close and yet turn on me in a flash. She would even knead me, which is supposed to be a sign of contentment. Thankfully, she was adopted before any damage was done.

Kinga was another puzzle to me. The first time I read to her, she made a motion as if to bite me but stopped short of actually doing it. Rightly or wrongly, I decided they were love bites and her way of asking me to resume petting her whenever I stopped. On later visits, she would rub against me when I entered the room and lie on a bed near me, but that was all. On the sixth day, she climbed in my lap and put her front paws on either side of my neck, like a hug, and nuzzled me. I bowed my head slowly so that we were cheek-to-cheek. No cat had ever done that before or since. She was adopted the next day. Was that her way of saying "Goodbye" or "Thanks for spending time with me"? I will never know, but it was an exquisite, magical moment.

The first two books I read were about dogs. The cats didn't seem to mind, but I decided I owed it to myself and the cats to read cat-themed books. The *Chicken Soup for the Soul* cat books were perfect for my purposes. I didn't have to remember the plot of a novel from one week to the next. Each story was short and self-contained. The stories have made me laugh out loud, and some have made tears blind my vision. Most importantly, they have broadened my education, understanding, and appreciation of felines.

The *Chicken Soup for the Soul* series has done something else for me. I have been writing for years, but sporadically and never professionally. Submitting stories to them has given me a creative outlet and a way to share my life experiences. Maybe one day they will select one of mine from the thousands of entries they receive. In the interim, I will continue to read to cats once a week and learn. Who knows? I might even become a cat person one day.

— Cheryl M. Taylor —

I Do Not Own Kittens

Kittens are angels with whiskers.
~Author Unknown

One July day, when Monté the magnificent tabby failed to pester me for more than two hours, I found him dead at the bottom of the basement stairs. Confused and devastated, I took his body to the clinic. His heart, the vet said, had a flaw.

When it was time to pick up Monté's ashes from the vet, my husband asked if there were any kittens to play with. Paul returned from the vet with a half-smile and told me all about the kitten he saw there. Since it had only been eight days, and I hadn't stopped crying, I bleated out my mantra between sobs, "I do not own kittens."

Kittens are small, fragile and delicate. They are magnets for perilous situations. One wrong step and, in the most literal sense, they are gone. I didn't need more heartache.

Yes, I worry too much. But that was my policy. For years, we had rescued adult cats.

But Paul wanted something different this time. Every couple of days, when he went on an errand, the car steered itself mysteriously toward the veterinary clinic, where two adorable ginger kittens lived. Every time, he told me about it.

Finally, I relented. This made him happy. Yes, I said, *you*, not me, may get a kitten. *You.*

But he did not bring home a kitten. On the day after my birthday,

Learning to Love the Cat | 277

he brought home *two* kittens. Plural. Two tiny balls of marmalade-colored fluff. Both fit in the same container, curled around each other.

"I do not own kittens," I told them with the solemnness reserved for judicial decrees. Then I leveled a finger at my husband's heart. "You two are *his*."

Paul thought that was hilarious. "It's okay, boys. You'll be cats soon enough. Then she'll claim you."

Every day, I told them, "I do not own kittens."

Rey, the tinier of the two, knew no fear. He didn't walk anywhere; he trotted, eager to greet all new experiences. He did not jump down. He jumped straight out like Superman and let gravity take care of the details. He snuggled, nestled and climbed into laps.

Beau, the shy and observant thinker, studied things from a distance and kept his own counsel. All contact was slight and fleeting, on his terms and no one else's. He did not snuggle, nestle or climb into laps.

Somewhere, possibly from a forgotten nook under the basement stairs, he found an old and hideous toy. Threadbare and weirdly illustrated, we gave the triangular toy a name: Byrd. He carried Byrd everywhere. When he felt an interest in playing, he set Byrd down, usually near the basement stairs, to maximize chasing potential, and then started to glare and meow.

No, no, that meowing said, *I am not bringing my favorite thing in the universe to you for your fun. Nay. Nix. I am going to stand here and howl until you, puny human, are brought to me and Byrd. Then, and only then, are you allowed to play with either of us.*

And so it went. Those were the rules. Beau enforced them. Byrd was under his jurisdiction and no one else's.

Four months after the kittens landed at our house, I went to the doctor for something else and came out with a diagnosis of cancer. Stage three cancer. No one looked me in the eye or gave me odds on anything.

My freefall into the land of nightmares then began.

In February, an awful post-chemo night when Paul was out of town, I was sick and kept getting sick. I didn't bother to go back to bed. I wedged myself into the narrow space on the bathroom floor and waited to see how many more rounds of violent illness there might be that night. Shaking, I rested my forehead on my shivering arms. And when I thought no one could hear me, I started to cry.

I cried like an animal caught in a trap — which, when analyzed, was exactly the case. I was caught in several traps. A trap called cancer. A trap called chemo. A trap called radiation.

In the middle of all that crying, I felt a soft weight drop onto my hair. Blinking, I reached until my fingertips brushed against fabric. I knew what it was without looking: Byrd.

Startled, I lifted my head and looked to make sure. Yes, I saw it. Byrd. Beau gave me Byrd. Beau presented me with the most precious thing in his world. He dropped Byrd right in my hair.

And then, seeing the precious gift I'd received, I cried again. But even to my ears, I sounded different. Softer. Edged with hope. I held Byrd and squeezed my eyes shut. When I opened them, I saw Beau's chin near my fingertips. His eyes were trained on me.

Beau studied me for several seconds in that unblinking fashion of his.

"You brought me Byrd," I said out loud to check if I were hallucinating. "You gave Byrd to me."

Never big on explanations, Beau said nothing. He lifted one paw, kind of pointed, and then stepped into the furrow of my arms. I stared and kept on staring, still unsure on the status of this hallucination. Beau gave me another glance, and then folded his legs and curled up in my arms.

It was a night of firsts.

He studied me. Maybe he was waiting for me to repeat the phrase: "I do not own kittens." Or maybe he was telling me that he was a big boy now. He was a cat. Or maybe he'd decided that he didn't belong to anyone. With the presentation of Byrd, he took custody of me.

I was now his human.

Deciding I felt okay with all of that, I set Byrd on top of him for safekeeping and cuddled Beau a little closer to me. Rey, never one for solitude, hopped over my head, jumped onto my shoulder and climbed down, nestling in next to Beau and Byrd. Within a minute or two, they were asleep.

I lay there on the floor clinging to the warm, soft contours of hope. A minute earlier, I had felt very much alone. Now, I felt the onset of courage. I was, after all, a newly inducted member of a pride. It was a tiny pride of minuscule lions, but still, they were mine, and I was theirs.

I closed my eyes and slept enough to dream of flying. I think we all did.

— Virginia Elizabeth Hayes —

A Cat with Purpose

You can't own a cat. The best you can do
is be partners.
~Sir Harry Swanson

Our rescued cat, Saffron, had never tolerated me. Whenever we shared the same room, she'd watch me suspiciously, her green eyes like slits, shoulders raised, balancing on the arm of the fireside chair. When alone, she took a relaxed stance, stretched out or curled in a ball on the rug by the hearth.

Don't get me wrong, I'm a cat lover, but accustomed to cats who actually like me — snaking around my legs for food, greeting me with a friendly meow as they strut, tails erect, into the house. Our old cat, Wayward, would purr like a road drill when I rubbed her tummy. She'd stretch out her arms and legs luxuriously whenever I approached. Enticing. Accepting. Like a furry Jezebel, luring my hands into her silky coat, drooling with pleasure. I cried buckets when she died.

Saffron was a different kettle of fish. I'd given up approaching her, trying to make friends. But the scratches on my hands bore witness to her dislike of me. Why, I'd no idea. The hatred was unwarranted. I always filled her bowl with freshly cooked tidbits. I'd never trodden on her tail or stepped on a paw.

One afternoon as I sat alone in front of a glowing fire, drowsy from good food, I must have nodded off. But I was roused by a movement in my lap. I opened one eye. No, it couldn't be. It must be some other ginger fur ball who'd sneaked in. I opened the other eye to reinforce that I wasn't still dreaming. Saffron padded her paws up and down gently, her eyes screwed shut, a dribble of ecstasy escaping her pink lips. Warily, I moved my hand toward her and stroked her, waiting for the baring of teeth or hissing, followed by sharpened claws. Nothing. My affection was accepted. I couldn't wait to tell my husband when he came home.

This became a daily occurrence, and I had no explanation for it until several months later when I was talking to my friend, Ana.

"I'm getting so fat," I told her. "There's hardly room for the cat on my lap. Saffron will soon revert to hating me again, and I'm a bit worried how she'll react to the baby when it comes. I've heard awful stories of cats getting into cots, sitting on the baby's head and smothering it." I shivered at the idea.

"Rubbish — that's an old wives' tale." Ana had met Saffron on many occasions and witnessed her feral behaviour toward me. "When did you say her behaviour changed?" A knowing look formed on her face.

"Not sure," I said, thinking back. "About the same time I fell preg…" My eyes opened wide. "You don't think it's anything to do with that, do you?"

"Who knows?" she said, laughing. "They say that cats have a sixth sense."

"You mean Saffron knew I was pregnant before I did? Oh, come on. Now I've heard it all."

I didn't tell my husband Mark about our conversation. He would have said I was bonkers.

The day drew nearer, and the nursery was ready. The crib had been trimmed in lemon and white. We chose neutral colours as we had decided not to find out if it was a girl or a boy.

At 4:15 a.m., we were roused from sleep by the cat padding up and down the bed, mewing loudly. At that moment, I realised my water had broken. Mark shot out of bed and dressed hastily, shooing out the cat. Things were happening fast. I was soon in the car and on the way to the hospital. Our son was born six hours later.

Kenzie was colicky and cried a lot. Mark and I took turns pacing the floor, shushing and lulling in an attempt to quiet our son, almost tripping over Saffron, who patrolled the landing. The moment we got back to sleep, Kenzie woke, screaming down the house. Saffron would run back and forth in distress, making a great din. Mark often got annoyed with her and shut her in the kitchen. Meanwhile, Kenzie screamed and screamed, his hot, little face all red and blotchy, eyes scrunched shut. I couldn't bear to see him in such distress; not even a pacifier would soothe him.

Both the midwife and the doctor insisted there was nothing wrong with our boy. Mark and I had taken to doing alternate nights, so at least one of us got some sleep.

One evening, I pulled the covers up to my chin, reveling in the fact that it wasn't my night. A few minutes later, I became vaguely aware that Kenzie had stopped crying. I let out a sigh of relief. It was short-lived, though, as he started up again. Amid the noise, I could hear my husband swearing at the cat. I must have dropped off to sleep because the next thing I knew, Mark was shaking me awake. The sound of Kenzie's fitful cries put me on high alert.

"Quick! Come with me. You have to see this."

Fearful, I leapt from the bed and followed. Saffron was doing her normal thing of patrolling back and forth to the nursery door, yowling.

"What is it? What's happened?"

Mark touched my arm. "Don't move. Just stay there."

I froze as he turned the handle on the nursery door. Saffron pushed her way through his legs, snaking under the stand of the Moses basket. I moved closer. I could just hear the cat's loud purring amid the wails from our child. Within seconds, the crying stopped. I looked at my sleep-weary husband.

"What the…?"

He raised a finger to his lips. "Just watch." Dropping to his knees, he reached under our now sleeping child's cot and pulled out a wiggling Saffron, who, claws extended, scrabbled to grip the carpet. With one arm behind his back and a squirming cat in the other, he closed the nursery door and then pointed a finger, beating time.

"One… two… three."

Kenzie's cry struck through the darkness. The cat struggled to be free. Mark let her drop to the carpet and reopened the baby's door. As before, the cat shot in, already purring, and the baby quieted.

"Can you believe it? When the cat's with him, Kenzie sleeps, and we've been shutting out poor Saffron the whole time. That's why Kenzie always sleeps in the daytime when he's downstairs — because his furry carer," Mark winked at me, "is in the room."

Mark was right. Saffron watched my every move while I bathed and fed our baby. He even alerted us a few times when our sleeping baby had a fever. Saffron was better than any nanny. Our baby was in a safe pair of paws!

— Sue Mackender —

The Collar Caper

*It is in the nature of cats to do a certain amount
of unescorted roaming.*
~Adlai Stevenson

I finished eating breakfast on my patio and opened the latch that held Butch's crate shut. Our red tabby purred and meandered out, unruffled by his short incarceration. He and I had performed this ritual for several months, with me locking in the stray so I could work in my garden or go for a swim without fear of the cat getting underfoot, or worse, biting me.

Even though he'd been dwelling on our patio, basking in the sun for months, I remained untrusting. Butch displayed an aggressive nature when he first wandered onto our pool patio. He sank his feline fangs into my thumb, which resulted in a trip to the Urgent Care Clinic. Since he wouldn't go away, my choice was either to have him removed by animal services or train him. So, I had improvised a plan I knew would take a great deal of time and patience.

Butch strolled out, rubbed his whiskers on the outside of the crate, did his downward-cat stretch, and then sashayed off to snooze serenely on my ottoman. At the door, I turned to see Butch's paws spread open into the air. He was sporting a turquoise collar around his neck and a nametag with my phone number engraved on it. I closed the door, content with my feline lodger.

Later that afternoon, Butch pawed at the sliding glass door, a signal he wanted his noon snack. If fed often enough, he was less likely to

Learning to Love the Cat | 285

patrol my neighbor's property and go hunting. My plan was to keep him fed, keep him safe, and keep him on my patio.

As I poured cat food into Butch's bowl, I noticed he wasn't wearing his collar. I searched the yard, under the bougainvillea and chain-link fence. The collar was gone. Reasoning that Butch had hooked the breakaway collar on the fence, I made a mental note to pick up another.

When my husband Tom and I returned from brunch that afternoon, I found Butch snoozing on the ottoman where I'd left him. But something was different. He was wearing a new collar with a bright blue, heart-shaped ID tag. The name "Bacardi"was emblazoned on it, along with a phone number. I did a double-take and called my husband. "This cat has been two-timing us!"

Tom stared at the nametag and laughed. "Butch, you miserable creature! You've been working the neighborhood."

Butch meowed and rolled over onto his side, enjoying being the center of attention. I found my cell phone, photographed the tag, and then dialed the number on the ID. A female voice came on the answering message. I left a message.

"Hi, just wanted you to know where your cat's been hanging out for the last six months. He's safe." I stared at Butch sprawled on my ottoman, like a king holding court. I left my address and then went back to working on my laptop. Deep down, I was disturbed Butch had another home. In fact, I was crushed after having spent so much time developing our relationship.

A few hours later, my doorbell rang. I looked through the front door's glass divider. I saw an attractive girl, about eighteen or nineteen. She smiled brightly and waved through the glass panel. "Hi, I'm the cat's mom."

I fought my jealousy and opened the front door. "Guess it's my fault he's here," I said. "I shouldn't have fed him." She followed me through the living room and out to the patio. Butch was lying on my ottoman. When he saw the girl, he went to her and rubbed against her leg. She bent down, stroked his back and scratched his ear. I waited to see if Butch nipped at her. He didn't. I wasn't sure how I felt about that.

"One time, he disappeared for five weeks," she said. "We wandered the streets yelling out 'Bacardi.' Neighbors thought we were a bunch of alcoholics. He was an indoor cat for five years. Then we put him outside."

"How old is he now?"

"Nine."

"Why is he outside?" I asked.

Butch sensed my anxiety. He rubbed against my leg. I didn't make an effort to pet him in case he chose this moment to demonstrate his loyalty for his first owner.

"He didn't get along with our other four cats," she said. "He likes being outside. We have four dogs. He gets along well with the dogs. In fact, he thinks he's a big dog."

"I know," I said. "Sometimes, he follows me around the pool like a dog."

That sounded too possessive.

Butch, now bored with being scratched by humans, strolled over to the fence to watch a woodpecker on the grass. Butch eyed the bird curiously, as if preparing to scale the fence and launch an attack.

"I gave him all his shots. I had him checked by a vet," I said.

The girl wasn't buying into my guilt trip. She hung her head sadly. "I just came back to the house to set the traps to catch the other cats."

"Other cats? Traps?" I said.

The girl and I walked over to the chain-link fence. "My mother passed away last year, and our house is too big for us. My father sold it. We're moving."

I felt my throat tighten.

"You'll be putting Butch... Bacardi... outside in a strange neighborhood?" I visualized Butch lost, confused, wandering the streets or being hit by a car.

The girl stared at me, as if making a painful decision.

"Do you want to keep him?" she asked.

"I can't. I'm allergic to cats," I said.

Butch looked up at me almost sadly, as if he understood every word we were saying. When I turned, he followed close by my feet. He strolled back to his ottoman and jumped up. I scratched his ear.

His gold-flecked eyes seemed to be pleading, "Say you'll adopt me."

I sighed. "Okay, I'll keep the cat," I said. "I'll take care of him."

A few weeks later, I drove by the girl's former home. Cordoned off with yellow tape barriers, the house was in the process of being torn down. There's something sad about seeing a house, once filled with life, being gutted.

This year marked Butch's fifth anniversary living with us. He has gone through seven collars, but has never come home with a different nametag again!

And in honor of his anniversary, we moved him to a screened-in patio with a cat condo built specially for him. He has an ottoman where he can watch the birds and squirrels and never have to fear predators or being hit by a car.

Butch taught us that perseverance, patience, and a little begging definitely pay off.

— Joyce Newman Scott —

Chapter 10

Miracles Happen

93

Journey of Love

*Miracles are not contrary to nature, but only contrary
to what we know about nature.*
~Saint Augustine

The allergy tests lit up my back and arms like tiny, four-way stop-lights. Angry, red welts flashed their terrible message — allergic to cats, allergic to dogs, allergic to fur. I cried because I knew what this meant. Our pets would have to go.

Our family of five lived on the Naval Air Station in Key West, Florida. My mother found neighbors willing to take our sweet dog, Tramp. My sister gave her guinea pig to one of her friends at school. But I begged my parents to let us keep my beloved cat, Grungy.

We had adopted Grungy six years earlier in Ankara, Turkey, from the Cat Lady, a kind soul who rescued feral felines. They sprawled over every inch of her sloped, brown yard. Thin and filthy, my choice lay tucked in a tight, little ball halfway up the hill.

"That's the grungiest looking cat I've ever seen," said my father, and the adjective seemed to fit the sorry-looking specimen. "Grungy Bey" (pronounced Grungee Bay) meant "Mister Grungy" in Turkish. My younger brother dubbed him "the Bey-Hey."

By the time he turned two, the Bey-Hey had used over half of his reputed nine lives. He survived a fall from a fourth-floor window ledge. He tore an ear and suffered multiple injuries in recurring cat fights. After one vicious, moonlit encounter, Grungy underwent surgery right on our kitchen table, his wounds neatly sutured by the helpful doctor who lived below us.

Grungy was twice lost and found, first in Rome when he somehow missed our return flight back to the States, and again when he finally arrived on the base in Providence, Rhode Island, and escaped from his carrier. For days, he swaggered around the airfields and mooched off the airmen until my dad learned about the self-appointed squadron mascot and retrieved him.

Two tours of duty later, Grungy faced a new challenge: Because of my allergies, he would have to be re-homed. My mother wrote an announcement for the local newspaper: "Wanted: Loving family for unique cat. Serious inquiries only." She added our phone number and placed the ad.

I prayed that no one would call, but several people did. Our parents decided to meet a young couple who lived two islands away on Boca Chica Key. They had no children, but the wife worked at home, so Grungy wouldn't be lonely while he adjusted to his new life.

I stood silent the day they arrived to see my cat. I didn't want to like the soft-spoken man or his pretty, dark-haired wife. To our surprise, Grungy allowed them both to pick him up and hold him. Each stroked his soft head and promised to take care of him. When I couldn't control my tears, I ran to my room.

Two weeks later, the woman called, distraught, to tell us that Grungy had somehow slipped out of their house. Neighbors and friends helped search for hours. They even called the police, but everyone gave up when darkness fell. Grungy was gone.

As the weeks passed, we tried not to speculate about our missing cat. We accepted a new normal with no dog barking at the doorbell and no guinea pig squealing for lettuce every time the refrigerator door opened. At least we knew the whereabouts of those former furry family members. Where could Grungy be?

Summer waned on the Keys and gave way to a warm Florida fall. One bright morning on my way to school, I stepped out of our duplex and nearly tripped over a matted, meowing wraith on the doormat. As he had been when I first found him, he was filthy and thin, but I didn't care. I scooped up Grungy and cried.

Somehow, my charmed cat had traveled from Boca Chica Key to Key West on a journey that spanned three bustling island towns and eight-and-a-half miles of elevated highway over the vast Atlantic. My brother, who had been right behind me, turned on his heel and marched into the kitchen with a succinct announcement for our mother.

"Guess what?" he said. "The Bey-Hey is back!"

And, so he was, permanently. Our parents decided that any cat who traversed nearly ten miles of ocean to be reunited with our family deserved to stay. The owners he left behind agreed and told us to keep him with their blessing.

Grungy became an outdoor cat, sleeping on our screened porch or under the carport. He was ours again, or perhaps we were his. He moved with our family twice more, first to Corpus Christi, Texas, and then to Fairfax, Virginia.

But his most interesting journey was the one he made alone across the Florida Keys to find his way back to us. How he managed such a miracle remains a mystery. Why he tried at all is easier — he tried because he loved us.

To this day, we remember the cat who walked on water to come home. And we never underestimate the power of love.

— Andi Lehman —

94

My Dad's Cat

The cat does not offer services. The cat offers itself.
~William S. Burroughs

I drove my car around the block for the third time and stopped again in front of the cat-rescue building, unable to take the next step. My dad's cat, Tuffy, rustled in her carrier next to me, banging her head against the sides.

"Settle down, Tuffy," I said. "I'm trying to figure out what to do with you."

Tuffy had been my dad's furry companion for the past fifteen years. She was a bear of a cat, with long, knotted fur and a cranky disposition.

The past year, when my dad was in and out of the hospital, I would go to his apartment and feed her. If I got too close she hissed, so I kept my distance.

"I know you don't want a pet," my dad said, handing me a card during a hospital stay. "Promise me you'll take Tuffy to this cat rescue after I die. They find homes for old cats."

He passed away that night, and the card now sat on the dashboard of my car like a request from heaven.

Tuffy had been a great companion for my dad, and I was grateful that she brought him comfort after my mom died. Shouldn't I take care of her now, even though my dad hadn't asked me to? I didn't want a cat, especially an old one that despised me. But if the cat rescue did find a home for Tuffy, how would I know she was happy? I couldn't stand to think of anyone mistreating her.

"Okay, Tuffy," I said, starting the car, "you're going home with me."

As I drove, I thought about my dad and how much I missed him. Before his health had declined, he helped me with home projects. Any time I couldn't figure out something, like how to install a new light fixture or change out cabinet hardware, he would delight in taking on the job.

As payback, I would bring him cookies the next time I visited. With Tuffy snuggled in his lap, he sometimes told stories of World War II and his time in the army. He managed to survive the second wave of the Normandy invasion, but was later wounded in Germany and became a POW. Fortunately, it was at the end of the war, and he wasn't mistreated. However, all he was given to eat each day was a piece of bread and cheese.

"Makes you appreciate everything we have now," he'd say. "Plenty of food. A warm bed at night. And my little Tuffy."

There was nothing little about Tuffy, but I didn't correct him.

At home now, I took in Tuffy's carrier and opened the door. She came out slowly and sat there, trembling.

"Are you cold, Tuffy? I guess you're used to eighty degrees in Dad's apartment."

I went upstairs and found a heating pad and a towel. "C'mon up, Tuffy."

Nothing. I realized that she had never climbed stairs. I was afraid if I tried to pick her up, she'd bite me. "Suit yourself then. I'm going to bed."

In the darkness, a loud wailing jolted me awake. Tuffy repeated the most pitiful cry I had ever heard. I sat up and cried myself. I went to the top of the stairs and looked down.

"I know how you feel, Tuffy. I miss him, too."

The next night, she cried at the bottom of the stairs again. The third night, she bounded up the stairs, alarming both of us. She jumped onto a chair, and then on top of a built-in cabinet by the window.

She soon claimed this as her spot, so I bought a soft cat perch and mounted it. She seemed to enjoy looking out the window as the afternoon sun bathed her in its warmth.

As the months went by, Tuffy adjusted more to my home and touch. She even surprised me by wanting to get in my lap while I was on the computer.

I helped her up. "You're my cat now, aren't you, Tuffers?"

She put her paw on one of the keys, and a photo of my dad popped up. Dumbfounded by what she had done, I put his photo back in its file and tried to make the same thing happen by hitting various keys. No luck.

"How did you do that, Tuffy?"

Although she let me pet her now, the one thing Tuffy wouldn't allow was brushing her fur to get out the knots. I took her to a professional groomer.

"What we do when fur gets this bad is shave the cat," the groomer explained. She showed me a photo. "We call this the lion cut."

I was hesitant. "I've never heard of shaving a cat."

"Oh, it's very popular, and it really helps," she said. "And your cat will look adorable!"

They bathed Tuffy first. She looked annoyed but didn't fight the groomer. Then they started shaving her. About halfway through, she began crying, hissing and struggling to get away.

"That's enough," I said. "She's too stressed." They stopped, and Tuffy calmed down. Her head looked like an old dust mop, and her shaved body like a plucked turkey. The pom-pom tail didn't help.

"Tuffy, you're a mess," I said, putting her in the carrier. "Thank goodness Dad isn't here to see what I've done."

As the months went by, Tuffy's hair grew back, and our affection for each other also grew. When I got home from work each night, I would give her a treat and sing, "I've grown accustomed to your face...." If I had a problem with the house, I would say, "What do you think Dad would recommend, Tuff-Tuff?"

One day, I noticed she was losing weight. She wasn't eating as much and struggled to get up and down from her perch. I took her to a vet. He explained that she was experiencing several health issues that affect older cats. Bottom line... she wasn't going to get better.

I knew what he was hinting at, but I wasn't ready to let her go.

In the following weeks, she grew weaker. She wasn't eating at all now, no matter what I offered. She couldn't make it to her litter box. I made an appointment with the vet and took her in.

The assistant gave Tuffy a shot to sedate her. She said I could stay and be with her as she went to sleep. When I was ready, they would take her into another room and give her another shot.

I petted her head. "Oh, Tuffy," I whispered. Tears blurred my eyesight as I stared down, stroking her head. She closed her eyes.

After a while, I motioned for the assistant to take her away. I stumbled into the waiting area, dazed. I saw the date on the counter and stopped. I'd been so worried about Tuffy that I had forgotten. Today marked a year since my dad had passed away.

Tuffy had helped me get through this year, and I had made sure she was well taken care of.

"She's your cat again, Dad," I whispered.

— Wendy J. Hairfield —

95

Little Kitten Paws

Cats' eyes seem a bridge beyond the one we know.
~Lynn Hollyn

When he came into our lives during the final six weeks of my husband's terminal cancer, several unusual happenings led us to believe the kitten was an angel in disguise. First of all, Larry had never been fond of cats, but he bonded quickly with this kitten who never left his side. It was heartwarming to watch their devotion to each other. There was something almost mystical about the bond they shared, which made the decision as to what to name the kitten an easy task — Little Larry, it was!

When our daughter Jacqui first saw the connection between her father and the kitten, she was in awe — so much so that she bought a little, red collar for the kitten with his new name engraved on the tag. Once she placed the collar around Little Larry's neck, we never removed it.

The kitten's favorite place to be was on Larry's chest with his furry, little head resting on my husband's frail shoulder. He did this faithfully until the moment Larry took his final breath.

Sadly, the kitten disappeared the night Larry died. This was surprising in that he was strictly an indoor cat because we lived out in the country where coyotes and other animals preyed on small pets. It was as though the angel kitten had either accompanied my husband to his heavenly home or had moved on to his next divine assignment.

I thought about him often, prayed that he was safe, and hoped that he'd find a way to let me know.

Miraculously, my answer appeared in the middle of the night several months after Larry's passing. I was awakened by little kitten paws walking softly across my bed. Now that Little Larry was gone, we didn't have a cat. But I knew without a doubt there was one on my bed that night. Strangely, I was not alarmed; to the contrary, I fell back to sleep with a contented smile on my face.

Upon awakening the following morning, I expected to find the kitten sleeping at the foot of the bed, but he wasn't.

When I told my son Chris about what had happened, he didn't seem to share my enthusiasm, but attempted to pacify me with a quick, "Nice!"

Later that morning, we realized that Little Larry must have known it would take something less subtle to reach Chris.

While I was finishing up the breakfast dishes, Chris offered to vacuum the family room since I had a few errands to run in town.

Taking advantage of the opportunity, I hurried upstairs to shower, thankful that I'd be getting an early start on my to-do list.

Before heading out the door, I yelled to Chris asking if he needed anything from town.

"No," he answered from the kitchen where he was apparently enjoying another cup of coffee before heading outside, "but come here for a minute."

Chris was sitting at the old, wooden kitchen table, carefully inspecting what appeared to be a small, red band.

"What's that?" I questioned, stepping closer to get a better look.

Then, "Oh, my gosh! Is that Little Larry's collar? Where did you get it?"

"That's what I was going to ask you," Chris countered. "I found it on the family-room carpet, just lying in plain sight."

We were both stunned! We knew the kitten was wearing his collar the night he vanished, and now Chris was holding it in his hand!

"I told you there was a cat on my bed last night," I reminded my son.

Immediately, we headed in opposite directions in search of our kitten, each wanting to be the one who found him. I ran upstairs and checked under all the beds and in the closets. Chris foraged through the entire downstairs. But, to our dismay, after nearly an hour of searching, we didn't find Little Larry that day or any day thereafter.

It's been nearly twenty years since we last saw our angel kitten on the night of my husband's passing. We will most likely never learn how his collar appeared mysteriously, but it adds to my certainty that there was something quite miraculous about that little cat who appeared just when Big Larry needed him.

— Connie Kaseweter Pullen —

96

Nine Lives

The mind of God may be glimpsed in the eyes of a cat.
~Celtic Saying

Phoenix, a tuxedo cat, graced my life with his presence when I turned thirty. I didn't want to adopt him, as he wasn't my first choice. He looked too sickly. But when I held him, he wrapped his front and back paws around me, holding onto me for dear life. So, of course, he became mine. He had an angelic quality about him from the very beginning. But sickness followed him throughout his life.

At eleven years old, he almost died when he ate pet food that was on recall. Unfortunately, I didn't hear that warning on the news before he was poisoned. After three weeks at the veterinary clinic and exploratory surgery, my cat had lost half his body weight and had to be fed through a feeding tube. Fortunately, Phoenix recovered fully.

At age eighteen, he had a life-threatening abscess in his mouth due to a genetic problem that finally surfaced in his old age. He underwent emergency surgery. Despite the concerns given his age, he handled surgery, as the doctor said, "with flying colors." During this time, Phoenix was also diagnosed with stage three kidney disease. But at his next checkup, his blood work showed that the kidney disease had reversed itself, and so he went from stage three back to stage one. I asked the veterinarian if this was possible, and I was told, "Not usually."

The veterinarian also found an ominous black tumor in his ear, which she feared might be cancerous. When he was checked again, the tumor had disappeared. The veterinarian checked the medical history from his last visit, and she confirmed that the suspected mass had been recorded as an area to be watched, and yet it was gone. Not long after that, a cold turned into pneumonia. Given his age at this point, he wasn't expected to recover. He needed a breathing treatment, but soon afterward he recovered again. We started calling him "The Miracle Cat."

Therefore, it came as a shock to me, despite his twenty-one years, that this cat was dead a day after my fifty-first birthday at a cabin I rented in Blue Ridge, Georgia. I had come inside to check on him, and he had a fixed stare that alarmed me. When I touched him, his body fell limp. I knew he had passed. But I had just euthanized my service dog two weeks earlier, so the timing was terribly unfortunate. I didn't have the emotional ability to handle yet another pet loss so soon.

I knelt down beside Phoenix and prayed: "Dear God, please don't take him now. He's been with me for so long. My birthday was yesterday. My dog died two weeks ago. I know we get only as much as we can handle, but I can promise you, I cannot handle this, not now. I need a break from heartbreak."

I touched Phoenix again, trying to figure out what to do. Suddenly, he breathed in dramatically, gulping in air as if he'd been drowning and had just risen to the surface. I was stunned and shaken by what I'd just witnessed. Even stranger, after what can only be described as a miracle, Phoenix no longer needed a daily dose of pain medication for arthritis. Phoenix had gone blind due to cataracts, but he explored the cabin immediately, one he'd never been to before, as if he could see every bit of it. He even looked at me again as if he was seeing me for the first time after being blind. This same miraculous circumstance continued when I returned home with Phoenix. He acted perfectly fine, as if he was taking a vacation from the usual symptoms of old age. He navigated the house beautifully.

Phoenix lived for another month after that, until I was more ready to accept that his remarkable life was over. I couldn't be sad. I'd be ungrateful if I chose to look at his life as a loss instead of as a blessing. I had never known anything in my whole life as inexplicable as this cat I called Phoenix. Apparently, I had named him well.

— Tamra Anne Bolles —

97

Intensely Inscrutable

*Looking at cats, like looking at clouds, stars or the
ocean, makes it difficult to believe there is nothing
miraculous in this world.*
~Leonard Michaels

My mom always called Thomas — our scrappy, skin-and-bones,
orange tabby — an "intense cat." As far as descriptions go, it
was a pretty good one. Tom played, hunted, fought, loved,
and ate intensely. The cat even managed to sleep intensely.
He would fall asleep into what my mom dubbed "cat comas." He'd
zonk out wherever he wanted to and wouldn't wake up for anything
except the sound of the food bucket being shaken.

Though he lived inside with us, Tom, a former stray, loved to go
outside. He would sit at the door and wait for a human to open the
door for him. He would bolt outside and stay out until he felt like
coming home. Sometimes, he'd be gone for a few hours, sometimes
a whole day, and sometimes even overnight. If we really wanted him
to come home, our best bet was to shake the food bucket and call his
name. If he were nearby and could hear the food rattling around in its
plastic container, then he'd come sprinting back from his adventures.
Sometimes, he couldn't hear it, or else maybe he'd ignore it. Either way,
we couldn't control him. Tommy did what Tommy wanted, although
he always came home eventually.

One August first, he didn't come home. I remember the specific
day because it was my sister's birthday, and we were heading to the

amusement park located about an hour away to celebrate. Thomas got out before we left. Usually, if we were going out for the day, we would try to keep him inside just to make sure he was in a safe place. But Tom, unaware of our plans, decided that he needed to spend the day in the great outdoors and made a leap for freedom when our front door cracked open. We called for him halfheartedly, but we knew that he rarely came home within the first few hours after getting outside. We shrugged our shoulders and figured he'd be fine. He always had been.

After a fun day at the park, we returned home late with no Thomas waiting on the porch. Figuring he decided to sleep outside, we didn't worry too much. But when the next evening, and then the morning after that, came and went, we began worrying. What could have happened to Tom?

Though terrible images flashed through our minds, we thought the most likely scenario was that another family in the neighborhood invited him in. They wouldn't know he already had owners (Tom forbade us to put a collar on him), so maybe they had opened their doors to the friendly, cute kitty. Being driven by food and perhaps smelling the delectable wet food they might have put out for him, Tom would have walked right into the strangers' house. After all, when he adopted us, he came waltzing into our house just for dry food.

Hoping that Tom was just living it up in a neighbor's house, we decided to put up pictures of him around the neighborhood. A few days passed without news. We were on the verge of going door-to-door with our flyers when we got a phone call.

"Hi, I'm calling about the missing cat named Thomas." It was a man calling. He lived about four or five houses down from us, but we didn't know him.

"Yes, do you have him?" we asked in excitement.

"No, but I know who might," he told us, and then explained that he saw his next-door neighbor with an orange cat in a carrier. We thanked him and hung up.

We knew the neighbor he spoke of: Mrs. B. She was a scary lady, rumored to raise baby bunnies in order to feed them to her snakes.

"Do you think she fed Tommy to her snakes?" my littlest sibling wondered with alarm in his eyes.

Our mom was quick to reassure him. "She's probably just keeping him for a pet because he's so cute." But she looked uncertain. We knew we'd have to confront Mrs. B.

For some reason, my mom and I were elected for the job. Holding hands, we made our way tremulously down the street. We rang the doorbell, and when Mrs. B. opened the door and saw us, she tried to close it immediately, which made her look mighty guilty to us. My mom and I exclaimed, "Wait!" in unison, and the door remained cracked open.

Mrs. B tried to deny it at first, but after a few questions, she broke down and admitted everything. "He kept peeing on my bushes. He left dead moles in my back yard. He was so skinny that I assumed he was a stray, so I took him away. You can have one of my dog's puppies to make up for it. Or I'll buy you a new kitten!"

My mom told her that Tommy was one of a kind, and we couldn't replace him. We asked where she had taken him.

That night, six members of my family went to the intersection, five miles from our house. We got out of the car, walked past the "No Dumping" sign, and shook the food bucket high above our heads. No Thomas appeared.

Thus began a month-long quest for Tom. We searched nearby neighborhoods, posted signs on streetlights, and answered dubious calls of orange-cat sightings. No Tom. We gave up the hunt when my older brother, who didn't live at home anymore but knew of our lost feline, sent a group text to the rest of us. Wanting to give us closure, he sent a picture he saw on the side of a cat-food bag that said, "Less than two percent of lost cats make it home." We figured Tommy was gone forever and mourned him.

We gave up on Tom, but he didn't give up on us. Near the end of September, fifty-two days after we lost him, an orange cat sat patiently on our porch. We saw him through the window, and with total disbelief, opened the door. He greeted us briefly and went straight to his food bowl. Proof that it was truly Tom, and he was really home.

We were excited, elated, and completely overjoyed. We petted him for hours, called my older brother, and even cracked open a can of wet food as a treat. Tom was part of the two percent. The most intense cat we had ever met, Tom had decided we were his family, and nothing would stop him from living where he wanted to live.

— Sarah Erstfeld —

98

Snowball

Now faith is the assurance of things hoped for,
the conviction of things not seen.
~Hebrews 11:1

M y family had moved into a new home situated on over two acres, including a spacious, fenced-in back yard. For some time, my older brother and I had been campaigning for a family pet. Now, at ages four and seven, we managed to convince our parents the time had come for adopting one.

Though my sibling and I were of like minds regarding the goal of having a furry family member, exactly what that meant to each of us was entirely different. I was excited and happy when my parents brought home the adorable and very wriggly Beagle puppy we named Snoopy. Despite the fun of playing with him and watching Snoopy explore his new yard, I *knew* this was really more my brother's pet than mine. I really, *really* wanted a cat!

Throughout the day on which Snoopy joined our family, I tried to show my gratitude for getting a pet while trying to hide my disappointment that he wasn't a cat. My parents must have surmised how I was feeling because they suggested that I pray about it. I think they meant I should pray about how to handle my disappointment, but I interpreted their suggestion differently. My parents were *brilliant*! I would pray for a cat.

I ran to my bedroom, knelt down by my bedside and clasped my tiny hands in prayer. With as much fervent sincerity as a four-year-old can muster, I pleaded with God to *please* send me a cat to love. Not more than a minute or two passed when I heard a faint but persistent scratching sound coming from the front door, which was just a few feet from my bedroom. Curious, I stood up, approached the open front door and peered through the screen.

At first, I didn't see anything unusual. Then I heard the soft scratching sound again, and looked down. There, sitting calmly before me on the porch, was a large, white cat with an expression on his face that seemed to say, "Ask, and ye shall receive!"

I was speechless… absolutely amazed! I opened the screen door to step onto the porch, and the kitty began rubbing against me and purring loudly. Looking around, I saw no one besides the cat. Gathering his considerable mass into my arms, I practically flew through the house and into the back yard where my parents and brother were playing with Snoopy. Quickly, I recounted to my surprised family what had happened.

So, Snowball joined our household that day, too. We became inseparable. My cuddly friend was extremely patient with the little girl who constantly hugged and kissed him. And since I thought baby dolls were boring, I was delighted when he chose to take long naps in my doll carriage. He was a wonderful companion, the first of many cats I have known and loved.

Although my parents always denied having anything to do with Snowball's arrival, as I grew older I suspected that maybe, just maybe, they might have. However, even if they did somehow arrange for him to appear on the porch at the very moment when I was praying for a cat, it would not diminish the miraculousness of a cat doing exactly what we want it to do exactly when we want it done. Amen!

— Linda Acock —

99

Pepper's Funeral

There is no more intrepid explorer than a kitten.
~Jules Champfleury

Several years ago, I decided to take a trip to the country to visit my friend Mary. Her kids and mine were going to have a play date while Mary and I spent the day chatting. Soon after we arrived, Mary went to check on her cat Pepper. He had gone out earlier in the day and never returned. It was not at all like her cat to wander away for a half-day without food or water breaks. We decided to get in the car and drive around the countryside looking for Pepper.

Up one lane and down another, we drove for over an hour when we suddenly spotted Pepper lying in the road. It was obvious the cat had been hit by a car. The kids were beside themselves with grief.

As we tried to comfort them, I suggested we gather up the dead cat and have a proper burial for it. It was going to be one of those teachable moments when the children would learn to grieve and yet celebrate the life of Pepper the cat and the joy she had brought to them throughout the years.

We got the kids involved in finding a proper casket — a box that Mary had on hand. We gave them crayons and markers to make the box look pretty and found some old material to use as a lining. Then we had them make invitations to deliver to the neighborhood children for the funeral and luncheon we would have the next day. It kept the kids busy and made them feel a little better about Pepper's demise.

Mary's husband Dave went into the back yard when he got home and dug a proper hole for the burial of Pepper. The rest of us dispersed to tell the neighbors that Pepper had died and invite them to the funeral and luncheon with their children.

The next day, my children and I again made the trip to Mary's house for Pepper's funeral. Several neighbors had come, and so we all solemnly processed out to the back yard with the kids acting as pallbearers. Dave gave a wonderful eulogy about the life and times of Pepper and all she had meant to them as a family. Each of the children placed a flower on the grave, and then we went into the house to have a nice funeral luncheon that the children had prepared. It was peanut-butter-and-jelly sandwiches, but we all ate and acted like it was a feast in honor of Pepper the cat.

By the time we had finished our luncheon, I decided it was time for us to gather up our belongings and head home again. Offering my condolences for the final time, I opened the door to leave and almost tripped over a cat who came racing into the house and jumped right into Pepper's bed. We never did find out whose cat we had buried.

— Christine Trollinger —

Missing Skittles

The thrill of coming home has never changed.
~Guy Pearce

"You carry in Skittles, and I'll take Percy," Marv said as he pulled our car up to our rustic vacation house in a sparsely developed area of the North Carolina mountains. "We sure don't want either cat to take off into these woods. I'm still not over the last time Skittles disappeared. He's so fast that we'd never catch him up here."

With Marv still recovering from surgery following a bad fall, we had decided the mountain air might speed his recovery and provide welcome relief from our hot Florida summer. While he recuperated by enjoying views of the Blue Ridge, I would finish up the edits on my upcoming book, due in three weeks.

Within a few days, we settled into our routines. While I sat at my laptop, writing, Percy, the elder, would locate the most comfortable spot in the house, only to be evicted from his perch moments later by Skittles, who had been a feral kitten originally. When Percy found another prime spot worth stealing, the dance began again. Eventually, they snuggled down together, all forgiven. Meanwhile, my husband lounged in his favorite overstuffed chair on the porch, reading, dozing, and gazing out at the beautiful vistas.

In the evenings, Skittles perched beside the screen overlooking the rugged terrain below our second-story porch. Amidst the sound of crickets and the flicker of fireflies, his eyes remained riveted on the happenings in the bushes below.

The leisure days of our little family of four, however, didn't last the full three weeks. The disruption began when I stepped outside after a light rain, slipped on a rock and sprained my ankle. But it was my daughter's brief visit with her Rottweiler on her way to Nashville two hours later that was to transform the remaining days of vacation.

Although the cats lounged lazily on the beds at the back of the house, the Rottweiler quickly picked up their scent. She was too fast to stop. A growl, a bark, and a wild dash of fur raced past as Skittles headed for the screened porch.

Amidst our scramble to grab the dog, protect the cats, and close doors, Skittle's feral-survivor mode kicked in. He clawed a hole through the screen, squeezed through, and leapt to the rocky patch of earth below.

In horror, we watched our orange-striped tabby scramble down the hill, into the bushes, and out of sight.

After a frantic search, my husband slouched onto the oversized, stuffed chair on the porch with fatalistic resignation. "He's gone. We won't see him again."

I gazed out at the dense canopy of trees surrounding our house. Would Skittles see the North Carolina woods as a giant Disneyland for cats? Would he think the dog was still in our house and be afraid to return? Would he even want to return to us? Or would the lure of new adventure draw him farther away?

"He's often outside in Florida," I said optimistically. "He'll come back. He likes to eat. And he loves Percy."

But he didn't come back that night. Nor the next morning.

We put out a bowl of food and a litter box and started praying. But he still didn't return. Another fretful day went by.

Each time I went to the door to call Skittles, Percy was close beside me, gazing out the door. I reached down to stroke Percy's soft, champagne-golden fur. "Where's your little friend, Percy?"

We alerted neighbors to our situation and listened anxiously to stories about bear sightings and lost cats that never returned.

The next morning, our neighbors reported seeing an orange tabby near their house. With few cats on the mountain, we were certain he'd seen Skittles.

Hobbling on my sprained and now badly swollen ankle, I searched the area, climbing through brush and up rocky slopes between our house and theirs. Marv and I took turns going down to their house to sit with a bowl of food. Later, I pushed my way through low-hanging branches with a trap and a can of tuna. But I knew Skittles was too smart to fall for it.

Meanwhile, I continued to work on the edits due in a couple of days.

Day five dawned with an inquiry from my editors, asking when I could send them my manuscript.

With only my phone for Internet and no printer in the mountains, we wondered what to do. I needed to return home to Florida to finish up my writing and send it to my publisher. But how could we leave? There'd been no more sightings of Skittles.

"I'll just stay here by myself," Marv said. "You could fly home."

"But how long can you wait? You're still weak. We can't scour every inch of the woods. What if he doesn't want to come back?"

Later, while cleaning the litter box, I scrunched up my nose from the stench. *This is so stinky,* I thought, *even though it's just Percy — not Skittles.*

A light went off in my head.

That's it! It smells like Percy!

With images of Hansel and Gretel floating through my mind, I hurried out the door with my bag of stinky litter and limped eagerly down the road to my neighbor's house. Scattering the litter that smelled like Percy, I made a trail from my neighbor's house to ours. I hoped Skittles would follow it home.

A couple of hours later, a lightning storm brought a pouring rain. I feared the smells would be washed away along with our last little hope. When the storm ended, I went to the back door and called forlornly to Skittles. Percy hovered by my side.

On the screened porch that evening, I talked with Marv about what to do. We were losing hope. Quietly, Percy stood peering through the screen at the steps to our front door. We heard a meow. And then another.

I studied Percy. "That meow wasn't Percy!"

Another meow. I raced to the front door and yanked it open.

Skittles stood on the steps.

"Skittles!"

Startled, he jumped back.

With heart racing, I held the door ajar quietly. Tentatively, Skittles inched back up, poked his head through the opening, scanned the room cautiously, and slipped inside.

Percy ran to him. Skittles nuzzled his head into the crook of Percy's neck. Percy licked his head.

After food and water, it was my turn to join the love fest. With a happy heart, I reached down to pet my little alpha cat. Skittles stretched his neck to curl his head lovingly into the palm of my hand.

Then Skittles spied Percy on his new perch. After a mutual stare, he went and pushed him off. The dance had begun again, and a loving home was restored.

—Linda W. Rooks—

Mike 108

A little drowsing cat is an image of perfect beatitude.
~Jules Champfleury

One recent Saturday morning, I stood in the middle of our local pet store surrounded by cat beds, tree houses, and squeaky catnip-filled mice. I was holding a two-pound ball of orange and white fluff barely eight weeks old. The kitten purred nonstop, like an idling motor, while I listened to instructions being given to me by the shelter volunteer. My daughter, Allison, waited impatiently at my side for her turn to hold the kitten.

I had arrived at the store looking for a male kitten to fill the hole in my heart after losing my cat, Jade, who had been my constant companion for eighteen and a half years. He had also been an orange and white cat, but he was short-haired. The coat of this kitten was a little bit longer than Jade's, but I couldn't help wonder if she was the one I was supposed to adopt. I had my heart set on another male cat. I prayed, *Please, Lord. Help me know if this is the cat who will heal my broken heart.*

Jade was "supposed" to be my son Russell's cat, but apparently, he took one look around our house and figured out quickly that Mom was the one he needed to suck up to. He never let me out of his sight for long.

When life took me on road trips away from home, Jade complained to the humans left behind. On one summer visit to Ohio to be with my family, my husband John videoed a conversation he had with Jade about my absence. Jade sat on his haunches at the foot of the bed and hollered like a grumpy old man.

John said, "Tell Mommy, Jade. Tell her what you think about her leaving us this way." And on cue, Jade would go into a tirade of meows and deep-throated hollers to let me know how displeased he was by my absence. Whenever I returned home from these trips, Jade would put me on "lockdown." He sat on my lap and refused to get up until he needed food, water, or the cat box. Forget it if I tried to leave him. He hollered loudly for me, even if he knew where I was.

Russell had selected Jade's name from a character in the *Star Wars* movies he loved so much. We laughed about the male kitten with the girl's name, but over time, we never thought much about the gender confusion his name caused.

Jade was also a constant source of strength for me through those years, especially, seven years ago when Russell unexpectedly died. As I grieved the loss of my only son, Jade comforted me. Nights when I couldn't sleep for crying, Jade curled up on the couch beside me as I stroked him. He'd purr, rumbling softly until drifting off to sleep. Soon after, I would drift off as I listened to his steady, peaceful breathing.

It somehow seemed appropriate then, that Jade passed away this year the day after what would have been Russell's thirty-fourth birthday. As sad as I am to have lost this beautiful companion, my son's cat, I have in my mind a picture of the two of them cuddled together in a corner of Heaven watching over our family.

After Jade's death, I thought I'd wait several months before searching for another cat, but John soon encouraged me to start looking for a kitten. He told me, "We could all use some joy in the house again."

The next day, I learned about the pet adoption sponsored by the local rescue shelter. Allison insisted on going with me, so the two of us headed out early Saturday morning to see what we could find.

Starting when Allison was in middle school, she's had unusual stories revolving around the number 108. That number always seems to pop up for her, especially during significant life events. After this had been happening for a while, she told us about it, but we were skeptical.

However, once she told us about 108, we began to see the number everywhere, too. In many ways the connections with the number seemed more a message of affirmation from God than a coincidence. In fact, one day, as I cleaned out a tub of discarded items from my past, I found the parking tag I had hung on my rear view mirror when I taught high school while pregnant with Allison. I laughed when I saw the number on it: 108.

On the day we returned home from Russell's memorial service, we passed a broken-down school bus on the side of the road near our house. The number of the bus? 108.

At the time, I pictured Russell nudging God in the arm with his elbow saying something like, "Hey, God. See that bus number 108 driving around down there? Wouldn't it be funny to make it break down at the intersection so Mom, Dad, and Allison can see it on their way home from the funeral?" And I imagined God answering, "You know, Russell, that would be a great joke." I'm sure the bus driver and the children he was transporting that day didn't appreciate the inconvenience of a broken-down bus, but it was a timely sign to us that God was with us in our darkest moment.

So now I stood in the middle of the pet store, with a warm, rumbling fluffball nuzzled up against me, trying to figure out if this was the kitten for us. If this was the kitten to help fill a family that was still so sad after seven years. Still missing our son. Now losing his cat. Would this kitten be able to fill our hearts with joy and love? But because I had come in search of a male, I had already picked out a name: Mike. That was the problem. This kitten was female.

The shelter volunteer continued to talk to me about the kitten I hadn't completely decided to keep. Vet instructions. Record of shots. Spayed. And a chip. She had been chipped.

The volunteer handed me a card with a lengthy series of numbers associated with her chip. She said, "This is a long number, so we normally stay focused on the last three digits. In this case, her number is 108."

Allison and I gasped at the same time. The confused worker looked at us as if she had committed some kind of unforgivable offense. Allison and I laughed as we tried to explain to her that everything was perfectly okay. In fact, it was more than okay; it was amazing.

Without hesitation, I completed the paperwork. Allison and I headed home with our new fur baby, Mike.

We once had a male with a female's name, and now we had a female with a male's name. As we headed home, we felt the closeness of God and His reminder that in the midst of our great sorrows, He walks beside us.

— Lori Durham —

Meet Our Contributors

Sylvia A. is a frequent contributor to the *Chicken Soup for the Soul* series. In choosing to use a pseudonym, she honors the tradition of anonymity in Alcoholics Anonymous. It's just one of the valued steps and traditions of the program that has kept her sober for twenty-one years and counting!

Linda Acock, a former elementary school teacher, enjoys: reading, gardening, cooking, playing board games, traveling, walking, and spending time with her husband and their kitties. Her goal is to write and publish children's books and a humorous adult-fiction series on which she has been working for some time.

Donna W. Adkins attended Asbury College and the University of Louisville. Her husband Jim is a retired minister. In December 2018 they celebrated fifty-nine years of marriage. Donna has had several songs published and is currently writing a book about their lives and experiences.

Valerie Fletcher Adolph is a published author, speech coach, historian and book reviewer. A number of cats have owned her over the last fifty years. At present only one named Cricket rules the household.

Monica A. Andermann lives and writes on Long Island where she shares a home with her husband Bill and their tabby, Samson. Her writing has been included in such publications as *Guideposts*, *Woman's World*, and *Ocean* as well as many titles in the *Chicken Soup for the Soul* series.

Valerie Archual is a blog writer, a children's book author and a previous contributor to the *Chicken Soup for the Soul* series. Although she loves writing, her favorite hobby by far, is spending time with her family (Tom Tom included) and creating memories, which, of course, are the best stories of all! Learn more at www.valeriearchual.com.

David-Matthew Barnes is a bestselling author, playwright, poet, and screenwriter. To date, he has written over fifty stage plays that have been performed in three languages in eleven countries. He is the author of twelve novels. His literary work has appeared in over one hundred publications.

Nancy King Barnes is a practicing registered nurse who lives with her husband in Rowlett, Texas. The *Chicken Soup for the Soul* series has served as a wonderful venue to express her life's experiences that God has provided. Writing is a hobby and she is thankful to Chicken Soup for the Soul for allowing her to share her heart.

Lainie Belcastro is elated to share her fifth story in the inspiring *Chicken Soup for the Soul* series! Her children's book, *Harriet's Heartbroken Heart*, for children coping with grief, is available worldwide. Via her storytelling character, Mrs. Terra Cotta Pots, she encourages children to plant their dreams! Learn more at www.lainiebelcastro.com.

Tamra Anne Bolles received her Bachelor of Arts in Journalism from the University of Georgia, and Master's of Education from Georgia State University. She has taught middle school for the Cobb County School District for twenty years in Northwest Georgia. Tamra enjoys kayaking, hiking, yoga and gardening. She plans to keep writing.

Sue Bonebrake received her Bachelor of Science in Education and M.A. degree from Northwest Missouri State University in 1969 and taught secondary and college English/Speech/Drama for almost thirty years. She and her husband have three children and three grandchildren. Now retired, they raise alpacas on a small acreage in northeast Iowa.

Veronica Bowman is a poet and writer. She and her husband share their country home with their much-loved rescue dogs, cats, and chickens. She enjoys reading, gardening, and cooking.

Betsy Boyd recently retired from a forty-year career as a high school English teacher and college counselor. She has been a member of the Story Circle Network, an organization that encourages women to write their stories, since 2008. She enjoys embroidery, travel, and hiking in the Great Smoky Mountains National Park.

A retired nurse, **Susan Grady Bristol** loves to write. She is a member of the Nebraska Writer's Guild and My Thoughts Exactly. She has been published in two other *Chicken Soup for the Soul* books and other anthologies. She teaches memoir writing at the local community college. Susan enjoys her grandchildren, traveling with her husband, and her friends.

Michelle Bruce is a retired registered nurse from Nebraska. Michelle and her husband, Jeremy, have four children and enjoy going to their many activities. She also enjoys refinishing vintage furniture, antiquing, and spending time with her numerous animals.

Thomas Canfield is a philosopher of sorts, contemplating such profound issues as the nutritional value of Twinkies and the merits of iced tea as opposed to the non-iced variety. He resides in the mountains of North Carolina.

Eva Carter has a finance background. She is retired and enjoys traveling, photography, and writing. She and her husband, Larry, live in Dallas, TX. This is her twenty-fourth story published in the *Chicken Soup for the Soul* series. E-mail her at evacarter@sbcglobal.net.

Nebula Award–nominated **Beth Cato** is the author of *The Clockwork Dagger* duology and the *Blood of Earth* trilogy from Harper Voyager. She's a Hanford, CA native transplanted to the Arizona desert, where she lives with her husband, son, and requisite cats.

Pastor Wanda Christy-Shaner is a four-time contributor to the *Chicken Soup for the Soul* series and has been published in *War Cry* magazine twice. She is a cancer warrior, animal rescuer, five-time missionary, and licensed minister. E-mail her at seekingtruth65@yahoo.com.

Elizabeth Citrowske received her Associates degree in Catholic Doctrine from the Institute of the Holy Doctors in St. Louis and her Bachelor of Theological Studies from St. Joseph's College online in April, 2019. She is excited for what the future holds now that she has graduated. She loves her faith, her family, and her boyfriend.

Angela Cleveland has fifteen years of experience as a school counselor and received the 2017 New Jersey School Counselor of the Year award. Angela lives in New Jersey with her husband Scott and pretty kitty Sydney. Learn more at www.AngelaCleveland.com and follow her on Twitter @AngCleveland.

Susan Cooper has written many articles and two books, *The Truth About Mold* and *Football Facts for Females*, and she is the editor and a contributor to a new anthology. She thrives on improv, Toastmasters, taekwondo, her husband Randy, and two cats. She and Randy are now writing a book for couples on growing their love.

Ange Crawford lives with her husband in Oregon's mid-Willamette Valley where she writes nonfiction and devotes herself to rescuing dogs, cats, and wildlife. Her humor essays have been published locally, nationally, and internationally. Ange enjoys supporting other writers as a judge for Oregon Writers Colony.

Sergio Del Bianco has a background in fine arts and psychology. He is an artist and writer, interested in the intersection of art, psychology, and the humanities. He resides in Europe with his spouse and growing family of rescue animals. E-mail him at sergiodelbianco@yahoo.com or through Twitter @DelBianco97.

At the time of publication, **Jaiden Deubler** is a student at Ohio Northern University. She is majoring in creative writing while pursuing a minor in public relations. She is also involved with Ohio Northern University's undergraduate literary magazine, *Polaris*.

Lori Durham is a retired English teacher who has previously published stories in *Guideposts* magazine. She enjoys traveling and working with youth. Originally from Cincinnati, OH, she resides in Brunswick, GA with her husband, John. E-mail her at ldurham132@gmail.com.

Rebecca Edmisten lives in Tennessee and has taught English and Theatre for twenty-one years. Her passions include her middle school daughters and writing for performance. Becky says that this Ogden Nash quote has always been her favorite tribute to the feline: "The trouble with a kitten is that eventually it becomes a cat."

Sarah Erstfeld is a reader, a writer, a teacher, and a learner. The two most important things to her are her faith and her family, with Disney coming in as a close third. She loves traveling, learning about other countries, and watching movies. She is happiest when she can stay home reading and spending time with her family.

Shelley Faulhaber enjoys spending quality time with her husband Derek, son Charlie, and niece Allana. Sharing books with the kids and watching their eyes light up over the plot of the story is really what she enjoys most.

Donna Fawcett is the former creative writing instructor for Fanshawe College in London, ON. She is an award-winning author, singer, songwriter, freelance magazine and newspaper contributor and a national conference speaker. Her novels *Rescued* and *Vengeance* both won Best Contemporary Novel in The Word Awards. Learn more at www.donnafawcett.com.

Jean Ferratier writes to honor and inspire others who face life challenges. She is a retired teacher who promotes self-development through her Clarity of Now Coaching practice. Jean is the author of *Reading Symbolic Signs: How to Connect the Dots of Your Spiritual Life* and a frequent contributor to the *Chicken Soup for the Soul* series.

H.M. Forrest is a freelance writer and editor who lives with her teenage son and exotic pets. She enjoys traveling with her son. Her stories have appeared in the *Chicken Soup for the Soul* series, *Writers Weekly*, and *Winter Whimsy*. She recently completed her first young adult fantasy novel. E-mail her at HMForrest1@gmail.com.

Barbara S. Foster has published many nonfiction articles and has taught "Writing for Publication" classes. She hosts a generic weekly television talk show and is also a Realtor. Barbara has raised seven children, has a dozen grandchildren and three great-grandchildren. She resides in Sterling, MA but is originally from Cincinnati, OH.

Dr. Carol L. Gandolfo received her doctorate in Clinical Psychology in 2000 and specializes in Developmental Disabilities and Forensics. She uses her training in forensics in much of her writing, but also enjoys writing about her famous cats. She enjoys writing, photography, painting, and spending time with her cats.

Julia Gousseva was born and raised in Russia but now lives in Arizona with her husband and son. She writes fiction and nonfiction stories, mostly set in Russia.

Karen Green is a freelance writer based in Southwestern Ontario with her husband and two girls. Her work has appeared in numerous print and online venues and she's the author of two books for young readers. Most days she can be found in her sunroom reading, writing, and drinking coffee.

Wendy J. Hairfield has a B.A. degree in Journalism, with honors, from Temple University. After a rewarding career in public relations and as a public information officer, she now enjoys writing, tennis, photography, and gardening. She has a daughter and stepson and lives in the Seattle area with her husband and two tortoises.

Virginia Elizabeth Hayes was born the youngest of nine girls and grew up to be a writer. Calling Missouri home, she lives with her husband and two cats. Her cartoon-memoir is called: *The Princeling Papers: or, How to Fight Cancer with Colored-Pencils and Kittens.*

Helen Heavirland is a nurse by profession, a bookkeeper by necessity, and an author by passion. She has published four books. She loves to learn and enjoys reading, international volunteering, hiking, observing wildlife, and watching the escapades of pets. Learn more at www.helenheavirland.com.

Lori Hein is a freelance writer and author of *Ribbons of Highway: A Mother-Child Journey Across America.* Her work has appeared in numerous publications including many *Chicken Soup for the Soul* books. Learn more at www.LoriHein.com.

Hailing from Acworth, GA, **Butch Holcombe** dreamed of being a published author. Those dreams became reality and he went on to create *American Digger Magazine*, now in its fifteenth year of publication. He considers himself a cat/dog person, but admits an affinity for squirrels. Please don't tell Frankie… it would crush him.

Mark A. Howe has been a full-time writer for eight years, mostly as a journalist in northern Indiana. A transplanted Kansan, he lives with his wife, Tonya, sons Matthew and Michael, their dog Josey and a pair of cats, Champ and Sport, who tolerate his existing in their world.

Leslee W. Kahler is a struggling author, mother of two and the ESL assistant at the local high school. Leslee has been a lifelong cat and animal lover and lives on a small farm in Pennsylvania with her family, four horses and eight rescue cats. She hopes to be a novelist one day.

Shannon Kernaghan and her husband once bought a house because their cats would love the screened porches and… they were right! Shannon's work appears in books, magazines, and newspapers. Learn more at www.ShannonKernaghan.com.

E.E. King is a painter, performer, writer, and biologist — She'll do anything that won't pay the bills, especially if it involves animals. Ray Bradbury said this of her stories: "marvelously inventive, wildly funny and deeply thought-provoking. I cannot recommend them highly enough."

Sarah LM Klauda is a professional writer, life coach, and social media manager. She lives in Baltimore, MD with her husband.

Joyce Laird is a Southern California freelance writer living with a house full of rescue fur-babies. Her features have been published in a wide range of magazines and she is a regular contributor to *Woman's World* magazine and the *Chicken Soup for the Soul* series. Joyce is also a member of Mystery Writers of America.

Deborah Leandra is a retired school teacher. She taught in the Texas public school system for twenty-four years. Her entire career focused on helping at-risk students. She is currently living in the Austin, TX area.

Ashley Ledlow used to work as an animal caretaker at the local shelter where she was delightfully deemed the cat lady by staff and customers alike. These days, she works as a waitress and continues to rescue any strays she finds.

Andi Lehman holds a degree in Communications from the University of Memphis. An author, editor, and popular speaker, she freelances in diverse markets. Andi enjoys writing stories and education programs about animals. "Journey of Love" is for her mom, who modeled compassion for all living things. Learn more at AndiLehman.com.

Alex Lester is a Canadian author who lives in Toronto.

Bobbie Jensen Lippman is a professional writer who lives in Seal Rock, OR with her robot named Waldo and her cat named Purrfect. Bobbie's work has been published nationally and internationally. She writes a human interest column for the *Newport, Oregon News-Times*. E-mail her at bobbisbeat@gmail.com.

Jessica Loftus, a seasoned clinical psychologist and national certified career counselor, owns a counseling practice in Palos Heights, IL. She and her husband co-author a blog, "Pet Ways to Ease Stress," which is featured on PsychCentral.com. E-mail her at jesiphd@gmail.com.

Carol L. MacKay's stories and poems have appeared in anthologies and magazines across North America, and on CBC Radio & TV. Her first picture book for children, *Lily in the Loft* (YNWP, Regina, SK), was published in 2017. Carol lives in Qualicum Beach, BC with her husband and their closet-opening cat, Victoria.

Sue Mackender grew up in Surrey, England and has three grown-up sons and eight grandchildren. Sue had been trying her hand at writing novels over the last ten years and has recently become the recipient of the Katie Fforde Bursary awarded as encouragement to new authors. When not tapping at her keyboard she enjoys music, Pilates and countryside walks.

Cat lover extraordinaire, **Irish Beth Maddock** is also an award-winning children's author. Her book, *The Great Carp Escape,* is available as a fundraiser for schools, churches, and charities in need. Irish plans to continue to do something about those ideas that get downloaded into her brain at 2 a.m. E-mail her at info@irishbethmaddock.com.

Irene Maran, a retired freelance writer, enjoys writing about life, family, and everyday topics humorously expressed in two bi-weekly newspaper columns in *The News-Record of Maplewood & South Orange* and *The*

Coaster of Asbury Park, NJ. She is also a storyteller in her hometown of Ocean, NJ.

Carol March lives in Albuquerque, NM, where she writes, teaches creativity and writing to new writers, and walks the desert and mountain trails with Zena. Her short fiction appears in magazines. Her fantasy trilogy, *The Dreamwalkers of Larreta*, is published by Ellysian Press. Read her blog at AWritersHeart.com.

Donna L. Marsh attended Tennessee Tech University before a career in cable TV. Now disabled, she writes, crafts, volunteers, studies the clouds, and occasionally strolls through cemeteries. She also spoils her dogs, enjoys time with her sons and their families, and is thankful for every moment she has with her parents.

Carole Marshall completed the University of Washington Certificate Program in Nonfiction Writing. She was a newspaper columnist and has written numerous features and health articles for *American Profile*, a national magazine. Carole has written three books and is also a poet and nature printer.

Nicole Ann Rook McAlister has studied journalism and pursues an avid interest in world religion and mythology. Nicole enjoys adventures in camping, sunrises on the beach, painting, crafting and all manner of such things. Several of her pieces have been on exhibit at the Whitesbog Historic Village in Browns Mills, NJ.

Kim Johnson McGuire received her Bachelor of Arts in Literature from University of California Santa Barbara in 1983. She has volunteered at animal shelters as a cat socializer for fifteen years. She works as a Pilates instructor and enjoys traveling, reading, and playing golf. She has two cute, quirky cats and lives on California's central coast.

Ann Morrow is a writer, humorist, and frequent contributor to the *Chicken Soup for the Soul* series. She and her husband live in South

Dakota and share their home with three dogs and two cats. Ann is currently writing her first middle-grade novel, which features a blind kitten. Learn more at annmorrow.net.

Teresa Murphy is a daycare teacher who lives in New Jersey with her husband and three children.

Linda O'Connell, a former teacher and frequent contributor to the *Chicken Soup for the Soul* series, writes from the heart, and enjoys a hearty laugh and walking on the beach. She snuggles with her mighty mouth cat when she is not doting on her three great-grandsons, all under four years old. Linda blogs at lindaoconnell.blogspot.com.

Andrea Arthur Owan is an award-winning inspirational writer, blogger, fitness pro, and chaplain in search of another feline that will tolerate two incorrigible dogs. Connect with her at andreaarthurowan.com, where she helps you live your best life — physically, emotionally, and spiritually. Follow her on Twitter @AndreaOwan.

Don Patton is a retired engineer living in Tucson, AZ with his wife Deborah and cat Rosie. He enjoys playing golf, visiting his native Northern California for fishing and boating, and reading and writing fiction and nonfiction.

Lori Phillips received her Bachelor of Arts in Communications/Journalism and her Master's in Education. She lives with her husband and children in Southern California. Lori enjoys writing, walking, yoga, meditation, and plant propagation.

Mindi Picotte has lived in beautiful places. Born and raised in the Upper Peninsula of Michigan, she earned a Master's degree in Nutrition Science from Montana State University, then sold everything and moved to New Zealand with a Kiwi chef. Now she's writing, reading, creating, and indulging in whims and in conversations with her cat, Alice.

Marsha Porter fell in love with writing when the 500-word essay was the punishment du jour at her Catholic school. Since then, she's written dozens of short stories, hundreds of articles and thousands of movie reviews.

Connie Kaseweter Pullen lives in rural Sandy, OR, near her five children and several grandchildren. She earned a B.A., with honors, at the University of Portland in 2006, with a double major in Psychology and Sociology. Connie enjoys writing, photography, and exploring nature. E-mail her at MyGrandmaPullen@aol.com.

Laura Rath is a Christian writer, blogger, and speaker and has been published in *The Upper Room* and *Candid Conversations*. She blogs at *Journey in Faith* (www.laurarath.blogspot.com) and writes for several Christian websites. Laura is a wife and mother and enjoys spending time with her family, reading and studying God's Word.

Beth Rice did not become a journalist like she'd planned, but her dad wouldn't let her give up on writing. She works as a content writer for DutchCrafters.com and is the author of the children's book, *I'm Adopted, I'm Special*. In her free time she enjoys reading, theater, movies and running.

Donna L. Roberts is a native Upstate New Yorker who lives and works in Europe. She is an Associate Professor and holds a Ph.D. in Psychology. Donna is an animal and human rights advocate and when she is researching or writing she can be found at her computer buried in rescue cats.

Michele Roch's most valuable life lessons come from her animals. Tiger was one of five cats sharing her life, and the most mischievous of them all. She currently shares her life with nine dogs, a bearded dragon, and two teenagers who all contribute daily to her continued education.

Janet Ramsdell Rockey has contributed to various *Chicken Soup for the Soul* books, *Heavenly Humor* collections (Barbour), and has authored two devotional books (Barbour). She lives in Florida with her family and two precocious cats.

Linda W. Rooks is a freelance writer and author of three books: *The Bunny Side of Easter*, *Broken Heart on Hold*, and *Fighting for Your Marriage while Separated*. Her writing has appeared in numerous national publications. Linda, Marv and their two cats enjoy a purrfectly lovely life together in Central Florida. Learn more at lindarooks.com.

J. A. Rost is a published author of cozy murder mysteries and romance novels. She also writes inspirational short stories and messages that are published on various websites and in magazines. Besides writing, her hobbies include volunteer activities and walking her dogs. Learn more at www.jarost-author.com.

Linda Sabourin lives in Arkansas where she rescues cats and kittens and hopes to create an official nonprofit rescue organization in the near future. She also goes to estate auctions and buys cool vintage stuff to sell on Ebay. You can follow her cat escapades on Facebook and Twitter under River Valley Cats!

Joyce Newman Scott worked as a flight attendant while pursuing an acting career. She started college in her mid-fifties and studied screenwriting at the University of Miami and creative writing at Florida International University. She is thrilled to be a frequent contributor to the *Chicken Soup for the Soul* series.

Susan A. Shumway graduated from Western Oregon State University in 2006 at the age of sixty-three. She is married to an artist and they share their love of creativity with five children, eleven grandchildren, and three cats. She has published several poetry books with a local poetry group and has been a member of a prose critique group for many years.

Leslie Silver studied journalism in college and improv comedy at Second City in Toronto. She is an avid solo traveler and adores Egypt and Iceland. New York City is her forever happy place. She recently wrote her first short play and is working on a personal essay collection. Logan & Adrianna know her best as Auntie Leslie.

Liz R. Sparkes resides on Vancouver Island with her family and an adorable but undisciplined Bengal cat named Dali. She is currently working toward obtaining her second bachelor's degree in English at Vancouver Island University. In her spare time, she likes to garden, travel, and experiment with cooking fun new recipes.

Janet Spicer is a writer and artist living in the Boston area with two cats, two teenagers, and one boyfriend. Her greatest joy is exploring foreign convenience stores in search of unusual snacks. She recently started a travel blog at janetspicergoes.blogspot.com to avoid working on her novel.

Danielle Stephens is a cat enthusiast and servant.

Esther Stevens recently waved goodbye to the fog and moved from sunny California to an even-sunnier Arizona. She has three adult daughters, three adult cats, and one adult husband. Esther loves coffee, writing, and lately… sleep. She hopes to someday snore louder than her husband. (One can dream.)

As a twenty-plus story contributor to the *Chicken Soup for the Soul* series, **Jean Haynie Stewart** is a freelance editor and shares stories about her life as a wife of more than fifty years, a mother of twin daughters, a grandmother of two incredible grands plus four "grandpets," at latest count, and the joys and adventures all of them bring.

Shannon Stocker has tremendous respect for the crazy cat ladies of the world. She's a picture book author, coma survivor, founder of the blog series, "InHERview" (www.shannonstocker.com), and proud author of several Chicken Soup for the Soul stories. Her world revolves around Greg, Cassidy, and Tye. Cat tweets embraced @iwriteforkidz.

Bonnie J. Taylor is an author and mother residing in Central Louisiana. Born and educated in New Jersey, Bonnie holds a Bachelor's degree in Social Science. Bonnie has three daughters and several rescue pets. She enjoys writing, gardening, and traveling with her children.

Cheryl M. Taylor is a retired Cardiac ICU nurse. She lives in Mississauga, Ontario with her husband, Murray, and their two Havanese. Her articles have appeared in various Daylily publications. Among her other interests are gardening, photography, and travelling. E-mail her at taylorcm@ rogers.com.

Susan Trewhella says she has never lived a day of her life without a cat. Since retiring from running a bookshop and health food store for twenty-one years, she spends time writing, gardening, and volunteering in literacy. She lives in Michigan with her husband Bill. They have four children and seven grandchildren.

Christine Trollinger is a freelance writer who lives in Missouri. She is a widow and has three children and has been published in several books in the *Chicken Soup for the Soul* series. She enjoys writing, gardening, cooking, and painting.

Renée Vajko-Srch grew up in France where she obtained her French Baccalaureate. She attended IBME in Switzerland, graduating with a degree in theology. She currently lives in the Ozarks with her husband and three sons. Her first novel will be coming out later this year. She blogs at www.motherhoodautismandgod.blogspot.com.

After receiving her bachelor's degree from the University of Colorado at Boulder, **Dani Watkins** pursued her passion and become a blogger and copywriter for those around the country. In her free time, she enjoys reading, writing fiction, biking, and cooking. She plans on publishing a memoir about life with epilepsy.

In 1960, **Judy Rebbeck Watten** accompanied her husband to Japan. She also lived in Hawaii, Taiwan, Ethiopia, Egypt and Panama. She was a silversmith for ten years, a potter for forty years and is passionate about reading, genealogy, glaze chemistry, her grandchildren, and memoir writing. E-mail her at RayJudyW@aol.com.

Dorann Weber is a freelance photographer and writer living in the Pine Barrens of Southern New Jersey. She's a contributor for Getty Images and her photos and verses have appeared on Hallmark cards and magazines. Writing her first story for the *Chicken Soup for the Soul* series ignited her passion for writing. She enjoys hiking with her family and dogs.

Kenneth Andrew White, born in the Lone Star state of Texas, has always had a vivid curiosity, unbound by a single subject. He delights in the pursuit of knowledge, not unlike his shadow stalking cat, out of sheer curiosity.

Susan Yanguas is a repeat contributor to the *Chicken Soup for the Soul* series. She authored the mystery novel *Bluff*, and her short stories have appeared in regional magazines. Currently, her most rewarding project is teaching a writing workshop at a local prison.

Meet Amy Newmark

Amy Newmark is the bestselling author, editor-in-chief, and publisher of the *Chicken Soup for the Soul* book series. Since 2008, she has published more than 150 new books, most of them national bestsellers in the U.S. and Canada, more than doubling the number of Chicken Soup for the Soul titles in print today. She is also the author of *Simply Happy*, a crash course in Chicken Soup for the Soul advice and wisdom that is filled with easy-to-implement, practical tips for enjoying a better life.

Amy is credited with revitalizing the Chicken Soup for the Soul brand, which has been a publishing industry phenomenon since the first book came out in 1993. By compiling inspirational and aspirational true stories curated from ordinary people who have had extraordinary experiences, Amy has kept the twenty-six-year-old Chicken Soup for the Soul brand fresh and relevant.

Amy graduated *magna cum laude* from Harvard University where she majored in Portuguese and minored in French. She then embarked on a three-decade career as a Wall Street analyst, a hedge fund manager, and a corporate executive in the technology field. She is a Chartered Financial Analyst.

Her return to literary pursuits was inevitable, as her honors thesis in college involved traveling throughout Brazil's impoverished northeast region, collecting stories from regular people. She is delighted to have come full circle in her writing career — from collecting stories "from the people" in Brazil as a twenty-year-old to, three decades later, collecting stories "from the people" for Chicken Soup for the Soul.

When Amy and her husband Bill, the CEO of Chicken Soup for the Soul, are not working, they are visiting their four grown children and their first grandchild.

Follow Amy on Twitter @amynewmark. Listen to her free podcast — "Chicken Soup for the Soul with Amy Newmark" — on Apple Podcasts, Google Play, the Podcasts app on iPhone, or by using your favorite podcast app on other devices.

About
American Humane

A merican Humane is the country's first national humane organization, founded in 1877 and committed to ensuring the safety, welfare, and wellbeing of all animals. For more than 140 years, American Humane has been first to serve in promoting the welfare and safety of animals and strengthening the bond between animals and people. American Humane's initiatives are designed to help whenever and wherever animals are in need of rescue, shelter, protection, or security.

With remarkably effective programs and the highest efficiency ratio of any national humane group for the stewardship of donor dollars, the nonprofit has earned Charity Navigator's top "4-Star" rating, has been named a "Top-Rated Charity" by CharityWatch and a "Best Charity" by Consumer Reports, and achieved the prestigious "Gold Level" charity designation from GuideStar.

American Humane is first to serve animals around the world, striving to ensure their safety, welfare and humane treatment—from rescuing animals in disasters to ensuring that animals are humanely treated. One of its best-known programs is the "No Animals Were Harmed®" animals-in-entertainment certification, which appears during the end credits of films and TV shows, and today monitors some 1,000 productions yearly with an outstanding safety record.

American Humane's farm animal welfare program helps ensure the humane treatment of nearly a billion farm animals, the largest animal welfare program of its kind. And recently, the historic nonprofit launched the American Humane Conservation program, an innovative initiative helping ensure the humane treatment of animals around the globe in zoos and aquariums.

Continuing its longstanding efforts to strengthen the healing power of the human-animal bond, American Humane pairs veterans struggling to cope with the invisible wounds of war with highly-trained service dogs, and spearheaded a groundbreaking clinical trial that provided for the first time scientific substantiation for the effectiveness of animal-assisted therapy (AAT) for children with cancer and their families.

To learn more about American Humane, visit americanhumane. org and follow it on Facebook, Instagram, and Twitter.

AMERICAN★HUMANE
FIRST TO SERVE

Editor's Note: Chicken Soup for the Soul and American Humane have created *Humane Heroes*, a FREE new series of e-books and companion curricula for elementary, middle and high schoolers. Through thirty-six inspirational stories of animal rescue, rehabilitation, and humane conservation being performed at the world's leading zoological institutions, and eighteen easy-to-follow lesson plans, *Humane Heroes* provides highly engaging free reading materials that also encourage young people to appreciate and protect Earth's disappearing species. To download the free e-books and learn about the program, please visit www.chickensoup.com/ah.

Thank You

We owe huge thanks to all of our contributors and fans. We were overwhelmed by the thousands of stories you submitted about your amazing cats. It takes a large team to turn all those submissions into a *Chicken Soup for the Soul* book: Our VP & Associate Publisher D'ette Corona, our Senior Editor Barbara LoMonaco, and our editors Jennifer Quasha and Crescent LoMonaco made sure they read every single one.

Susan Heim did the first round of editing, D'ette Corona chose the perfect quotations to put at the beginning of each story, and editor-in-chief Amy Newmark edited the stories and shaped the final manuscript.

As we finished our work, D'ette Corona continued to be Amy's right-hand woman in creating the final manuscript and working with all our wonderful writers. Barbara LoMonaco, Kristiana Pastir and Elaine Kimbler jumped in at the end to proof, proof, proof. And, yes, there will always be typos anyway, so feel free to let us know about them at webmaster@chickensoupforthesoul.com, and we will correct them in future printings.

The whole publishing team deserves a hand, including Executive Assistant Mary Fisher, Senior Director of Marketing Maureen Peltier, VP of Production & Special Projects Victor Cataldo, and our graphic designer Daniel Zaccari, who turned our manuscript into this beautiful book.

Sharing Happiness, Inspiration, and Hope

Real people sharing real stories, every day, all over the world. In 2007, *USA Today* named *Chicken Soup for the Soul* one of the five most memorable books in the last quarter-century. With over 100 million books sold to date in the U.S. and Canada alone, more than 250 titles in print, and translations into nearly fifty languages, "chicken soup for the soul®" is one of the world's best-known phrases.

Today, twenty-six years after we first began sharing happiness, inspiration and hope through our books, we continue to delight our readers with new titles, but have also evolved beyond the bookstore with super premium pet food, television shows, a podcast, video journalism from aplus.com, movies and TV shows on the Popcornflix app, and licensed products, all revolving around true stories, as we continue "changing the world one story at a time®." Thanks for reading!

Share with Us

We all have had Chicken Soup for the Soul moments in our lives. If you would like to share your story or poem with millions of people around the world, go to chickensoup.com and click on "Submit Your Story." You may be able to help another reader and become a published author at the same time. Some of our past contributors have launched writing and speaking careers from the publication of their stories in our books!

We only accept story submissions via our website. They are no longer accepted via mail or fax. Visit our website, www.chickensoup.com, and click on Submit Your Story for our writing guidelines and a list of topics we are working on.

To contact us regarding other matters, please send us an e-mail through webmaster@chickensoupforthesoul.com, or fax or write us at:

Chicken Soup for the Soul
P.O. Box 700
Cos Cob, CT 06807-0700
Fax: 203-861-7194

One more note from your friends at Chicken Soup for the Soul: Occasionally, we receive an unsolicited book manuscript from one of our readers, and we would like to respectfully inform you that we do not accept unsolicited manuscripts, and we must discard the ones that appear.

Changing the world one story at a time®
www.chickensoup.com